Managing Pollution

Managing Pollution

Economic Valuation and Environmental Toxicology

Edited by

Clive L. Spash

Lecturer in Environmental and Ecological Economics, University of Cambridge, UK, Director of Cambridge Research for the Environment (CRE) and President of the European Society for Ecological Economics (ESEE)

and

Sandra McNally

Environmental Science and Policy Research Group, Centre for Ecology and Hydrology, Monks Wood, Abbots Ripton, Huntingdon, UK

Edward Elgar

Cheltenham, UK • Northampton MA, USA

Published by
Edward Elgar Publishing Limited
Glensanda House
Montpellier Parade
Cheltenham
Glos GL50 1UA
UK

Edward Elgar Publishing, Inc.
136 West Street
Suite 202
Northampton
Massachusetts 01060
USA

A catalogue record for this book
is available from the British Library

Library of Congress Cataloguing in Publication Data

Managing pollution : economic valuation and environmental toxicology / edited by Clive L. Spash, Sandra McNally.
    p. cm.
   Includes bibliographical references and index.
    1. Pollution—Economic aspects—Case studies. 2. Pollution—Government policy—Case studies. I. Spash, Clive L. II. McNally, Sandra, 1972–

HC79.P55 M36 2001
363.73'7—dc21

2001018188

ISBN 1 84064 558 X

Printed and bound in Great Britain by MPG Books Ltd, Bodmin, Cornwall.

Contents

Figures

Tables

Contributors

Floor Brouwer   Agricultural Economics Research Institute (LEI-DLO), The Hague, Netherlands.

Mark Dickie   Department of Economics and International Business, University of Southern Mississippi, Hattiesburg, MS, USA.

Richard Dubourg   Entec Uk Ltd and Centre for Social and Economic Research on the Global Environment (CSERGE), University College London and University of East Anglia, Norwich, UK.

Katherine E. Falconer   Scottish Natural Heritage (SNH), Edinburgh, UK.

Ian D. Hodge   Department of Land Economy, University of Cambridge, UK.

Douglas Macmillan   Agricultural and Rural Economics Research Group, Department of Agriculture, University of Aberdeen, UK.

Giuseppe Munda   Department of Economics and Economic History, Universitat Autònoma de Barcelona, Spain.

Ståle Navrud   Department of Economics and Social Sciences, Agricultural University of Norway, Aas, Norway.

John Powell   Countryside and Community Research Unit, Cheltenham and Gloucester College of Higher Education, Cheltenham, UK.

María Xosé Vázquez Rodríguez   Department of Applied Economics, University of Vigo, Spain.

Marta Romo   Department of Economics and Economic History, Universitat Autònoma de Barcelona, Spain.

Clive L. Spash   Department of Land Economy, University of Cambridge and Director of Cambridge Research for the Environment, UK.

Preface

This book arose from a request by an environmental toxicologist in the Institute of Terrestrial Ecology about how economists addressed pollution and toxic chemical problems. He felt there was a need to communicate the content and meaning of economic approaches to his colleagues. Despite efforts of both environmental and ecological economists, there remains a divide between natural and social sciences which is both artificial and often detrimental to environmental policy. Standard methods of higher education and professional training tend to narrow intellectual visions rather than encouraging interdisciplinary thought. Thus, Sandra and I both felt a volume which pulled together on-going research in economics that was attempting to address issues related to environmental pollution could help fill the communication gap, even if only by a small amount. The contributors were encouraged to relate their work to toxicology and the approaches found in the natural science literature on the issue they were studying. The aim was to show how economists make use of and select scientific information.

The work included here is largely from within the economic sub-discipline of environmental economics. That is, most of the authors are trying to build upon the framework of mainstream neoclassical economics. The main methodology employed for analysing pollution problems in this area has been cost–benefit analysis. Thus, the book shows how various methods are being applied to assess the benefits of pollution control and some of the difficulties that arise when trying to apply them. There are exceptions in the volume where institutional issues or alternative approaches such as multiple criteria analysis are raised as being more relevant. The introductory chapter also attempts to place the environmental economic approach in a broader context and to suggest how it faces various challenges and limitations. As that chapter also explains, the collection of papers attempts to show the diversity of work in terms of models, methods, pollutants addressed and geographical regions under study.

Clive L. Spash
Cambridge
February 2001

Acknowledgements

The compilation and editing of this set of papers has been greatly aided by the assistance of Claudia Carter who has taken great pains to offer support in the often difficult tasks of getting responses from busy academics, making various word processing and graphics files compatible, and double checking manuscripts. Thanks to the authors and especially one who completed their work while going through personally difficult times. The work of the staff at Edward Elgar is also appreciated, especially in copy editing which managed to find errors even after several checks here. Finally, during the putting together of this volume debate and thinking about valuation issues was greatly aided by participation in the Concerted Action on Environmental Valuation in Europe (EVE) funded by Directorate General XII of the European Commission under the Environment and Climate RTD Programme, contract no. ENV4-CT97-0558.

1. Evaluating the impacts of pollution: an introduction and overview

Clive L. Spash

CONTENT AND CONTEXT

This introductory chapter sets the context within which each of the contributions falls. The aim is to show how different approaches to the management of pollution are being developed by economists while drawing out some of the common themes and problems. Economists are concerned by a wide range of pollutant impacts on the environment as they affect human welfare and not just human health, although this has formed the primary focus of regulatory authorities. The selection in this volume shows economists addressing environmental management of a variety of problems from health impacts to land contamination to ecosystems damages.

The interaction between natural science information and economic analysis can be difficult to manage as several contributors explain (Dickie, Spash, Navrud, Falconer and Hodge). In fact, varying degrees of scientific knowledge are employed in economic analyses, although all economic studies have some basis in an understanding of environmental impacts of pollutants. However, the gap between natural and social sciences, when addressing the same issue, often remains large. The studies here show how economists are grappling with the use of scientific information. One drive behind this book was to present a range of ongoing work by economists addressing environmental pollution so that natural scientists working in the areas of ecotoxicology, epidemiology and ecology might gain an understanding of typical economic practice. At the same time the volume aims to provide an opportunity for some reflection by economists as to how they use scientific information and what might be the future role of economic analyses. Thus, a range of case studies has been selected to exemplify the range of methods employed by economists as well as the type of subjects being addressed.

Economic approaches to the environment have focused upon the inclusion of monetary estimates of damages in the decision process. Questions have been raised as to the extent to which this is feasible, meaningful and politically or philosophically acceptable (Sagoff 1988; O'Neill 1993; Adams 1995;

Foster 1997). The current volume is not directly related to this debate although the questions remain relevant and have implications for the validity of different approaches, especially in a policy context. Thus, in this chapter the opportunity is taken to reflect upon such issues as they relate to the work presented in the book. For example, three chapters directly discuss the application of monetary valuation in the area of health risks (Dickie, Dubourg and Rodríguez, Powell). However, monetary valuation in this area has also led to severe criticism. The result of putting monetary amounts on morbidity and mortality is to discriminate on the basis of the current income distribution. This means accepting that the value of a statistical life will be weighed differently due to variations in lifetime earnings, current income or living standards, and so willingness or ability to pay. Most controversially, in contributing to a cost–benefit analysis (CBA) of the enhanced greenhouse effect, Pearce et al. (1996, p. 197) claimed the value of a statistical life in India could be set at around $120 000 while in developed countries the value would be 'a best guess of $3.5 million' and ranging up to $9 million. The implication that human life or injuries might be treated in this way was criticized as unjust discrimination and has proved politically unacceptable. Some attempts might then be made to address 'equity' as income distribution and to do a sensitivity analysis but this is far from likely to placate the critics or address their concerns.

Part of the problem here is that mainstream economics, following the objective scientific tradition, has tried to divorce socio-economic analysis from the political and ethical dimensions of policy. Thus environmental values are regarded as objective facts to be revealed (Spash 1997). Economic analysts, who are trained at best to show some regard to income distribution issues as of secondary significance, neglect and are often surprised by their work's political reception. This has led some economists to explore a variety of alternatives such as: adopting politically set targets and then discussing whether these can be achieved at least cost (for example, Brouwer); trying to develop a range of physical impact indicators without weights and restricting analysis to the impacts of regulatory regimes for economic agents (Falconer and Hodge); and developing multiple criteria analysis and life cycle assessment of products and processes (Munda and Romo). Thus there is some divergence between economists about the extent to which monetary valuation should be applied and to which their own analysis should strive to be independent of politics and ethics.

A generally favoured alternative is to advise from the perspective of cost-effectiveness to achieve given targets rather than determining targets via a full CBA. Yet, assessing costs can prove as difficult as assessing benefits and many costs of an environmental project can require non-market valuation techniques. For example, the costs of a project may involve imposing risks of morbidity or mortality. Thus, cost-effectiveness is best regarded as a constrained form of environmental monetary valuation and can as a result lead to exactly the same difficulties as found under a full CBA (for example, valuation of life). In reading through the contributions to this volume you will be able to reflect upon how far political and ethical dimensions can be regarded as separable from economic analysis.

The characteristics of the work presented in this volume are summarized in Table 1.1. As this shows, the case studies address different media (air, land and water) and pollutants. Air quality has formed a major concern being most easily linked to human health impacts (Dickie, Dubourg and Rodríguez). The change in Europe from local smog due to household coal combustion to the long-range transportation of pollutants from centralized electricity production has altered this relationship and the type of impacts. Acidic deposition became the first sign of this change and remains a significant factor impacting many ecosystems (Spash, Navrud, Macmillan). Awareness of the dangers of chemical wastes has encouraged a strong regulatory approach at various points in the past while economists have had relatively little to say on the matter. Thus the discussion here is of particular interest (Munda and Romo, Powell) and the idea that a purely science-based approach could be ineffective raises questions as to how socio-economic analysis can help. In contrast, the area of farming has been one where economists have played a major part in discussing production systems and regulation (for example, the Common Agricultural Policy). The view of farming is changing from merely food provision to management of a rural economy nested within environmental systems that are valued in a variety of ways (such as maintenance of ecosystems functions, and provision of habitat for rare species). Hence a move towards integrating environmental and socio-economic indicators may provide an alternative way in which to assess rural policy towards such problems as pesticide use (Falconer and Hodge).

As Table 1.1 also shows, among the commonly discussed economic methods employed for environmental CBA, the contingent valuation method (CVM), production analysis (for example, quadratic and linear programming), avoided costs and hedonic pricing (HP), are discussed and applied by contributors. In terms of the standard methods recommended by environmental economists, the production approach has been regarded as an important way of using scientific dose-response information and linking this with economics. The idea has been to use the existing results of scientific research on cause–effect relationships and plug these into existing economic models of production processes. In practice the integration requires tailoring both models and can mean commissioning new research. Due to the expense that this can imply, alternative methods of economic assessment may be sought. However, the potential is for ongoing scientific work to be conducted with an eye to economic and policy requirements without adding significantly

Table 1.1 Components of the research reported in each chapter

Author	Physical model(s)	Assessment method(s)	Impact target(s)	Main pollutant	Pollutant medium	Region of study
Dickie	Dose-response	Avoided cost	Human health	Lead	Air	USA
Dubourg and Rodríguez	Dose-response/ subjective risk	CVM	Human health	Particulates (PM_{10})	Air	Spain
Spash	Dose-response	Production function, programming models	Agricultural crops	SO_2, NO_x, O_3	Air/land	USA and Europe
Macmillan	Dose-response	HP, CVM	Salmon fisheries	SO_2	Air/water	Scotland
Navrud	Critical load	CVM	Freshwater fisheries	SO_2	Air/water	Norway
Powell	Subjective risk	HP, CVM	Human health and welfare	Toxic waste	Land/water	Hungary
Munda and Romo	Life cycle	MCA	Systems functions	Solid waste	Land/air/water	Spain
Brouwer	Input-output	Cost-effectiveness	Water ecosystems and Human health	Nitrates	Land/water	Europe
Falconer and Hodge	Hazard indicator	Linear programming	Human health and ecosystems	Pesticides	Land/water	UK

4

to the cost. This requires a level of communication between disciplines, which is too often absent.

Hedonic pricing appears in two of the case studies in this volume and both times in conjunction with CVM. The dual application can appear in order to validate results which might be questioned as lacking robustness if only derived on the basis of one method. The HP approach uses the value of environmental characteristics implicit in market prices such as housing, land or wages. The aim is to separate out the aspect of the environment under analysis from the overall price. For example, variations in air quality due to tropospheric ozone within an airshed can result in price differentials in houses by location. If other factors affecting house prices can be controlled for, the influence of ozone concentrations can then be isolated and evaluated. Difficulties arise in modelling all the potential factors influencing the market price (for example, for housing) and in obtaining data that allows all the factors to be measured with enough detail to conduct statistical analysis.

A currently popular method of obtaining monetary estimates, contingent valuation, is employed by several of the contributors to this volume, although this has also proved to be a controversial technique. The rise in popularity of CVM is in part due to the possibility of a potentially wide range of applications and more inclusive resulting value. In the latter regard the method attempts to assess the value associated with direct use of an environmental attribute/entity but also value associated with preserving personal potential future use (option value), with personal expectations of use by future generations (bequest value), and with personal welfare from knowing the attribute/entity exists (existence value). These last three types of value have often been incorrectly classified as 'non-use' values, but are in fact all related to an individual's personal welfare and uses or functions associated with an attribute or entity. Thus, they are more appropriately termed indirect use values, or, as in the United States, 'passive use values' (Arrow et al. 1993). As other methods are solely assessing direct use values, the potential to provide estimates of indirect use values has promoted CVM. However, despite this apparently large breadth of value categories being included within the method, there are values which fall beyond its scope and in fact beyond standard economic analysis. These are discussed further at the end of this chapter.

APPROACHES FROM ENVIRONMENTAL COST–BENEFIT ANALYSIS

Primary Impacts of Pollution: Human Health

Mark Dickie provides the opening contribution, 'Environmental toxicology and health risk assessment in the United States: economic and policy issues'.

This chapter starts with a critical review of the natural science approach to human health impacts. As with the following chapter, the focus is upon dose-response methods.

Dose-response function estimations via scientific experiments are seen to require extrapolation from limited data. Very high doses used on animals in the laboratory are translated to estimate the impacts of low doses on humans in the general environment. For example, chemicals may prove carcinogenic generally in rodents but have no effect on humans, leading to a false positive result. Alternatively, the laboratory tests may fail to detect any carcinogenic impact on rodents but upon release the chemical proves to be carcinogenic for humans, a false negative. Additional complications arise because humans are highly variable in response within the species, as compared to across species. Thus, a conversion factor for interspecies adjustment of dose is required and the choice of factor affects the final risk estimates substantially. The most sensitive human may be more sensitive than the most sensitive non-human.

Both quantitative (dose-response) and qualitative (hazard assessment) extrapolation are controversial. Exposure through one route may fail even qualitatively to reflect the toxicity of exposure via a different route. Other aspects of uncertainty in assessing risks from human chemical exposure arise due to multiple and cumulative exposures and the different toxicity of exposure within a population, for example, children versus adults. Toxicity assessment is an inexact science constrained further by the cost of bioassays, so that human health risks from most chemicals remain unquantified.

Government agencies must then take the available data and decide whether and how to regulate chemicals. Risk management attempts to cross the divide between science and policy, the laboratory and the world, the bioassay and economic welfare impacts of resource reallocation. In practice, Dickie argues, risk managers err on the side of caution and protecting public health and the intentional overstatement of risk is normal. The commonly portrayed dichotomy between science and policy is in fact a blurred and indistinct division.

This leads to what Dickie terms a precautionary principle where caution leads to a probable overestimation of exposure risks. In the US, for example, arbitrary factors thought to reflect uncertainty are used to make humans more sensitive than the test evidence. The population at risk from exposure is also argued to have been arbitrarily set without being related to data. For example, in the past the United States Environmental Protection Agency (US EPA) relied upon 'a fictitious "maximum exposed individual" whose unrealistically high exposures strained any appearance of scientific credibility' (Dickie).

Much discretion in regulating toxic chemicals occurs within the US because risk assessment only tries to determine whether a chemical poses an appreciable risk to a sensitive individual. Thus, some US agencies and programmes trade off health risks with expected benefits from chemical production while others exclude CBA and economic considerations from regulatory decisions. The regulation of lead in the US is used as a case study to illustrate the points made about the relationship between toxicology and economic assessment. Dickie argues that the economic analysis, while uncertain, does aid policy making and results in a different regulatory standard.

A central aspect of the debate discussed by Dickie is the role of science in environmental regulation. The model of scientists providing objective 'true risks' of exposure to chemicals is seen to be a fallacy. While scientific input to the decision process is essential, the role of that information must be judged in the light of the institutional structures from which it arises. Thus, scientific and economic information will be used differently in different agencies, as Dickie notes. The problem is how best to develop processes for decision making which are able to address multiple goals (safety, efficiency, equity, fairness and ethical responsibility) while avoiding capture and manipulation by vested interests.

Richard Dubourg and Maria Rodríguez, in 'Calculating morbidity benefits from reducing air pollution: a Spanish case study', provide an example of how economics is being applied to human toxicology. This chapter considers the potential benefits of reduced human morbidity from improving air quality in the city of Vigo, north-west Spain, which suffers from acute air pollution problems. The epidemiological evidence linking air pollution with specific types of respiratory morbidity was examined. Ambient concentrations of particulate matter and ozone were related to the number of hospital admissions for pneumonia and chronic obstructive pulmonary disease (COPD), the number of visits to emergency rooms for COPD, and the number of days when activity was restricted or particular minor symptoms were experienced. This evidence was combined with the results of the first CVM survey of respiratory morbidity to be undertaken in Spain. The study tried to focus only upon the costs of 'pain and suffering' and excluded such damages as the costs of treating illness and lost wages. The authors describe how the survey was specifically designed to be compatible with existing epidemiological exposure-response functions in order to construct a 'monetized health damage function'.

More specifically, the CVM survey attempted to value the morbidity impact of pollution arising from particulate matter (PM_{10}) in Vigo. Primary care specialists helped the authors 'translate' various epidemiological 'endpoints' into health impacts, which were felt to be more meaningful to survey respondents. Thus respondents were presented with brief descriptions of representative 'illness episodes', which gave details of the likely symptoms, restrictions and duration of the epidemiological endpoints. These descriptions ranged from impacts associated with 'restricted activity days' to hospital admission due to induced illness. In accordance with the hypothetical scenario approach used in CVM, respondents to the survey were required to imagine that they experience each 'illness episode'. They were then asked to estimate their maximum willingness to pay (WTP) to prevent each episode from occurring. At the same time they were meant to focus solely upon pain and suffering and exclude their own concerns about treatment costs, lost wages or the institutional structures providing treatment. Thus, the respondent was placed in the artificial position of being asked to accept that they could avoid illness, and any treatment, by making a payment. Such an approach is commonly referred to by practitioners as the 'magic wand', because payment is assumed to remove the impacts of illness instantaneously, as if by magic.

The statistical relationship was examined between the stated WTP, the type of illness and personal characteristics of the respondents such as income and educational levels. In general, the results accorded with expectations, for example, a positive relationship between WTP and income levels. There was some evidence of an 'information effect' where those with more experience of a respiratory illness better appreciated its impacts and therefore had a higher WTP to avoid such an illness.

Mean WTP estimates were combined with dose-response coefficients from epidemiological studies. These coefficients were based upon estimates of the physical relationship between particulate matter and epidemiological endpoints, that is, epidemiological exposure-response functions. The authors then computed their monetary damage function, which linked the level of particulate matter to health costs (excluding the costs of treating illness and the loss of wages due to illness). Rather than wanting to estimate the total value of reducing PM_{10} levels to zero, the authors note that the costs of reducing levels by a given percentage is required for comparison with the costs of pollution control measures. They therefore estimated the economic benefit of a 10 per cent reduction in PM_{10} levels for Vigo.

Dubourg and Rodríguez acknowledge various difficulties with this approach. They point to factors which may cause estimates of value to be understated. For example, their study excluded the costs of treating illness, and of the increase in mortality associated with PM_{10}. As noted by Dickie and the authors themselves, exposure-response functions ignore the fact that some groups in the population, such as elderly people and children, are more vulnerable to PM_{10}-related illness than others. This means that the coefficients as estimated in the epidemiological studies can fail to give an accurate picture of the risk exposure actually faced by individuals. While awareness is raised as to the potential importance of such an error, the magnitude and overall direction of the error from these and similar problems remains unclear.

As with other CVM studies, the estimates of monetary damages are sensitive to analytical assumptions, such as treatment of a few large WTP bids, or 'outliers', and adoption of a linear monetary damage function. A very large difference was reported in the mean and median WTP to avoid all illness episodes. The median values were usually only 25–30 per cent of the mean value, indicating a few large bids at the upper end of the distribution. In effect, this implies that a few individuals are exerting a disproportionate influence on mean WTP affecting the total estimated value of pollution reduction. Such an influence is then greatly magnified when the mean is multiplied by the entire affected population. Exactly how such 'outliers' should be treated remains a matter of some controversy in CVM studies. This suggests an important role for sensitivity analysis.

Another issue related to sensitivity of the results is an implicit assumption that there is a linear relationship between the level of pollution and WTP to reduce pollution. One result is that, in this analysis, the WTP to reduce PM_{10} by 10 per cent is always the same regardless of whether PM_{10} levels are high or low. However, both the physical impact of PM_{10} and the perceived value of its reduction might be expected to vary, depending on the current pollution level. Sensitivity analysis might be used to identify a range of pollution levels where the findings are most relevant or, more appropriately, to test a variety of functional forms to show the sensitivity of the results.

The study illustrates the extent of effort which goes into conducting a CVM study, for example, ensuring that individuals understand the questions. Yet debate continues over many aspects of survey design. The hypothetical scenario is often criticized without thought, but scenarios should aim to be believable and realistic. Some doubts arise in this regard when considering the current state of practice in health economics CVM survey design where illness is cured instantly, if you pay. Another concern often raised with regard to the CVM is the choice of an appropriate bid elicitation method. This study employs open-ended questions although the current trend is for dichotomous choice or closed phrasing (as recommended by some expert panels). Whether such aspects of survey design should be controlled by external peer pressure regardless of practical experience, or the context of the case study, is highly questionable. For example, Willis has argued against the dichotomous choice format within the British context, while accepting it might be appropriate for the US. Thus, as with other contributions to this book, questions arise as to what is expected of economic versus natural science analysis of environmental issues and how far analysts are able to address criticisms. These are topics raised again at the end of this chapter.

Secondary Impacts of Pollution

The dose-response approach is also the subject of the chapter 'Air pollution and agricultural crop damage: can Europe learn from the United States?'. This attempts to draw on the more extensive experience of the US EPA in using data from the natural sciences for economic valuation studies. In particular a major research programme running for about a decade was established in the 1970s to inform US policy on the secondary impacts of pollution; this was the National Crop Loss Assessment Network (NCLAN). Primary impacts are those affecting human health as discussed by Dickie, while secondary impacts are those affecting such things as materials, crops and forests, and more generally ecosystems.

Various air pollutants have been identified as a potential influence on commercial crops including sulphur dioxide (SO_2), nitrous oxide (NO_x), ozone (O_3) and carbon dioxide (CO_2). In particular, ozone in the lower atmosphere has been identified as a serious cause of crop loss in the US and seems likely to be creating similar losses in Europe. In this chapter the methods which can be applied to assess the economic damages from air pollution are critically reviewed. The methods typically require measuring pollutant concentrations, relating these to physical crop damages, and estimating the reactions of the agricultural sector and consumers to give welfare changes in terms of consumers' surplus and producers' quasi-rents. The approach taken by the European dose-response programme is shown to have neglected lessons learned by researchers in the US.

A key problem in pollutant impact assessment, which applies across economic approaches to environmental valuation, is the extent to which information can be used in different contexts. Thus, on the scientific side NCLAN faced the difficulty of using dose-response functions derived by different methods (laboratory, closed chamber, open chamber and field trials) growing various cultivars and at a variety of locations across the continent. This raised the same type of questions as are now discussed by economists in the context of transferring monetary damage estimates. Variations in experimental approach are known to influence results and thus data from one method are non-comparable with that from another. In addition, laboratory conditions are too artificial for practical application of the results, leading to the adoption of approaches which come close to field conditions but which still allow some scientific control.

One type of crop might be of interest, such as potatoes, but which cultivars are analysed will determine whether potatoes in general are regarded as resistant to given toxins. Some cultivars are resistant and others susceptible to significant damage which prevents definition of an aggregate dose-response function, but research resources mean that only a limited number of cultivars can be tested. Thus, concentration falls upon the most commonly used cultivars. In addition, varying climatic, edaphic and farm management conditions mean that the same cultivar can respond differently to the same pollutant exposure. Pollutant exposure itself is difficult to define and the measure chosen will affect the functional relationship derived.

Economists are therefore relying upon scientific information which is highly uncertain before they even begin to introduce their own uncertainties. On the economic assessment side there are many choices to be made affecting the derived monetary benefits from pollution control. A range of models may be chosen from simply taking the existing market price for a commodity through to conducting duality modelling. Each approach makes different implicit assumptions about how the market is operating. Even where the same approach is chosen, various choices in simulation, statistical analysis and aggregation will create great scope for diverse results. As with the scientific model the transfer of results across different regions raises another set of information transfer issues. Crop damages for farmers of potatoes in Idaho are difficult to transfer to Ontario and the consequences of doing so are unclear. Yet the pressure from agencies responsible for developing policy is to do more of this information transfer in order to avoid the costs of original research.

Overall NCLAN provides a picture of attempting a best-practice approach to dose-response estimation and the transfer of scientific data. In Europe, perhaps due to subsidiarity and a lack of a federal structure, there now exists a diverse set of dose-response results and most are non-comparable due to their design differences. In addition, emphasis has been placed upon natural science research to the exclusion of economic analysis. The demands placed upon the plant scientists by the economists under NCLAN resulted in a reorientation of the research and a focus upon the transferability of scientific functions across regions. Interestingly a similar debate about transferring information is now being conducted with regards to economic assessments.

In his contribution, 'Monetary valuation of the toxic impacts due to acidic deposition in Scotland', Douglas Macmillan is also concerned with the secondary impacts of air pollution. Although there have been a number of studies which have estimated the costs of acidification to human health, visibility, forest growth and building materials, there has been little attempt to value the benefits of abatement to semi-natural ecosystems. This partly reflects the difficulties of establishing a reliable dose-response function linking reductions in SO_2 to long-term ecological change, but also the non-market nature of the benefits arising from environmental recovery. Macmillan has attempted to produce reliable monetary benefit estimates for recovery in the semi-natural environment of the Scottish uplands. Specific objectives were: (i) to identify impacts from acidification; (ii) to construct accurate physical dose-response functions; (iii) to link the dose-response functions to appropriate economic models in order to estimate both market and non-market benefits of recovery; and (iv) to investigate the influence of uncertainty concerning future environmental recovery following abatement.

Macmillan employed two CBA methods. HP was used to estimate the direct benefits to anglers of reduced acidification in Galloway, while the CVM estimated the benefits in Scotland for improved biodiversity. The resulting estimate from the CVM of £8–12 billion contrasts with the £4 million from the HP study. Macmillan concludes that a narrow focus on specific user values can grossly underestimate the value of environmental improvement. This shows how a range of valuation estimates can be obtained depending upon how narrowly the environmental change or relevant population is defined and again identifies a role for sensitivity analysis.

The HP study estimated the 'direct-use benefits' to salmon anglers of reducing acidic deposition using three steps to construct a cause–effect relationship: (i) prediction of the effects of reduced acidic deposition on water quality and fish population status; (ii) linking changes in fish population status to fish catch; and (iii) prediction of the effect of higher catch on the market value of access to the salmon fishery. The latter relationship was established through estimation of an HP function. Since salmon beats are only infrequently traded in the open market, there were relatively few data from which to develop an HP model for the Galloway fishery. Instead, results were obtained from a model developed for all UK salmon fisheries by Radford et al. (1991). From the estimated relationship between the sale value of salmon beats and the average catch for each boat, a 10 per cent increase in salmon catch was estimated to create a 5.5 per cent increase in the market value of the fishery. A major assumption in this study is that the function estimated for all UK salmon fisheries was transferable to the specific case of the Galloway fishery.

The CVM study aimed to evaluate the benefits arising from an improvement in the biodiversity of polluted areas for an aggregation of indirect use and direct use values, without any breakdown. Respondents were shown pictures which were meant to convey implications for biodiversity of different levels of acidic deposition. These pictures illustrate the way in which scientific information on biodiversity is simplified for the purposes of a CVM survey. The CVM was conducted via a postal questionnaire where respondents were asked whether they would be prepared to pay a specified amount (that is, dichotomous choice). Different groups of respondents were asked whether they would be willing to pay different amounts. An 'optimal bid design method' was used to determine the number of bid amounts, the actual bid-level values and the sample size corresponding to each bid value. The dichotomous choice approach to CVM requires a large sample size and thus Macmillan collected 1820 responses (from 3000 mailed questionnaires) while Dubourg and Rodríguez, using an open-ended question, interviewed 448 people. A logistic regression model was used to relate the probability of a 'yes' response to the bid level and other explanatory variables. Results were stated to be in line with expectations. From this estimation, the WTP for each scenario was estimated by integration.

Macmillan argues that omission of indirect use values would significantly underestimate the benefits of controlling the emissions which lead to acidic deposition in Europe. However, he argues that CVM is often regarded as less credible than HP since estimates of indirect use benefits are more controversial (and less tangible). While Macmillan reviews problems discussed in the literature with regard to CVM, a similar review could be made of HP. For example, Macmillan's study found problems with data availability, aggregation and the use of cross-sectional data. Other problems with HP models are outlined by Hanley and Spash (1993). In the context of this study, they include the assumption that the market value of salmon beats perfectly reflects the availability of salmon catch and that this is revised as catch levels change over time. There are also some statistical issues that can greatly affect results such as the correct functional form of the HP model. Though the problems associated with CVM are more obvious, especially to the non-specialist, the potential for error is at least as great in an HP study. This raises the question as to the extent to which the results from different valuation methods should be used in policy analysis.

The policy problem of acidic deposition is also the concern of Ståle Navrud in 'Linking physical and economic indicators of environmental damages: acidic deposition in Norway'. This chapter provides an exploration of the uses being made of natural science versus economic information. Navrud argues that there are two distinct ways of introducing the sustainability concept in decision making, either as an exogenous variable in the form of physical indicators or as an endogenous variable in economic models, that is, economic indicators. These two approaches are termed here 'strong sustainability' and 'weak sustainability', respectively. This chapter is an attempt to provide links between these two concepts, by using the indicator of critical loads to describe the environmental change to be valued in a CVM survey. The goal was to integrate strong sustainability concerns with the damage function approach of environmental economics. The case study presents results on the willingness to pay of the Norwegian population for increased freshwater fish stocks which result from reducing exceedance of critical loads for sulphur.

A similar approach to that of Macmillan is employed using four main steps. First, air dispersion models are used to estimate how changes in pollution emissions affect atmospheric concentrations. Second, calculations are made as to how changes in atmospheric concentrations of pollutants affect acidic deposition and concentrations at the target (soil, water). Third, dose-response functions are used to calculate the impacts on affected ecosystems (for example, fish stocks). Fourth, economic damages are estimated using CVM.

The second and third steps consist of calculating changes in critical load exceedance and its impact on fish stocks.

In-person interviews of 1009 Norwegian households was carried out using both open-ended and dichotomous choice formats. Many respondents stated zero WTP because they thought that the countries causing the depositions should pay, rather than because they had no utility from increased fish stocks. Treatment of these protest zero bids then created a problem for the analysis, but as Navrud notes: 'this type of protest behaviour is found in most CV studies'. Results from the two formats were used to give a range estimates of the WTP.

Next, Navrud discusses the use of benefit transfer techniques to calculate European welfare gains from reducing acidic deposition. There are two main approaches. First the unit value at the study site (Norway) is assumed to be representative for the policy site (Europe) either with or without adjustment for differences in income levels. Second, a benefit function is either estimated at the study site and transferred to the policy site, or estimated from several study sites using meta-analysis. Once a function is available then values for variables at the policy site can be obtained to estimate WTP. Navrud concludes that reliable estimates for CBA could be obtained from a benefit function approach. However, some assumption would be required to use the results of the current work including that the marginal WTP is constant, that is, independent of the current level of acid deposition, and that Norwegians are representative of all Europeans with regards to WTP for reducing fish damages.

Primary and Secondary Impact Assessment

In 'Prioritizing toxic chemical clean-up in Hungary using monetary valuation', John Powell also refers to benefit transfer, but he is primarily concerned with providing economic information to improve the approach being taken to regulate pollution. Estimates of the number of contaminated sites in Hungary vary widely from 3000 to 12 000 and the Ministry of the Environment has reasonable levels of information on only 175 'priority' sites. Estimated clean-up costs for even the two-thirds of these sites on a priority list far exceed the budget of the decontamination programme established in 1996. One site alone has an estimated clean-up cost of £10 million while the annual budget is only £3 million. Decontamination of sites must therefore be prioritized. This chapter examines the potential for estimating the social and environmental benefits from removing health risks and environmental impacts, derived using market and non-market valuation techniques, in order to rank contaminated sites. Quality and quantity of information required are both issues that need careful consideration in a transition economy where financial resources, scientific and economic information, and environmental expertise are low. The study investigates the extent to which limited economic valuation information can improve the decision over the removal of toxic waste.

An initial issue which arises and tends to be at best implicit in economic valuation work is the institutional context. There are problems with trying to decide upon decontamination of land where ownership is uncertain and priorities for resource use in this area are low. However, contamination is more than a historical problem of past lack of responsibility because new sites are being created, partially due to the pressure for industrial and material growth. Economists are familiar with the incentives created by the free market system for private firms and individuals to externalize any costs possible, including environmental costs. Thus, government intervention is necessary, but how this should be guided remains unclear. A purely natural science approach to assessing the risks seems inadequate because risk is largely associated with human impacts which must then relate to socio-economic indicators.

In fact, Powell argues that a natural science risk assessment procedure is flawed and that an explicit acknowledgement of socio-economic factors is required. He uses a case study to suggest how this might be achieved. However, the reliance on purely monetary estimates of individual preferences about contaminated sites, which he employs, can also be viewed as inadequate. Once wider concerns of socio-economic values are touched upon the incommensurability of economic, social and ethical values arises. This problem applies equally to all monetary valuation methods such as the property value approach or CVM, both of which Powell employs. All such methods are also dependent on individual knowledge and perception of environmental hazards, and public understanding of toxicity. Thus a range of issues are relevant to risk management involving expert versus public opinion. This is where economists conducting CVM studies are found discussing the provision of information and how to inform an often ignorant general public about complex environmental problems in relatively short surveys. The alternative of relying upon scientific experts seems equally problematic and undemocratic.

While Powell shows how benefits may be relatively large, the question of whether individual preferences reflected via monetary payments are a good approach to ecotoxicology is not addressed. The recommendation is again made for using benefit transfer. The reasoning is that enforcement agencies can save money by avoiding original research. However, there is no reason to believe a priori that public preferences about one toxic waste dump should match those of a different public about a different site. Thus, the issues raised by earlier chapters seem to confront the analyst in Eastern Europe even more explicitly.

Alternative Assessment Methods

In 'Combining life cycle assessment and multicriteria evaluation: comparing waste management options in Spain', Giuseppe Munda and Marta Romo move away from the standard approach to pollution evaluation taken by economists. Using the example of waste management systems in northern Spain, they compare different systems with energy recovery, including several subsystems like transport, plant management and electricity production. The chapter addresses a theoretical and empirical analysis of different waste management alternatives. The theoretical issue tackled is the use of a multicriteria evaluation approach in combination with a life cycle assessment framework because the two approaches are thought to be complementary and mutually reinforcing. Life cycle assessments generate indicators of potential impacts on the environment and humans. In the life cycle assessment, the following impact categories were considered: toxicity for humans, greenhouse gas releases, eutrophication, acidic deposition, ozone layer depletion, smog, energy consumption and solid waste generation. Multicriteria methods can be used to aggregate such indicators in order to arrive at a final evaluation. The promise of multicriteria is to avoid reduction of indicators to a common unit of measurement, as normally practised by environmental economists using money.

This chapter contrasts with the approach suggested by Powell. Multicriteria analysis (MCA) is recommended with detailed analysis of life cycle implications of waste management systems. The chapter gives technical details as to the conduct and performance of the approach and some of the possibilities this holds. An interesting aspect of this type of MCA is the potential to explicitly address distributional criteria and maintain several non-equivalent measures of performance through to the final report. As in the case of reporting sensitivity analysis, the outcome is then seen within a broader context and the hope is that results will be used as a package rather than single numbers being plucked for use out of context.

The final two contributions relate economic analysis of environmental pollution to the policies which might be employed for controlling that pollution. Brouwer takes a broader view than some of the other studies in the book and reflects upon his experience in 'Cost-effectiveness analysis for nitrate pollution control in the European Union'. Nitrate pollution is a problem heavily related to farm practices, that is, the use of nitrogen fertilizers and intensive animal farming. He considers cost-effectiveness of pollution control at two levels. First is the relative cost-effectiveness of different taxation policies. Second, he considers a cost-effective response from a farmer's point of view. These issues are especially relevant in the context of various

European Union directives that are expected to reduce nitrate pollution in all member states.

Differences in the physical nature of the nitrate problem across Europe are reviewed before discussing the cost-effectiveness of different regulatory approaches. In particular, product taxes are compared with farm-level taxes on nitrogen surpluses. Although Kleinhanss et al. (1997) provide evidence for considerable reductions in fertilizer use if a levy reaches 50 per cent, the policy would only have a very limited impact within 'hot spot' areas where producers often engage in intensive livestock production. In contrast, Helming (1997) shows that a tax on nitrogen surpluses at the farm level is much more cost-effective than a product charge. This emphasizes the importance of the regional distribution of pollution when considering policies at a national or international level.

At the individual farm (or firm) level, when regulations are introduced on nitrate leaching, farmers can respond either by altering the intensity of production or by changing farm management techniques. Brouwer reviews the merits of the different options open to farmers and outlines the different ways economists look at this question. For example, one option is simply to compare farms following 'sustainable management practices' with a control group. A more formal economic approach, such as that used by Schleef (1996), is to use a linear programming model to consider the cost-effectiveness of different options open to farmers. Options considered by Schleef include transportation of animal waste, renting land, and changing the feed diet of livestock. Brouwer's general conclusion is that farmers often have management options which allow for a more cost-effective way to reduce nitrate pollution than by reducing livestock numbers, but this is neglected when devising policy.

Falconer and Hodge, in 'Pesticide policy design and decision-making in the United Kingdom: information, indicators and incentives', discuss issues relating to both the chapter by Brouwer and that of Munda and Romo. That is, they are concerned with both the pollution impacts of farming and its regulation, but also the use of indicators in economic assessment and for policy guidance. They focus upon the construction and role of indicators in environmental policy using the example of agricultural pesticide regulation. This has become particularly relevant in European countries following the implementation of the 1980 European Drinking Water Directive. In addition, the Fifth European Union Environmental Action Programme proposed a reduction in the use of plant protection products as a major objective for the agricultural sector. Falconer and Hodge show how the use of environmental indicators can contribute to the identification of cost-effective policy options to reduce the overall use of pesticides.

The chapter begins with a discussion on the nature of the pesticide problem, before explaining the role and then the construction of environmental indicators. Generally, environmental indicators synthesize information collected by other types of impact assessment methodologies. They are then seen as potentially fulfilling several roles as decision aids which include: providing a simple framework within which to start assessing the social and environmental impacts of damage, allowing clear identification of the relative hazards of different products (for example, by pesticide users), and providing a basis on which to differentiate regulatory regimes for diverse products.

Issues in the construction of indicators are explored at a general level and via the case of pesticides. The general discussion includes data availability and assumptions, impact variability in time and space, aggregation and weighting of components and how to incorporate economic information. Weighting of different aspects of environmental damage in constructing an environmental indicator raises the question as to what extent the results from economic valuation studies can be employed. The pesticide indicator in the case study involves ranking a selection of the most commonly used arable pesticides on the basis of their potential impact on the environment. The simple summation of very different components (from hazards to bees through to human health) further emphasizes the weighting problem.

Finally, Falconer and Hodge use their case study to examine the correlation between the volume of pesticide use, financial costs of farm production inputs and ecological hazards. They show that the impact of a pesticide tax may differ greatly depending on whether it is linked to spray costs (for example, if it is implemented on an *ad valorem* basis), or to quantities such as the number of units used, or differentiated according to the adverse environmental potential of the product.

ISSUES IN CURRENT ECONOMIC ASSESSMENT OF POLLUTION

Several different aspects of the way in which economists are trying to address pollution problems can be identified among the various case studies. Most prominent appear to be the validity of results and methods, the use of information, and sensitivity analysis. In addition, the work presented in this volume requires some qualification in terms of what is expected from economic valuation. Thus, this section returns to the issue, mentioned earlier in the chapter, of the theoretical limits to economic valuation.

Convergent and Conduct Validity

One approach to validating the results from economic or scientific studies is to repeat the work. This can be done under identical conditions to see if results can be repeated or under controlled variations to identify the variety of conditions which affect results. The strict approach requires controlling for all unwanted influences so clear cause–effect relationships can be identified. This is rarely possible in scientific fieldwork or socio-economic studies.

In economic valuation work the results from using two different methods is sometimes compared, for example HP and CVM, in order to test convergent validity. Convergent validity concerns the extent to which different methods for valuing a given environmental change produce similar results. Thus, if an HP study gives a similar result to a CVM study, the analysis is regarded as converging on a single answer. This can raise several difficulties because the implementation of any one method requires several choices affecting the resulting monetary estimates. Sampling, data analysis and survey designs all introduce possible bias and errors into the monetary estimates. Controversy surrounds whether open-ended formats (Dubourg and Rodríguez) or dichotomous choice formats (Macmillan) should be used in asking bid questions, and over the use of WTP versus willingness to accept (WTA). Convergent validity studies often seek to define acceptable bounds within which estimates should fall and also common terms and conditions which studies should meet. Thus, Cummings et al. (1986) defined a set of 'reference operating conditions' and used plus or minus 50 per cent overlap in estimates of consumers' surplus as signifying convergence.

More recently, the National Oceanic and Atmospheric Administration (NOAA) commissioned a panel (including Nobel prize winning economists Arrow and Solow) to judge whether CVM was a valid technique for measuring passive use values associated with natural resource damage assessment. The resulting report both endorsed the method and set down a series of recommendations for conducting a CVM survey which were meant to be definitive (Arrow et al. 1993). However, a volume of studies critical of CVM and many of the recommendations of the NOAA panel was also produced at the same time (Hausman 1993). The NOAA guidelines assumed survey redesign could avoid all the problems and questions raised by CVM research over the preceding 20 years.

The NOAA report has been criticized for failing to consider all the relevant arguments and for being limited to a specifically American context. For example, one key recommendation was to use a referendum (dichotomous choice) format where the respondent is asked whether they would pay $X and must answer 'yes' or 'no'. As Willis (1995, p. 127) has pointed out:

> The NOAA Report failed to consider in detail arguments against the use of referendum formats. There is no definitive evidence that referendum models out-perform open-ended (OE), payment card (PC), and iterative bidding (IB) formats for public goods. There is simply no 24-carat gold standard against which results

from different methods can be compared. Further, people in Britain are unfamiliar
with voting on tax propositions, compared with people in the USA…

As an experienced CVM practitioner, Willis concluded against the exclusive
adoption of referendum formats in Britain. There are other areas where the
NOAA recommendations are unsatisfactory and open to question. For
example, some of the difficulties facing a CVM practitioner are the extent to
which budget constraints and substitute goods should be stressed; how
framing, choice of bid vehicle and elicitation method can be decided when
opposing parties have an interest in the analysis; and when an adequate
amount of information has been provided. Also, among their controversial
recommendations was the blanket use of WTP, despite noting that WTA is
theoretically required for damage assessment. As Knetsch (1994) has noted,
the NOAA panel argument that 'conservative values' are in some sense to be
preferred and will be forthcoming under WTP formats is a poor defence and
the results are likely to 'compromise the valuations and seriously distort
incentives' (p. 356).

More generally, while the NOAA guidelines did include some sensible
suggestions for survey conduct (many recognized good practice) they also
neglected a series of questions raised by psychologists, among others. These
research issues include: mapping CVM responses in relation to factors such as
equity and ethical considerations in order to understand contingent perceptions
of the environment; understanding the processes by which people arrive at
their stated intentions to pay or accept payments; and the effect of information
provision (Willis 1995). This implies neglect of the social construction of
preferences. As Vatn and Bromley (1994, p. 132) note: 'Societal processes
form the context within which individual preferences are both developed and
supported. Valuing that fails to recognise the pre-eminent role of context in
preference formation will fail to produce coherent valuation estimates'.

The Role of Information

Information provision and environmental education
Information is discussed in environmental valuation work in two broad
contexts. First is the concern over the level of ignorance among members of
the general public about environmental issues and in particular those they are
being asked to value. Second is the interaction between scientific and
economic information and the extent to which information can be used out of
its original context. This applies both to economists using scientific
information and to policy makers using the results of one study at another time
and location.

The limited extent of public knowledge over the environment is of obvious concern if they are to make judgements informing policy on the basis of their preferences (as assumed in CBA). In revealed preference studies, individuals are assumed to be well informed about the environmental issues of concern. For example, there would be no reason to expect that air pollution would influence house prices if the general public were unaware of the pollution problem in the first place. The information issue has become controversial with the use of CVM because the analyst must decide the extent, type and format of information respondents should be given about the environmental entity to be valued. This problem is exacerbated when an environmental change being valued is something about which respondents are generally unaware, for example, as shown for understanding of biodiversity degradation in the UK even among highly educated groups (Spash and Hanley 1995). In such cases the valuation process becomes an educational process and forms the view of respondents, perhaps dramatically changing their perception of an issue. If CVM is a process of providing information which changes preferences, then the sample results cannot be extrapolated because they are no longer representative of the general population.

One reaction to this kind of problem is to argue in favour of deliberative processes for valuation. These may be seen as supplementing existing methods such as CVM (Brouwer et al. 1999). Alternatively, the point of the monetary valuation exercise may be diminished by the deliberative process and seem a rather technical abstraction from the pluralism of discussion. Thus, the argument has been made in favour of accepting that some choices can be made without monetary pricing (Vatn and Bromley 1994; O'Neill 1997). This encourages a wider discussion of deliberative institutions for value articulation.

Information and benefit transfer
An aspect now being developed which some authors (Powell, Navrud) raise is the scope for benefit transfers. The attraction of benefit transfer is the potential to reduce costs. If, for example, the mean WTP, or a benefit function, estimated in one location were transferable to another location, this would avoid the need for more original research. However, a robust transfer technique might result in sizeable costs of its own in order to check for the validity of making such a transfer in the first place.

There are various methods for testing the benefit transfer approach. The general principle is that site-specific benefit estimates based on a particular method (such as HP, CVM) are compared with the estimates which would result from function or mean value transfer from another site. As Bergstrom and DeCivita (1999) point out, there are several potential sources of error due to differences in context between sites. Hence site valuation will be influenced by the specification and measurement of environmental changes and the availability of substitutes and complements with respect to site attributes. According to Brouwer and Spanninks (1999), significant influences on individual preferences should be accounted for by the benefit function and be of similar magnitude across sites. These are regarded as necessary conditions for the validity of benefit function transfer. The essential concern is for comparability across site characteristic such as: the type of users, the quality and quantity of environmental changes. In addition, the quality of the studies which produced the original functions or estimates must be questioned.

The approach is used in the US to supplement CBA (Bergstrom and DeCivita 1999). The general principle is also more commonly practised than many realize because economists typically borrow scientific information from other contexts even when conducting original economic valuation work, as shown in the chapters of this volume. In addition, existing numbers are often used out of context in policy circles. This is of concern because there are numerous potential problems which can make such transfers of information, whether dose response or economic, questionable (Spash). However, very little published evidence exists concerning the validity of transferring point estimates of the monetary value of environmental benefits or complete benefit functions from one site to another (Brouwer and Spanninks 1999). The research which has attempted to evaluate the performance of benefit transfer suggests that this practice can lead to serious errors in estimation (Downing and Ozuna 1996; Kirchhoff et al. 1997). Thus the validity of benefit transfer remains highly controversial.

Although existing research implies that the welfare measures produced by benefit transfer are inaccurate, compared to original case-specific research, the degree of accuracy has been regarded as adequate by Bergstrom and DeCivita for helping set broad policy priorities. However, where decisions threaten to produce irreversible losses of rare environmental attributes, a primary study is deemed preferable. Hence, in the chapter by Macmillan, where an HP function was transferred, the result would then be regarded as providing an order of magnitude for the benefits to anglers of reducing pollution by acidic deposition. Indeed, in the light of the many other problems with valuation methods, any welfare measure will be only a crude estimate of the value of an environmental change (or some components of that change). This has led some economists to look towards specific forms of multiple criteria analysis as a potentially more informative approach where original information can be preserved (Munda and Romo).

Sensitivity Analysis

While many analysts agree that conducting data runs to show how sensitive results are to changing specific variables is a good idea, very few actually present such data. As Merrifield (1997) notes, the coverage given to the topic in CBA texts is limited and the topic is more often ignored altogether. Yet sensitivity analysis could provide a considerable amount of information concerning the robustness of results.

As was mentioned earlier, for example, the treatment of outliers in CVM studies can have a large influence on aggregated WTP values. More generally, CVM practice is inconsistent with regard to how different motives to bid are treated in data analysis. Thus some zero bids are regarded as 'protest bids' and excluded from data sets while motivational questions are absent from screening of positive bids (such as outliers). This creates considerable potential for variation in results from the same data set. There appears to be a neglected role for sensitivity analysis in such work. Thus, mean WTP, preferred as a basis for welfare estimates, should be compared with a median WTP estimate. This might also enhance the credibility of such studies.

More generally, results can be difficult to interpret because single numbers are given after a poorly described aggregation process. Results can be highly sensitive to factors such as population size and discount rates. For example, a recent report from the UK Department of Environment, Transport and the Regions (1999) used a 25 per cent discount rate in aggregating the results of a CVM study. This is extremely high compared to any CBA or public policy appraisal process but there was no sensitivity analysis on this factor in the report. The only comment in this regard was a footnote which mentions a 5 per cent change in discount rate causing a 10 per cent reduction in WTP. Thus, if the relationship were linear, something in the order of a 40 per cent reduction in WTP was made to the final results over the more normal 6 per cent discount rate used in UK public policy appraisals. The study employed a panel of experts (Ian Bateman, Nick Hanley, Michael Hanemann, Susana Mourato, Richard Ready and Ken Willis) and 'an approach that is more likely to produce conservative results' (p. 12). This was the largest CVM study ever conducted in the UK (with a sample of 10 640 public interviews) and was used to inform a decision by the Treasury as to whether they should implement a tax on aggregates extraction (which has not yet happened). A policy maker reading the executive summary would never come across the sensitivity of the results to the discount rate or other factors.

There is some risk of both unintended and deliberate data manipulation in the complex calculations, often implicit, in a benefit assessment exercise. Merrifield (1997) argues that sensitivity analysis can make a CBA more informative, can discourage abuse and make inadvertent bias more transparent. He also believes that it would help prevent the practice among public officials of ignoring those CBA results which are unpalatable to special interest groups. The outcome would also move studies away from concentration upon single numbers and lead to the provision of data within ranges, although single numbers might still be defended within this context. The drawback for the policy process is that the complexity of environmental valuation would no longer be something which might be relegated to an annex of a report. As Merrifield (p. 91) notes, each additional factor added to a sensitivity analysis at least triples the number of tables reporting net present values. However, if the outcome was far greater transparency in the conduct of CBA, and public policy, then this could be a small price to pay. Either way, the current practice of doing little or no sensitivity analysis and relegating decisions over key factors to footnotes seems unjustifiable.

Limitations to Economic Valuation

A category of values can be recognized which are by definition outside of the economic calculus to evaluate. The category is mentioned here in order to qualify the discussion over the extent to which economic techniques can achieve a comprehensive valuation of the costs and benefits of environmental pollution. Non-economic values can be related to notions of intrinsic value outside of good for human ends, and non-consequentialist and non-utilitarian reasoning about the environment. For example, a species may be valued as a food source and because it is beautiful and because of its potential to benefit science, but it may also be valued separately from all these uses or aspects of its nature which create good consequences for humans. Economists employ an ethical theory (teleology) which places the ultimate criterion of morality in some non-moral value (for example, welfare, utility and happiness) that results from acts. This theory then judges acts as only having value if they lead to good consequences (instrumental value), and sees the only intrinsic value as being in the consequences of these acts. In contrast, alternative ethical theories (for example, deontology) attribute intrinsic value to features of the act themselves. For example, killing a human is wrong even when the outcome is judged to be better. The act is judged on its own rather than by the outcome. Such values are exemplified by concerns for justice, human rights, the rights of animals and religious convictions.

One aspect of this alternative approach to valuing the world around us is that some things are not for trade, sale or exchange. The refusal to trade can be particularly relevant when environmental degradation affects human health, animal welfare and ecosystems' functioning and structure. In these cases intrinsic values in non-human animals, plants or ecosystems may be recognized by individuals as constraining economic trade-offs. Studies show a substantial minority of respondents to CVM surveys for biodiversity and wildlife claim rights-based beliefs (Spash 1998, 2000). The extent to which such preferences are liable to arise in other contexts, or be applicable to other economic valuation methods, is unclear. However, excluding such respondents to a CVM as protest bidders, because their behaviour diverges from the accepted economic model, seems at least unscientific.

The discussion of intrinsic values has been rather limited in environmental economics. The idea has been expressed that existence values in CVM might capture non-utilitarian values and are a sign of concern for non-human intrinsic values or rights (Pearce et al. 1989; Pearce and Turner 1990). However, while an individual's WTP for such things as species preservation, or biodiversity, may be showing respect for non-human intrinsic value, this fails to measure the intrinsic value of that species. In the same way, the maximum amount of money one person may be willing to pay to prevent the loss of another person's life fails to reflect the value of that life. Pearce (1998, p. 363) has stated that 'willingness to pay for non-use may well capture so-called "ethical" preferences'. In contrast, non-utilitarian and more generally non-consequentialist reasoning seem particularly relevant restrictions upon the applicability of environmental valuation. As Lockwood (1999) explains, an individual can simultaneously be prepared to trade some entities and regard others hierarchically while relating different conceptions of value to different entities (that is, intrinsic value, instrumental value and no value at all). There are multiple values which can be expressed in relation to the environment and no reasons why these should all be reducible to WTP. Environmental philosophers have attempted to raise awareness of the policy relevance of refusals to make trade-offs on ethical grounds (Holland 1995; O'Neill 1993). As Holland (1995, p. 22) notes: 'to be asked to trade one's principles, even hypothetically, is likely to seem inappropriate and even morally disreputable'.

Another way in which economic approaches are limited is with regard to life support functions and ecosystem functions. The functions which ecosystems perform are many and varied. Only a minority of these fall within the framework where they can be bought and sold in markets subject to private ownership. Among the most important functions performed by ecosystems are maintenance of climatic stability and nutrient cycles. Avoiding the loss of species habitats and sites of scientific interest will help maintain biodiversity. Biodiversity of ecosystems, genes and species is seen as an important aspect of nature and a key to sustainable economic systems.

CVM may be able to place monetary amounts on some aspects of species value or even ecosystem diversity but is unable to address many of the concerns raised by the need to maintain ecosystem functions and protect biodiversity. Where an identifiable output or service can be related to an ecosystem function and this output or service is connected to a marketed commodity, a production analysis approach may be able to assess the economic value of changes in ecosystem functions. However, environmental impacts can be complex, highly uncertain or unknown, such as the loss of a site-specific species which has never been classified. The general perception that biodiversity is equated to species is too simplistic and tends to ignore genetic and ecosystem diversity. However, the issue goes beyond merely a lack of information.

In the case where the functions are essential for life they then, by definition, have no substitutes and cannot be traded. Hierarchical and non-compensatory expressions such as lexicographic preferences are then logical expressions of value rather than exchange or trade values (Lockwood 1999). More generally, as Brown (1984) has noted, functional values are outside of typical preference structures in economics because there is little sense in regarding them as matters of consumer choice, for example, discussing a preference for having or destroying the ozone layer. This reasoning has led some, including a few who have rejected the notion of ethical refusals to trade, to accept that ecosystems have a set of values which are outside economic valuation, that is, they are primary or above other values (Gren et al. 1994). In addition, Common and Perrings (1992) have shown, using resource models, how efficiency in resource allocation is neither a necessary nor a sufficient condition for sustainability of resource use, and have noted the importance of ecosystem resilience. They emphasize that this implies an approach which 'privileges the requirements of the system above those of the individual' (p. 32) and that this involves ethical judgements. Common and Perrings then regard consumers as sovereign only as long as they avoid threatening the general system and so the welfare of future generations. Thus, the ethical categories of limitation on economic valuation and those from ecology become linked. Those regarding some ecosystem functions as having a primary or functional value are in fact implicitly attributing an intrinsic value to survival, that is, survival is then an end in itself regardless of reference to any other entity.

CONCLUDING REMARKS

Environmental valuation in economics has expanded dramatically since the 1980s due in part to the growing public policy concern over environmental management. The use of CBA for environmental assessment has become focused around the CVM because of its potential to address so many issues and provide a more inclusive value. At the same time, many questions have been raised as to the meaning and limitations of monetary valuation of the environment. The environmental economist in the neo-classical tradition prefers to avoid political and ethical questions and exclude these from the analysis, but this seems impossible given the beast with which we are grappling. Thus, the issues raised in this chapter, which are apparent in the work presented in this volume, show that the approach economists are and have been taking to environmental issues will need to change. Some aspects of that change should be to acknowledge explicitly the sensitivity of results, their context specificity and the limited category of values that economists generally address and supply to the policy process. This may then encourage more novel research and wider attention to alternative processes of expressing environmental values. If those values which cannot be captured in a monetary calculus are ignored, they will continue to be lost just as the environment has been and is being degraded, damaged and destroyed due to the neglect of pollution. The challenge is to recognize that pollution impacts on multiple and non-comparable values, and that we need to design institutional processes which allow for the expression of different discourses.

REFERENCES

Adams, J.G.U. (1995), *Cost-benefit Analysis: Part of the Problem, Not the Solution*, Oxford: Centre for Environmental Policy and Understanding, Green College.

Arrow, K., R. Solow, P.R. Portney, E. Leamer, R. Radner and H. Schuman (1993), *Report of the NOAA Panel on Contingent Valuation*, Washington, DC: Resources for the Future.

Bergstrom, J.C. and P. DeCivita (1999), 'Status of benefit-transfer in the United States and Canada: a review', *Canadian Journal of Agricultural Economics*, **47**(1): 79–87.

Brouwer, R., N. Powe, K. Turner, I.J. Bateman and I.H. Langford (1999), 'Public attitudes to contingent valuation and public consultation', *Environmental Values*, **8**(3): 325–47.

Brouwer, R. and F.A. Spanninks (1999), 'The validity of environmental benefits transfer: further empirical testing', *Environmental and Resource Economics*, **14**(1): 95–117.

Brown, T.C. (1984), 'The concept of value in resource allocation', *Land Economics*, **60**(3): 231–46.

Common, M. and C. Perrings (1992), 'Towards an ecological economics of sustainability', *Ecological Economics*, **6**: 7–34.

Cummings, R.G., D.S. Brookshire and W.D. Schulze (1986), *Valuing Environmental Goods: An Assessment of the Contingent Valuation Method*, Totowa, NJ: Rowman & Allanheld.

Department of the Environment, Transport and the Regions (1999), *The Environmental Costs and Benefits of the Supply of Aggregates: Phase 2*, London: Department of the Environment, Transport and the Regions.

Downing, M. and T. Ozuna (1996), 'Testing reliability of the benefit transfer approach', *Journal of Environmental Economics and Management*, **30**(3): 316–22.

Foster, J. (ed.) (1997), *Valuing Nature? Economics, Ethics and Environment*, London: Routledge.

Gren, A.M., C. Folke, K. Turner and I. Bateman (1994), 'Primary and secondary values of wetland ecosystems', *Environmental and Resource Economics*, **4**(1): 55–74.

Hanley, N. and C.L. Spash (1993), *Cost-benefit Analysis and the Environment*, Aldershot, UK: Edward Elgar.

Hausman, J.A. (ed.) (1993), *Contingent Valuation: A Critical Assessment*, Amsterdam: North-Holland.

Helming, J.F.M. (1997), 'Impacts of manure policies for the Netherlands', in F. Brouwer and W. Kleinhanss (eds), *The Implementation of Nitrate Policies in Europe: Processes of Change in Environmental Policy and Agriculture*, Kiel: Wissenschaftsverlag Vauk, pp. 235–51.

Holland, A. (1995), 'The assumptions of cost–benefit analysis: a philosopher's view', in K.G. Willis and J.T. Corkindale (eds), *Environmental Valuation: New Perspectives*, Wallingford: CAB International, pp. 21–38.

Kirchhoff, S., B.G. Colby and J.T. LaFrance (1997), 'Evaluating the performance of benefit transfer: an empirical inquiry', *Journal of Environmental Economics and Management*, **33**(1): 75–93.

Kleinhanss, W., H. Becker and K.-H. Schleef (1997), 'Impacts of agri-environmental policy measures on nitrogen emissions from agriculture', in E. Romstad, J. Simonsen and A. Vatn (eds), *Controlling Mineral Emissions in European Agriculture: Economics, Policies and the Environment*, Wallingford: CAB International, pp. 137–55.

Knetsch, J.L. (1994), 'Environmental valuation: some problems of wrong questions and misleading answers', *Environmental Values*, **3**(4): 351–68.

Lockwood, M. (1999), 'Humans valuing nature: synthesising insights from philosophy, psychology and economics', *Environmental Values*, **8**(3): 381–401.

Merrifield, J. (1997), 'Sensitivity analysis in benefit–cost analysis: a key to increased use and acceptance', *Contemporary Economic Policy*, **15**(July): 82–92.

O'Neill, J. (1993), *Ecology, Policy and Politics: Human Well-being and the Natural World*, London: Routledge.

O'Neill, J. (1997), 'Managing without prices: on the monetary valuation of biodiversity', *Ambio*, **26**: 546–50.

Pearce, D. (1998), 'Valuing risks', in P. Callow (ed.), *Handbook of Environmental Risk Assessment and Management*, Oxford: Blackwell Science, pp. 345–75.

Pearce, D.W., W.R. Cline, A.N. Achanta, S. Frankhauser, R.K. Pachauri, R.S.J. Tol and P. Vellinga (1996), 'The social costs of climate change: greenhouse damage and the benefits of control', in J.P. Bruce, H. Lee and E.F. Haites (eds), *Climate Change 1995: Economic and Social Dimensions of Climate Change*, Cambridge: Cambridge University Press, pp. 178–224.

Pearce, D.W., A. Markandya and E.B. Barbier (1989), *Blueprint for a Green Economy*, London: Earthscan.

Pearce, D.W. and R.K. Turner (1990), *Economics of Natural Resources and the Environment*, New York: Harvester Wheatsheaf.

Radford, A.F., A.C. Hatcher and D.J. Whitmarsh (1991), *An Economic Evaluation of Salmon Fisheries in Great Britain: Summary Report*, Portsmouth: Centre for Marine Resource Economics, Portsmouth Polytechnic.

Sagoff, M. (1988), *The Economy of the Earth: Philosophy, Law, and the Environment*, Cambridge: Cambridge University Press.

Schleef, K.-H. (1996), *Impacts of Policy Measures to Reduce Nitrogen Surpluses from Agricultural Production: An Assessment at Farm Level for the Former Federal Republic of Germany*, Braunschweig, Bundesforschungsanstalt für Landwirtschaft, Institut für Betriebswirtschaft, Arbeitsbericht.

Spash, C.L. (1997), 'Environmental management without environmental valuation?', in J. Foster (ed.), *Valuing Nature? Economics, Ethics and Environment*, London: Routledge, pp. 170–85.

Spash, C.L. (1998), 'Investigating individual motives for environmental action: lexicographic preferences, beliefs and attitudes', in J. Lemons, L. Westra and

R. Goodland (eds), *Ecological Sustainability and Integrity: Concepts and Approaches*, Dordrecht, The Netherlands: Kluwer Academic Publishers, vol. 13, pp. 46–62.

Spash, C.L. (2000), 'Ecosystems, contingent valuation and ethics: the case of wetlands re-creation', *Ecological Economics*, **34**(2): 195–215.

Spash, C.L. and N. Hanley (1995), 'Preferences, information and biodiversity preservation', *Ecological Economics*, **12**(3): 191–208.

Vatn, A. and D.W. Bromley (1994), 'Choices without prices without apologies', *Journal of Environmental Economics and Management*, **26**(2): 129–48.

Willis, K. (1995), 'Contingent valuation in a policy context: the National Oceanic and Atmospheric Administration Report and its implications for the use of contingent valuation methods in policy analysis in Britain', in K.G. Willis and J.T. Corkindale (eds), *Environmental Valuation: New Perspectives*, Wallingford: CAB International, pp. 118–43.

2. Environmental toxicology and health risk assessment in the United States: economic and policy issues

Mark Dickie[*]

INTRODUCTION

Policy analysis of environmental health risks in the United States rests on a division of labour between risk management and risk assessment. Risk management concerns analysis, design and implementation of policy, while risk assessment uses available scientific evidence on toxicity and exposure to describe and quantify the health threat associated with a given chemical. Environmental toxicology often provides the critical evidence used in risk assessment. Yet toxicological evidence yields uncertain predictions of human health hazards, and the uncertainty promotes controversy about appropriate methods to assess risk. Critics concerned with public health contend that risk assessments fail to account adequately for effects of multiple and cumulative exposures, or for populations such as children whose exposure or susceptibility may be unusually high. Proponents of economic efficiency, on the other hand, argue that risk assessments routinely exaggerate threats to human health and may support regulations yielding minor health benefits at substantial cost.

This chapter examines economic and policy issues arising from the use of environmental toxicology to assess health risk in the US. Assessment of environmental risks to children, an issue of current policy interest (US EPA 1998c), is emphasized at several points. The chapter argues that the philosophy and practice of risk assessment hinders use of economic analysis to inform policy decisions. A guiding doctrine of risk assessment in the US is to handle uncertainties in the toxicological evidence using the precautionary principle: when in doubt, err on the side of overstating risk to promote

* The US Environmental Protection Agency partially funded the research described here under C R 825921-01-0 to the University of Southern Mississippi. The research has not been subjected to Agency review and therefore does not necessarily reflect the views of the Agency, and no official endorsement should be inferred.

protection of public health. The precautionary principle runs counter to the economic perspective of balancing public health against costs and benefits of using chemicals. Despite the divergent perspectives, however, economic analysis and risk assessment can be used together to analyse policy options, as illustrated by the recent risk assessment and economic analysis of residential lead standards (US EPA 1997, 1998d).

The chapter continues with a non-technical overview of basic principles and practices of toxicology, followed by a discussion of major scientific uncertainties hindering precise estimation risks to humans. How the US Environmental Protection Agency (EPA) addresses these uncertainties in assessments of health risk is examined. The divergent perspectives taken by risk assessment and economic analysis, and the way these differences are reconciled according to the statutory guidelines and discretionary authority of different programmes in the US federal government, are discussed. Key points are then illustrated with a case study of the risk assessment and economic analysis which the US EPA has used to support proposed standards for residential lead. The final section draws some conclusions.

BASIC PRINCIPLES AND PRACTICES OF TOXICOLOGY

How Toxic Effects Occur: Pharmacokinetics and Pharmacodynamics

The mechanisms causing toxic reactions to xenobiotics (foreign substances) often are not known precisely, but a broad outline can be sketched using basic principles of pharmacokinetics and pharmacodynamics. Pharmacokinetics concerns absorption, transport and excretion of xenobiotics, while pharma-codynamics addresses actions of xenobiotics in living organisms.

Chemicals enter the human body through oral ingestion, inhalation or dermal absorption, and then may be absorbed into the bloodstream and distributed throughout the body, possibly causing toxicity in organs or tissues distant from the portal of entry. Some portion of a xenobiotic may be excreted, some stored in fat, blood or bone, and some metabolized, chiefly in the kidneys and liver. Metabolites then may meet any one of the same three fates – excretion, storage or further metabolism. Metabolic reactions usually convert non-polar (fat-soluble) molecules into more polar (water-soluble) ones, because the kidneys, which are the main excretory organ for xenobiotics, are best at eliminating water-soluble compounds.

Because excretion, storage and metabolism take time, frequency and duration of exposure, as well as dose, are important determinants of toxicity. Exposures therefore are classified by route – ingestion, inhalation or dermal absorption – as well as by size of dose and temporal pattern of exposure. Dose usually is measured relative to size, typically milligrams per kilogram (mg/kg) of body weight for oral ingestion. As shown in Table 2.1, frequency and duration of exposure are classified broadly as acute, subchronic or chronic. Effects of exposure in turn are classified by their immediacy, reversibility and duration.

Table 2.1   Temporal classification of exposure

Impact	Explanation
Acute	Single or repeated exposures within a 24-hour period
Chronic	Multiple exposures, usually daily for a significant fraction of lifetime
Subchronic	Multiple or continuous exposures for about 90 days

The fraction of a chemical excreted or stored does not cause toxicity (although stored substances may cause toxicity later if remobilized); the remainder of the substance and its metabolites may harm health. Under the prevailing view, a foreign substance causes toxicity by binding to a receptor – a molecule or group of molecules that recognizes the toxicant by its physical and chemical properties (Kamrin 1988) – through a 'lock-and-key' mechanism in which a given xenobiotic 'fits' a given receptor (Philp 1995). The location of receptors for a specific substance is thought to determine the site of toxicity, while the number of receptors available for binding determines the degree of toxicity for a given dose.

Toxicity Varies Widely Between Organisms

The toxicity of a chemical varies widely over living organisms, both between and within species. The dose required for a given degree of toxicity may vary by up to four orders of magnitude between rats and mice (Kamrin 1988), and significant variation also exists among subjects of the same species. Variability among humans probably is far greater than variability among laboratory animals bred for genetic similarity, and some toxicologists believe that variation among humans exceeds variation between humans and experimental animals.

Factors contributing to human variability are shown in Table 2.2. Age affects toxicity, largely because defence mechanisms are weaker in the very young and very old. Deterioration of cellular and immune defences, for example, contributes to higher incidence of cancer in the elderly. Additionally, some toxic effects can occur only while an organ is developing, and so are restricted to the young. Chemical injury causes greatest harm during prenatal development (ATSDR 1997), but development of many organ systems, particularly lungs and nervous systems, continues after birth and may be disrupted. Developmental toxicity includes adverse effects from exposures before conception (to either parent), during prenatal development, and up to sexual maturation. Effects may be manifest at any time during the organism's life. The ability to metabolize and excrete some toxicants differs between children and adults, with children usually less (though occasionally more) able to detoxify chemicals. Also, because children have more future years of life than do adults, they have more time to develop delayed effects triggered by current exposure.

Table 2.2   Major determinants of variability of human responses

Age	Sex	Health Status
Previous Exposure	Genetic Differences	

Dose Response

Toxic responses differ in their relationships to dose. One key distinction is between quantal and graded responses. Mutagenesis, carcinogenesis and teratogenesis are quantal responses (positive or negative coded as zero or one) whose frequency in a population, but not severity in an individual, increases with dose. Mutagenesis refers to the formation of mutations in genetic material, and contributes to other toxic effects, particularly carcinogenesis, that is, the growth of tumours resulting from abnormal growth or reproduction of cells. Teratogenesis – the formation of birth defects in offspring – can result from mutagenesis or other mechanisms. Graded responses, on the other hand, are those where severity increases with dose.

Key features of a dose-response function are the presence or absence of a threshold, slope and curvature. Until the 1950s, a basic principle of toxicology held that all toxins had thresholds, based on the idea that a poison must first overcome natural defence mechanisms before causing toxic effects. Current thinking is that most systemic toxicants have thresholds, while the threshold concept is inapplicable to carcinogens and mutagens. Mutations begin at the molecular level in a single cell, and multiple, sequential alterations in the DNA of a single cell and its progeny are thought to lead to cancer. Thus, extremely low doses of an electrophilic carcinogen, which reacts with DNA, may be sufficient to induce mutations and therefore cancer. Epigenetic carcinogens such as dioxin, however, are not genotoxins and may have a threshold because they operate by a different mechanism (Philp 1995), causing local injury and cell proliferation (Presidential/Congressional Commission 1997).

In the absence of a threshold, slope and curvature of dose-response functions are critical for assessing low-dose effects. If the dose-response function is convex to the origin, or sublinear, at low doses, then risk declines rapidly as exposure falls. But risk is proportional to dose if the function is linear. Current models of genotoxicity imply low-dose linearity, with irreversible DNA damage proportional to the amount of a carcinogen in contact with a cell.

Assessing and Quantifying Toxicity

The rodent bioassay is prominent among methods used to assess toxicity. Bioassays are classified by temporal pattern of exposure (acute, subchronic or chronic) and/or by type of toxicity. For example, chronic studies often focus on carcinogenicity, while assessments of reproductive toxicity (which includes adverse effects on reproductive systems including alterations in organs, endocrine systems or pregnancy outcomes) often span two generations of animals. Bioassays usually are not designed to test for a specific toxic effect hypothesized in advance, such as development of cancer in a particular organ, but rather search for any toxic effects a substance may produce.

Owing to variability among organisms, bioassays usually test animals of both sexes, and often involve more than one species. To support assessment of dose-response functions, two or more doses are used. For testing carcinogenicity, only high doses are administered: low incidence makes use of low doses impractical. As a rule of thumb, the number of animals required for testing equals three times the inverse of the incidence rate (Philp 1995). Cancer incidences at low exposure on the order of 10^{-4} to 10^{-6} imply that tens of thousands or even millions of animals would have to be tested (Kamrin 1988). Such tests are plainly impractical, and therefore high doses are used to induce cancer in 30 to 70 per cent of animals tested. One treatment group is administered an extremely high dose to assess the potential for carcinogenicity. This 'expected maximum tolerated dose' or EMTD is the highest dose not resulting in serious toxicity (for example, excess mortality) other than cancer. A common procedure has been to administer one-half the EMTD to a second treatment group, but revised guidelines recently proposed by US EPA (1996a) call for two additional treatment groups at doses below the EMTD. Specifically, the guidelines call for three treatment groups and one control group each including 50 animals of each sex, tested for 18 to 24 months.

There are two general approaches to assessing dose-response functions. Biomechanical models simulate toxicity mechanisms, while empirical curve-fitting models simply fit observed data. Various measures used to summarize dose-response functions are shown in Table 2.3. For threshold chemicals, the critical measure is the NOAEL (no observed adverse effect level), defined as the highest dose at which no deleterious effects are observed (or the LOAEL if a 'no effect' dose is not detected). Exclusive focus on the NOAEL has been criticized, however, because it is a point estimate conveying no information about the slope of the dose-response function or about variability in responses, factors that affect confidence in the NOAEL as a threshold. If the dose-response function is steep or toxic responses highly variable across subjects, exposures slightly above the NOAEL may cause significant toxicity.

Table 2.3   Summarizing dose-response quantification

Abbreviation	Description
NOAEL	(No observed adverse effect level): The highest exposure level without statistically or biologically significant increases in frequency or severity of adverse effects
LOAEL	(Lowest observed adverse effect level): The lowest exposure level with statistically or biologically significant increases in frequency or severity of adverse effects
ED_{10}	(Effective dose – 10): The dose estimated to produce the toxic effect in 10 per cent of test subjects (quantal response), or to produce 10 per cent of the maximal effect (graded response)
LED_{10}	The lower 95 per cent confidence interval on the ED_{10}
q_1	The estimated slope of the dose-response function in the linearized multistage assessment

An alternative to the NOAEL is a 'benchmark dose' such as the LED_{10}. The LED_{10} is the lower limit of the 95 per cent confidence interval surrounding the ED_{10}, which in turn is the dose estimated to cause toxicity in 10 per cent of subjects tested. The LED_{10} accounts for variability in responses and adjusts for sample sizes and other features of study design. For example, larger samples would tend to yield lower estimates of the NOAEL, but would have narrower confidence intervals as well. Also, the LED_{10} applies to functions with or without thresholds, because its estimation does not hinge on absence of an effect.

The major problem in quantifying the dose-response functions for carcinogens is extrapolating from high doses used in bioassays to the low doses to which humans are exposed. Curve-fitting models familiar to economists, such as probit and logit, have been used for extrapolation, as have biomechanical models. Most federal agencies in the US have used 'linear multistage assessment'. The multistage model assumes that development of cancer requires a sequence of steps and yields a dose-response function of the form:

$$P(d) = 1 - \exp[-(q_o + q_1 d + q_2 d^2 + \ldots + q_k d^k)]$$

where P denotes probability of cancer at dose d, q_i, $i = 1, \ldots, k$ are parameters, and k represents the lower of the number of dose groups or the number of biological stages of carcinogenesis. The slope of this function at low doses is easily verified to be q_1, a constant, and therefore the function is linear at low doses. The linearized assessment, then, forces $q_2, \ldots, q_k$ to be zero.

SCIENTIFIC UNCERTAINTIES IN TOXICITY ASSESSMENTS

Scientific uncertainties in toxicity assessment arise from several sources. Three critical extrapolations are subject to great uncertainty: (i) animal-to-human extrapolation, (ii) high-to-low dose extrapolation, and (iii) route-to-route extrapolation. Additional uncertainties concern human variability (including differences between adults and children), effects of multiple and cumulative exposures, and significance levels of statistical tests. This section outlines uncertainties and reviews evidence bearing on them.

Animal-to-human Extrapolation

Extrapolating results of animal bioassays to estimate human risks raises two basic questions. First, what do results for animals imply for humans? Second, if results differ between two animal species, what can be inferred about human risk? Qualitatively, both questions concern whether results of toxicity tests in animals carry over to humans. Quantitatively, the issue is comparability of dose-response functions between animals and humans.

Fundamental biological mechanisms are similar among closely related organisms like mammals (Grobstein 1981), but there are many potentially relevant differences in anatomy and physiology. Rats, for example, have a forestomach, breathe exclusively through the nose and have a different anatomy of the lung and a more permeable skin than do humans. Differences between humans and animals are particularly striking for assessing reproductive and developmental toxicity, because reproduction and development differ in fundamental ways between humans and laboratory animals. On the other hand, mechanisms of carcinogenesis through DNA alterations appear the same across species.

The concordance (proportion of test results in agreement, whether positive or negative) between rats and mice in carcinogenicity assays is 0.70 (Lave et al. 1988), suggesting a lower concordance between rodents and humans. Experimental results indicate that all 23 recognized human carcinogens are carcinogenic in laboratory animals, with tumours occurring at the same site in humans and animals in 18 cases (Presidential/Congressional Commission 1997). Thus, the sensitivity (proportion of human carcinogens found to be carcinogenic in tests, 'true positives') of animal bioassays for carcinogenicity is quite high. But the value of a test also depends on its specificity (proportion of chemicals not carcinogenic to humans found to be not carcinogenic in tests, 'true negatives'). For example, a test that labelled all chemicals as carcinogenic would necessarily identify all human carcinogens, and thus be 100 per cent sensitive, though its specificity would be low. Of chemicals tested in the National Toxicology Program, 65 per cent are rodent carcinogens (Lave et al. 1988), suggesting that high sensitivity may arise partly from a high rate of positive results. In particular, one strain of mice is widely used in carcinogenicity bioassays because of its tendency to develop tumours in response to a variety of agents, possibly leading to many false positives (Philp 1995).

While qualitative implications of animal bioassays for human toxicity are not fully resolved, quantitative extrapolation also is controversial. Interspecies adjustment of dose is required to adjust for differences in size, pharmacokinetics and length of life, and the conversion factor chosen substantially affects final risk estimates (Hertz-Picciotto 1995). Even after interspecies adjustments, dose-response functions differ markedly among experimental animals (Grobstein 1981), and the species most relevant for human extrapolation usually is unknown.

An additional complicating factor is that human variability in susceptibility exceeds the variability in laboratory animals bred for genetic similarity. Thus, even if it were known that humans and animals were on average equally susceptible, the most sensitive human likely would be more sensitive than the most sensitive animal. This difference hinders estimation of low-dose effects and threshold levels in humans.

High-dose to Low-dose Extrapolation

High- to low-dose extrapolation is a second major source of scientific uncertainty, particularly for carcinogenicity assessments. Critics have argued that testing animals at the EMTD and other high doses causes elevated rates of cell reproduction to repair tissue damage. Rapid cell proliferation raises chances for spontaneous mutations leading to cancer. While chronic cellular damage is known to induce cancer in some cases, it appears doubtful that high doses in themselves cause many laboratory cancers (US EPA 1996a). In fact, most carcinogens identified by the National Toxicology Program induce tumours in organs without cellular toxicity; cellular toxicity usually is not observed at one-half the EMTD, though increased tumour incidence usually is; and toxicity or cell proliferation often occurs without carcinogenicity.

While a chemical-inducing cancer at high doses is thought to be carcinogenic at low doses, its relative degree of carcinogenicity depends on the dose-response function. High doses are routinely extrapolated downward by two or three orders of magnitude (Hertz-Picciotto 1995) and sometimes even by six orders of magnitude (Kimm et al. 1981). Different models fitting observed data equally well (recall that only two or three doses may be administered) may predict risks at low doses that differ by orders of magnitude. Empirical evidence bearing on the accuracy of these extrapolations is available only for a few chemicals, but it seems that risk predictions are fairly accurate. Researchers have used low-dose extrapolation to predict human risks at exposure levels lying between high laboratory doses and low environmental exposures, and resulting estimates are reasonably close to excess cancer mortality among exposed humans (Hertz-Picciotto 1995).

Route-to-route Extrapolation

Route-to-route extrapolation is required when humans are exposed through more or different routes than are experimental animals. For example, pesticides may enter through ingestion, inhalation or absorption. Air pollution may be inhaled, or after deposition may be ingested or absorbed dermally. Animal experiments rarely cover all possible routes of exposure; air exposure studies are particularly difficult and expensive to conduct for animals (Kamrin 1988). Yet data obtained from one route of exposure may not indicate even qualitatively the toxicity associated with other routes, owing to pharmacokinetic differences at different portals of entry (Philp 1995). Moreover, there is no generally accepted method for quantitative extrapolation from one route to another.

Multiple and Cumulative Exposures

Uncertainty arises about effects of chemical mixtures, because humans are exposed to a variety of chemicals, while toxicity assessments usually are conducted on a chemical-by-chemical basis. Effects of chemical mixtures may be antagonistic (less toxic than the sum of individual chemicals' toxicity), additive (as toxic as the sum), or synergistic (more toxic than the sum).

Advocates of stricter regulation express concern about possible synergistic effects, but available evidence generally fails to support this fear. Effects of chemical mixtures appear to be antagonistic or additive at low doses, though possibly synergistic at high doses. Giving laboratory animals low doses of chemicals with different toxicity mechanisms, or different target organs, seems to cause no cumulative effect beyond that induced by the chemicals separately (Presidential/Congressional Commission 1997). Chemicals with similar mechanisms and target organs usually show antagonism. For example, prior exposure to dioxin reduces response rates to a second carcinogen. As an example of synergism at high doses, the relative risk of lung cancer mortality from smoking is about five, while the relative risk from occupational exposure to asbestos is in the 10 to 12 range. The risk from both exposures is not 15 to 17, however, but 50 to 60.

Effects in Children

Health risks to children from exposure to toxic chemicals may differ qualitatively or quantitatively from risks to adults because of differences in pharmacokinetic and pharmacodynamic processes (Bearer 1995). Yet little evidence exists on the unique susceptibility of children, or on whether current animal models and animal-to-human extrapolation methods adequately capture pharmacokinetic processes in children.

Statistical Significance

Problems arise in assessing actual levels of statistical significance when bioassays do not hypothesize a specific effect (for example, a tumour in a particular organ) in advance, but rather search for any adverse effect that may occur (Lave 1982). An increase in tumour incidence for one sex–species–site combination in a typical two-species assessment that is significant at the 1 per cent level when viewed as a single hypothesis test only, implies a significance level of 7–8 per cent once the multiple comparisons are accounted for (US EPA 1996a).

Compound Effect of Uncertainties

The compound effect of these uncertainties produces orders-of-magnitude uncertainties in the assessment of human health risk. Toxicologists concede that toxicity assessment is 'rather inexact' (Kamrin 1988), or for low-level exposures 'very inexact' (Philp 1995). Bioassays also are expensive and time-consuming, implying that resources are unavailable to test any but a few chemicals. For example, the typical two-year, two-species carcinogenicity bioassay cost $1 million in 1991, and required five years to execute from preparation through data analysis (Philp 1995). Human health risks from most chemicals remain unquantified.

FROM TOXICOLOGY TO POLICY: ANALYSIS AND MANAGEMENT OF RISK

Despite scientific uncertainty in estimating human health risks, government agencies must decide whether and how to regulate potentially hazardous chemicals. Regulatory decisions will not be ideal by any criterion, if only because the actual frequencies of adverse human health effects at low exposures remain unknown. If risk is overestimated, regulations may be too stringent, causing consumers and businesses to forgo beneficial uses of products without appreciable improvements in public health. If risk is underestimated, on the other hand, lax regulations may allow frequent and severe illness.

Policy analysis in the US generally follows the risk assessment/ management paradigm set out by the National Research Council (1983). Risk assessment bridges the gap between science and policy: it is a systematic characterization of human health risk based on available scientific evidence concerning toxicity and exposure. Risk management, in turn, concerns policy design and implementation. A broadly accurate if somewhat simplistic view is that risk management integrates economic and social concerns with the scientific output of risk assessment.

This division of labour may suggest that risk assessors would provide risk managers with the most scientifically defensible estimate of actual risks faced by the population, along with measures of the variability or uncertainty in estimated risks. Risk managers then would choose how to regulate, balancing protection of public health against other social objectives. Given the imprecision of risk estimates, risk managers often might choose to err on the side of protecting public health, implementing more stringent regulations than would be justified by the best estimate of risk. In some circumstances, however, risk managers might regulate less stringently.

The actual conduct of risk assessment precludes any such rational division of labour. Risk assessments often fail to produce the most scientifically defensible estimates of risks faced by different subpopulations, but rather provide risk managers with upper-bound, worst-case estimates. The intentional overstatement of risk almost assures that risk management decisions will err on the side of protecting public health. While many would view this outcome as desirable, the process of reaching it blurs the distinction between science and policy. The measurement of uncertainty is a scientific issue of risk assessment, but making prudent allowance for uncertainty is a policy decision that properly belongs to risk management.

Four Components of Risk Assessment

Risk assessment in the US consists of the four steps shown in Table 2.4. According to risk assessment guidelines, priority is given to studies of humans over studies of animals (US EPA 1993, 1996a) in hazard assessment (addressing qualitatively whether, how and in what circumstances a substance may adversely affect human health) and in dose-response assessment (concerning quantitative relationships between exposure and adverse effects). As a practical matter, however, human data often are unavailable or are judged to be inadequate (US EPA 1993), particularly if they do not support toxicity (US EPA 1996a). According to proposed guidelines for cancer risk assessment (ibid.), positive results (favouring carcinogenicity) from either a human or an animal study establish that a substance is a human carcinogen. Animal data with negative results for two species, absent contradictory findings, establish that a substance is not likely to be a human carcinogen, but negative results from a human study are insufficient. Animal data have been favoured by other agencies as well. The Food and Drug Administration (FDA) approved aspartame as a sweetener on the basis of low toxicity in laboratory animals, despite the absence of any substantial human data. Yet cyclamates were banned on the basis of carcinogenicity in rodents, despite epidemiological evidence of a long history of safe use in humans. Hence, to date the 'critical study' with most influence on a risk assessment usually is an animal study (US EPA 1993), and thus toxicology often provides the key data for the first two steps of risk assessment.

Table 2.4   The four steps of risk assessment in the United States

Step	Description
1. Hazard assessment	Determine whether/how an agent may harm human health
2. Dose-response assessment	Quantify the relationship between exposure to an agent and the frequency or severity of toxic effects
3. Exposure assessment	Estimate the degree of human exposure to the agent
4. Risk characterization	Summarize the evidence concerning the risk to human health from exposure to the agent

Epidemiology, the study of disease in human populations, is the main alternative to toxicology, although controlled laboratory studies of humans are possible for minor and reversible toxic effects (US EPA 1998a). Epidemiology has linked several well-known toxicants to human effects, including tobacco to lung cancer, asbestos to lung cancer and other lung diseases, benzene to leukaemia, and vinyl chloride to a rare liver cancer (Kamrin 1988; Philp 1995). Epidemiology plainly avoids the need for animal-to-human extrapolation, and also may mitigate uncertainties from unknown human variability and low-dose extrapolations: a large, representative sample might span most of the range of human variability, while observed exposures typically are much lower than those used in laboratory animals. Still, epidemiological data often come from occupational exposures of workers, a non-representative sample with relatively high exposure. Epidemiological studies have trouble measuring exposure accurately and controlling for concurrent exposures and other confounding influences, and thus are less able to detect toxic effects and to establish causality.

In view of the imprecision of predicting human risk from toxicological data, a major challenge of risk assessment is addressing uncertainties in the scientific evidence. As discussed below, risk assessments apply the precautionary principle of protecting public health when in doubt. In other words, the treatment of uncertainty is designed to reduce chances that risk is understated – with the inevitable result of increasing chances that risk is overstated.

Hazard Assessment

To determine whether a substance threatens human health, risk assessors often must address uncertainties about one or more of the three critical extrapolations: (i) from animals to humans, (ii) from high to low doses, or (iii) from one route to another. The treatment of each uncertainty favours a finding of toxicity. Animal toxicity is taken as evidence of toxicity in humans, even when the chemical is toxic to only one of two species tested. In assessing cancer risk, a key question is whether carcinogenesis at high doses implies carcinogenesis at low doses. Risk assessment guidelines answer this question in the affirmative, an assumption that is consistent with available evidence for genotoxic carcinogens, but not for epigenetic carcinogens such as dioxin. Uncertainty concerning route-to-route extrapolation is resolved qualitatively by assuming that toxicity by one route implies toxicity by any other (US EPA 1993), at least if the chemical is absorbed to give an internal dose (US EPA 1996a).

Dose-response Assessment

To quantify relationships between exposures and adverse effects, risk assessors again must confront uncertainty in animal-to-human and high-to-low-dose extrapolation. Issues of route-to-route extrapolation, and of quantifying effects of multiple exposures or chemical mixtures also may arise. The treatment of these uncertainties favours overestimation of risk. There is no generally accepted method for quantitative extrapolation between routes. Multiple exposures and chemical mixtures often are ignored, when considered effects are assumed additive. However, the Food Quality Protection Act of 1996 requires the EPA to assess all routes of exposure, and the cumulative effects of exposure to all substances with toxicity mechanisms similar to the pesticide in question.

Animal data usually are available for more than one species, raising the question of which species to use in extrapolating to humans. Ideally, a biological rationale would indicate the species most representative of human health responses (US EPA 1993, 1996b), but such a rationale often is lacking. The most sensitive species tested then is chosen for the extrapolation. The next step is to adjust the experimental dose for physical and biological differences between the animal species and humans. Preferably, pharmacokinetic information for the chemical in question would be used for interspecies adjustment of dose, but as a practical matter this information is rarely available. The resulting uncertainty is resolved in a manner thought to be health-protective, through the use of default conversion factors (US EPA 1996a). The default adjustment used by the EPA for oral ingestion (ibid.), for example, is to multiply the animal dose (mg/kg) by a factor of body weight to the 3/4 power. The rationale is that physiological processes, and daily intakes of food and water, tend to maintain proportionality with body weight to the 3/4 power.

Once the species is chosen and the dose adjusted, dose-response assessment differs according to assumptions about the presence of a threshold and the slope and curvature of the function. For non-cancer effects, thresholds usually are assumed. Dose-response functions may be linear (as they often are for neurotoxins, US EPA 1998a) or non-linear (as often assumed for reproductive toxicants, US EPA 1996b). A summary measure of the dose-response function like the NOAEL or the LED_{10} is deflated, typically by two orders of magnitude, to compute a reference dose, RfD (or a reference concentration, RfC, for inhalation):

$$RfD = NOAEL \div (UF \times MF)$$

An RfD also can be defined using the LED_{10} in place of the NOAEL in this formula. The term *UF* represents an order-of-magnitude uncertainty factor. As shown in Table 2.5, *UF* = 10 when extrapolating from data on humans, to account for variation in sensitivity not reflected in the sample (10H). When extrapolating from animal data, *UF* = 100, reflecting an additional order of magnitude uncertainty (10A) to account for potentially greater sensitivity in humans than in animals. The term *MF* represents a 'modifying factor' with a default value of unity ($0 < MF \leq 10$) that is adjusted according to professional judgement about scientific uncertainties at hand. Thus, the RfD is typically 100 times less than the NOAEL or the LED_{10}. If LOAEL is used, another 10L uncertainty factor is used to make the uncertainty factor 1000, and if no chronic exposure data are available yet another 10S safety factor is applied.

Table 2.5   Uncertainty and modifying factors used in environmental risk assessment

Factor	Description	Used when extrapolating from	Used to account for
10H	Tenfold uncertainty factor	Prolonged exposure/ healthy humans	Variation in human sensitivity
10A	Additional tenfold uncertainty factor	Long-term exposure of animals	Possibly greater sensitivity in humans
10S	Additional tenfold uncertainty factor	Less than chronic exposure	NOAEL may be higher for chronic exposure
10L	Additional tenfold uncertainty factor	LOAEL instead of NOAEL	Unknown gap between NOAEL and LOAEL
MF	Modifying factor $0 < MF \leq 10$	Not based on extrapolation	Scientific uncertainty in study and data

These factors are arbitrary adjustments thought to span the range of scientific uncertainty with a margin of safety: they are not based on scientific evidence that humans are ten times more sensitive, or ten times more variable in sensitivity, than the most sensitive animal species. Moreover, the NOAEL used in computing the RfD pertains to the 'critical effect', which is the toxic outcome with the lowest NOAEL. Presumably, avoiding the critical effect implies avoidance of other toxic effects with higher thresholds. Together with the uncertainty factors, this means that exposure to the RfD is unlikely to pose appreciable risk of any adverse effect for even the most sensitive humans. In general, the RfD is similar to a measure of 'acceptable daily intake' (ADI) used in other countries. EPA defines the RfD as an estimate (with uncertainty spanning perhaps an order of magnitude) of a daily exposure to the human population (including sensitive subgroups) that is likely to be without an appreciable risk of deleterious effects. An acute RfD pertains to the absence of adverse effects from a one-day exposure, while a chronic RfD pertains to the absence of chronic effects from daily exposure over a lifetime.

The Food Quality Protection Act of 1996 (FQPA) requires an additional tenfold safety factor to account for potentially greater sensitivity or exposure in children, unless reliable data indicate that a different level is safe for children. Applying a separate safety factor for children in effect removes part of the population that the 10H and 10A factors are meant to protect, and presumably would justify a reduction in those factors.

For cancer, the US EPA assumes linear dose-response functions unless no gene mutations occur and there is conclusive evidence of non-linearity (US EPA 1996a). Under existing guidelines, risk analysis is based on a measure denoted q_1^*. This is the upper 95 per cent confidence interval limit on q_1, the slope of the dose-response function in the linear multistage assessment. New guidelines proposed by the US EPA (1996a) dispense with linear multistage assessment, however, and recommend the simpler but in effect nearly identical procedure of drawing a straight line from a point of departure to the origin (zero dose, zero effect). The guidelines recommend the LED_{10} as the point of departure for extrapolation, for consistency with non-cancer assessments, and because an excess tumour rate of 10 per cent is near the limit of detection. The resulting estimator is believed to be an upper bound, inherently protective of health without any order-of-magnitude adjustments for human variability (US EPA 1996a).

Exposure Assessment

After using toxicological evidence to assess qualitatively the potential of a chemical to harm human health and quantitatively the dose-response function, the third step of risk assessment is estimation of human exposure (US EPA 1992). Human exposures are undoubtedly highly variable. For example, recent concern has focused on potentially higher exposures in children. Relative to size, children eat more food, drink more water, and breathe more air than do adults. Hand-to-mouth activities and proximity to the ground and floor further increase children's exposure to some toxicants.

Data on actual human exposures are expensive to collect and often are unavailable. In the absence of hard data, past risk assessments often relied on a fictitious 'maximum exposed individual', whose unrealistically high exposures strained any appearance of scientific credibility. Now less extreme measures are used (US EPA 1993, 1998b). Where possible, the US EPA attempts to construct distributions of exposure for the population, and draws a 'high-end exposure estimate' from the upper tail of this distribution.

Risk Characterization

A key element of risk characterization is to combine information on the toxicity of a chemical with information on human exposures to assess the need for regulatory concern. For chemicals with threshold effects, a common procedure is to compare the reference dose to the estimated exposure dose (EED). To the extent that the RfD exceeds the EED, regulatory concern is likely to be small. An alternate approach is a 'margin of exposure' (MOE) analysis, indicating the margin by which the 'no effect' dose exceeds the human dose:

$$MOE = NOAEL \div EED.$$

Again, the LED_{10} may be used in place of the NOAEL in this formula. If $MOE > (UF \times MF)$, then RfD > EED. A margin of exposure analysis often is used for threshold effects, and recently proposed guidelines call for its use when credible evidence indicates the cancer dose-response function is non-linear (US EPA 1996a).

For chemicals without threshold effects, risk is characterized as a probability. The probability of developing cancer, P, is expressed as:

$$P = Q \times EED$$

where Q denotes the slope of the dose-response function at low doses (q_1^* from linearized multistage assessment, or the slope of the straight-line extrapolation). This estimate may be compared to some *de minimis* level of risk such as 10^{-6} to assess the need for regulatory concern.

Recent legislation, including the FQPA as well as the Safe Drinking Water Act of 1996, requires consideration of children in conducting risk assessments. Some toxicologists believe that, with the possible exception of neurotoxicity (an adverse change in the structure or function of the central or peripheral nervous system), the differences between children and adults are likely to be greater for exposure than for susceptibility. Yet there is no consensus as to whether current procedures adequately account for the relative susceptibility of children.

TOXICOLOGY, RISK ASSESSMENT AND ECONOMICS

Risk assessment is not designed to provide precise estimates of actual health risks, but rather to determine whether a chemical poses any appreciable risk (Hertz-Picciotto 1995), even to highly exposed, highly susceptible individuals. This viewpoint is difficult to reconcile with the focus on efficiency that characterizes economic perspectives on regulation.

The divergent policy perspectives of economics and risk assessment are reconciled in a variety of ways according to statutory guidelines and discretionary authority of different federal agencies and programmes. At one extreme, some statutes dictate setting health-based standards without consideration of costs or benefits, while other statutes direct agencies to protect health while considering cost or technological feasibility standards. Finally, some statutes allow benefits of using a chemical to be balanced against health risks. Perhaps the most prominent example of a health-based standard is the Delaney clause of the Food, Drug and Cosmetic Act, which directs the FDA to ban any food additive found 'to induce cancer in man or animal'. Under the Clean Air Act, primary, national ambient air quality standards are set to protect public health, including sensitive population groups, with an adequate margin of safety. The Occupational Safety and Health Act allows consideration of feasibility, however, by setting a goal of assuring that no employee suffers material health impairment from regular exposure over a worklife, 'to the extent feasible'. Similar qualifying language appears in the Safe Drinking Water Act, under which maximum contaminant limits are determined on the basis of health considerations only, but standards are set to reflect cost and technological feasibility. Cases where benefits (whether or not expressed in monetary terms) are considered include regulating drugs (as opposed to food additives), where the FDA weighs benefits as well as risks. The Federal Insecticide, Fungicide, Rodenticide Act calls for 'taking benefits into account' in regulating pesticides, although the Food Quality Protection Act of 1996 partly restricts the consideration of benefits.

The importance of economic considerations in regulating toxic chemicals thus varies considerably across agencies and programmes of the US federal government. In cases where economic analysis of regulatory options is warranted, however, it is quite difficult to develop required information from a risk assessment. Two key problems arise. First, measures of risk computed in risk assessments are poorly suited to economic analysis, and second, the uncertainty in risk assessment is so great that the sign of net benefit estimates may change over the range of estimated risk, as shown in Table 2.6. Also, assessments often measure subtle physiological functions that are difficult to value economically, like lung function.

Economic analyses often focus on estimating aggregate benefits of reducing the probability of adverse health effects. Measures such as MOE and RfD are not probabilities, and fail to support estimation of probabilities for small risks unless the dose-response function is linear. Estimating aggregate benefits requires information on the population distribution of risk, or at least the risk faced by the average individual. But risk assessments estimate individual risk, not a population distribution of risk accounting for differences in susceptibility and exposure. The individual risk estimate is not a best estimate of average risk, but instead is an upper-bound estimate for a highly susceptible and/or highly exposed individual. The uncertainty inherent in toxicity assessments

Table 2.6   Problems in using risk assessment results in economic analysis

Output of risk assessment	Desired input for economic analysis
Risk estimate subject to order-of-magnitude uncertainty	Risk estimate whose uncertainty alone does not determine sign of net benefits
Individual risk	Distribution of population risks
Upper-bound estimate of risk	Central estimate of risk
Risk measured as RfD or MOE	Risk measured as probability of adverse effect
Measures of subtle changes in physiological function	Effects meaningful to individuals

further complicates economic analysis: nearly any net benefit estimate will change sign as risk estimates vary by orders of magnitude.

RESIDENTIAL LEAD: A CASE STUDY

The US EPA recently proposed standards for remediation of residential lead hazards. The Agency conducted a risk assessment and an economic analysis of alternative standards to reduce hazards (US EPA 1997, 1998d). The risk assessment and economic analysis are unusually well integrated and perhaps for this reason played a key role in setting the standards. This section presents a case study of the risk assessment and economic analysis. The main intent of this section is not to critique the analyses, but rather to highlight some key issues raised previously, including: (i) the joint use of economic analysis with risk assessment, (ii) how economic analysis can inform policy decisions, even when uncertainty in the underlying risk assessment determines the sign of net benefits, and (iii) the role of children's health in policy.

Background

Toxic effects of lead have been noted since ancient times, and now are well known. Exposure to lead adversely affects the central nervous system, kidneys and red blood cells, and lead poisoning has long been recognized as a particularly serious environmental threat to child health. Children's behaviour increases exposure to lead-contaminated dust and soil, and their developing nervous systems increase their susceptibility to neurotoxic effects. Lead poisoning persists today primarily because of exposure in the home, where lead-based paint remains one of the largest sources of exposure, along with lead in dust and in soil. Although lead-based paint was banned in 1978, many children still live in homes with at least some lead paint. According to data from a 1987 survey of the US housing stock conducted by the Department of Housing and Urban Development (HUD), over 80 per cent of houses in the US have some lead paint (though mostly in small areas). About 15 to 20 per cent exceed federal guidelines for lead in dust or in soil. Similarly, over 80 per cent of public housing units built before 1980 have some lead-based paint.

The Residential Lead-Based Paint Hazard Reduction Act of 1992 (also known as Title X of the Housing and Community Development Act of 1992) established Section 403 of the Toxic Substances Control Act. Section 403 requires the EPA to promulgate regulations to identify hazards from lead-based paint and lead-contaminated dust and soil. The proposed standards do not require property owners to take any action, but rather define conditions under which the EPA recommends action to reduce lead hazards. If a child lives in the home, the EPA recommends remedial action whenever a particular lead hazard exceeds the relevant standard. Separate standards are defined for areas of interior and exterior paint, for dust lead loads and for soil lead concentrations. Each standard is associated with one or two specific interventions to be taken when the lead level exceeds the standard. Effectiveness of interventions is measured by post-intervention lead levels, and duration is measured in years.

Both the risk assessment and economic analysis consider lifetime effects of exposure occurring during childhood, from birth to age six years, over the 50-year period from 1997 to 2046. The risk assessment estimates residential lead levels before and after potential interventions, maps ambient lead levels into blood lead levels, and maps blood lead levels into health effects. The primary health effect considered is reduced IQ, chosen as a surrogate for a variety of neurological effects lacking adequate metrics, and to facilitate economic valuation. The economic analysis provides cost and benefit estimates for each standard considered, with benefits measured as damages avoided by interventions.

Risk Assessment of Residential Lead Hazards (US EPA 1997)

The risk analysis relies on human data, although animal studies generally confirm epidemiological results for lead toxicity. Baseline exposure is modelled using the HUD survey, while baseline blood lead levels are taken from the 1992 National Health and Nutrition Examination Survey. In the absence of intervention, blood lead is assumed to remain at baseline levels, although this assumption seems doubtful in view of recent trends. Regulatory and voluntary actions have produced major reductions in children's blood lead levels in the US. Average blood lead has fallen from over 20 micrograms per decilitre (μ/dl) in 1970, to less than 5 μ/dl today. The currently defined toxic dose is 10 μ/dl. Reducing and finally phasing out lead in gasoline contributed significantly to the decline.

Risk assessors used two models relating blood lead to ambient lead. The Integrated Exposure, Uptake and Biokinetic Model (IEUBK) simulates physical and biological processes, while the 'Empirical' model is a statistical, epidemiological model. Multiplying the change in blood lead from either model by 0.257, based on the results of Schwartz (1994), yields the estimated average change in IQ. The two models differ markedly in predicted changes in blood lead levels and consequent IQ changes. Specifically, the IEUBK model predicts a much larger decrease in blood lead from any given decrease in ambient lead.

Economic Analysis of Residential Lead Standards (US EPA 1998d)

In the economic analysis, interventions are triggered by the birth of a child in a home where the level of lead in soil, floor dust, windowsill dust, exterior paint or interior paint exceeds the corresponding standard. Depending on its duration, the intervention is repeated as necessary to keep lead levels below the standard as long as a child under age six lives in the home. Interventions cease when a young child is no longer present. The analysis uses projected future birth rates and projected demolition rates of housing.

Standards for lead in soil, in floor dust and in windowsill dust are varied while standards for interior and exterior paint are held constant at HUD guidelines. Each standard is compared to the estimated ambient lead level in the home, and the household is assumed to take the intervention appropriate to any standard exceeded. Costs of intervention are estimated based on unit costs. Benefits are estimated by linking the IQ changes predicted by the risk assessment to lifetime earnings, using estimated relationships between IQ and educational attainment, employment and earnings. The analysis also accounted for lead-induced changes in special and compensatory educational costs, but earnings effects of IQ changes amount to 98 per cent of estimated benefits.

The EPA estimates the present value of lifetime earnings of the average US new-born to be about $240 000, while the estimated total effect of IQ on earnings is 2.4 per cent per IQ point, based on the work of Salkever (1995). The total effect includes the direct effect of IQ on earnings, holding schooling and probability of employment constant, as well as indirect effects arising from greater schooling and higher employment probabilities associated with higher IQ. After accounting for costs of additional schooling associated with higher IQ, the EPA estimated that each IQ point is worth about $800 of discounted lifetime earnings.

Table 2.7 summarizes the results where costs and benefits are discounted at 3 per cent. As shown, the sign of estimated net benefits depends on which risk assessment model is applied. At the proposed standards, net benefits are $107.2 billion (1995$) based on the IEUBK model, and –$10.5 billion based on the Empirical model. The greater responsiveness of blood lead to ambient lead in the IEUBK model leads to higher marginal benefits at any ambient lead level, which in turn causes the standards maximizing net benefits to be much tighter. Maximal net benefits remain negative under the Empirical model.

Table 2.7   Results of economic analysis of residential lead standards

	IEUBK model results		Empirical model results	
	Standards maximizing net benefits	Proposed standards	Standards maximizing net benefits	Proposed standards
Floor dust standard	40 μ/ft^2	50 μ/ft^2	80 μ/ft^2	50 μ/ft^2
Window sill dust standard	100 μ/ft^2	250 μ/ft^2	310 μ/ft^2	250 μ/ft^2
Soil standard	250 ppm	2000 ppm	4350 ppm	2000 ppm
Net benefit	$173.2 bn	$107.2 bn	–$8.9 bn	–$10.5 bn

Several features of the economic analysis warrant comment. First, the analysis is somewhat misplaced: the policy option chosen by the EPA is information provision, not mandatory remediation, yet costs and benefits were estimated for interventions. Second, some key assumptions skew costs and benefits estimates. The EPA assumed that all households needing intervention undertake it coincident with the birth of a child, biasing net benefits upward. Ignoring the trend decline in blood lead also overstates benefits, while neglecting quality-of-life impacts of IQ as well as other health effects of lead understates benefits. Third, the importance of possible biases should not be overstated, because the analysis did not aim to estimate the absolute level of net benefits, but to compare net benefits of different standards.

Finally, although the uncertainty in the risk assessment precludes precise determination of the standards maximizing net benefits, or even the sign of net benefits, the economic analysis is informative about policy options and seems to have played a major role in setting the proposed standards. The proposed standards lie between the standards that maximize net benefits for the two risk assessment models, and proposed standards seem to have been chosen with attention to the slope and curvature of the net benefit function. For example, more stringent soil standards boost estimated costs markedly, and at an increasing rate, in both risk assessment models. Similarly, the floor dust standard is set quite near the level that would maximize total benefits under the IEUBK model. This outcome makes economic sense because the cost function for floor dust abatement in both risk assessment models, as well as the benefit function in the Empirical model, is relatively flat.

CONCLUSIONS

Toxicological evidence yields uncertain predictions of human health risk from exposure to potentially hazardous chemicals in the environment. Risk assessments handle the uncertainty based on the precautionary principle of promoting health protection, by minimizing chances that risk will be understated at the expense of likely overstatement. The precautionary principle is at odds with the economic approach of balancing costs and benefits of reducing health risks, and measures of risk produced in risk assessment often are not conducive to economic analysis. Moreover, the uncertainty in estimated risk may preclude precise estimation of net benefits, even apart from uncertainties in benefit estimation. None the less, recent work supporting proposed residential lead standards shows that it is possible to combine economic analysis and risk assessment to inform policy decisions.

Several factors explain the successful combination of risk assessment and economic analysis of residential lead hazards, and the apparent impact the two analyses had on policy decisions. The risk assessment estimated health benefits in an economically meaningful metric (IQ) without arbitrarily inflating results to account for uncertainty. Divergences between IQ changes predicted by the two risk assessment models were less than orders of magnitude. The economic analysis did not aim for an up-or-down policy decision based on the sign of net benefits, but sought instead to compare the consequences of policy options.

It seems doubtful, however, whether close collaboration between risk assessors and economists will be the norm in the immediate future. While economists may hope that risk assessment methods will change to suit the needs of economic analysis – primarily by estimating population risks as probabilities of health effects that individuals value – it may also be useful to adopt economic methods to the output of risk assessment. It would be interesting to determine, for example, properties of a social welfare function that rationalizes the precautionary principle. More practically, economists could investigate using RfDs or MOEs to estimate probabilities (or, possibly, directly valuing different thresholds), and could develop methods to convert measurements of physiological function into health status attributes meaningful to individuals.

REFERENCES

Agency for Toxic Substances and Disease Registry (ATSDR) (1997), *Healthy Children – Toxic Environments*, Atlanta, GA: US Department of Health and Human Services, Public Health Service.

Bearer, Cynthia F. (1995), 'How are children different from adults?', *Environmental Health Perspectives*, **103**: 7–12.

Grobstein, Clifford (1981), 'Saccharin: a scientist's view', in Robert W. Crandall and Lester B. Lave (eds), *The Scientific Basis of Health and Safety Regulation*, Washington, DC: The Brookings Institution, pp. 117–29.

Hertz-Picciotto, Irva (1995), 'Environmental risk assessment', in Evelyn O. Talbott and Gunther F. Craun (eds), *Introduction to Environmental Epidemiology*, Boca Raton, FL: CRC Press, pp. 23–38.

Kamrin, Michael A. (1988), *Toxicology: A Primer on Toxicology Principles and Applications*, Chelsea, MI: Lewis Publishers.

Kimm, Victor J., Arnold M. Kuzmack and David W. Schnare (1981), 'Waterborne carcinogens: a regulator's view', in Robert W. Crandall and Lester B. Lave (eds), *The Scientific Basis of Health and Safety Regulation*, Washington, DC: The Brookings Institution, pp. 229–49.

Lave, Lester B. (1982), 'Methods of risk assessment', in Lester B. Lave (ed.), *Quantitative Risk Assessment in Regulation*, Washington, DC: The Brookings Institution, pp. 23–54.

Lave, L.B., F.K. Ennever, H.S. Rosenkranz and G.S. Omenn (1988), 'Information value of the rodent bioassay', *Nature*, **33**(6): 631–3.

National Research Council (1983), *Risk Assessment in the Federal Government: Managing the Process*, National Academy of Sciences, Washington, DC: National Academy Press.

Philp, Richard B. (1995), *Environmental Hazards and Human Health*, Boca Raton, FL: CRC Press.

Presidential/Congressional Commission on Risk Assessment and Risk Management (1997), *Risk Assessment and Risk Management in Regulatory Decision-making*, Final Report, Vol. 2, Washington, DC.

Salkever, D. (1995), 'Updated estimates of earnings benefits from reduced exposure of children to environmental lead', *Environmental Research*, **70**: 1–6.

Schwartz, J. (1994), 'Low-level lead exposure and children's IQ: a meta-analysis and search for a threshold', *Environmental Research*, **65**: 42–55.

US Environmental Protection Agency (1992), *Guidelines for Exposure Assessment*, Washington, DC, Federal Register 57: 22888-22938.

US Environmental Protection Agency (1993), 'Reference dose (RfD): description and use in health risk assessments', Background Document 1A, Integrated Risk Information System, Washington, DC.

US Environmental Protection Agency (1996a), *Proposed Guidelines for Carcinogen Risk Assessment*, Office of Research and Development, Washington, DC, EPA/600/P-92/003C.

US Environmental Protection Agency (1996b), *Guidelines for Reproductive Toxicity Risk Assessment*, Office of Research and Development, Washington, DC, EPA/630/R-96/009.

US Environmental Protection Agency (1997), *Risk Assessment for the Section 403 Rulemaking*, Chemical Management Division, Office of Pollution Prevention and Toxics, Washington, DC.

US Environmental Protection Agency (1998a), *Guidelines for Neurotoxicity Risk Assessment*, Washington, DC, EPA/630/R-95/001Fa.

US Environmental Protection Agency (1998b), 'EPA's risk assessment process for tolerance reassessment', Office of Pesticide Programs, Staff Paper No. 25.

US Environmental Protection Agency (1998c), *The EPA Children's Environmental Health Yearbook*, Office of Children's Health Protection, Washington, DC.

US Environmental Protection Agency (1998d), 'Economic Analysis of Toxic Substances Control Act Section 403: Hazard Standards', Draft Analysis for Proposed Rulemaking, Economic and Policy Analysis Branch, Economics, Exposure and Technology Division, Office of Pollution Prevention and Toxics, Washington, DC.

3. Calculating morbidity benefits from reducing air pollution: a Spanish case study

Richard Dubourg and
María Xosé Vázquez Rodríguez*

INTRODUCTION

Air pollution issues have recently come to the forefront of discussions about environmental policy. The principal reasons for this have been twofold. The first is the emergence of a growing body of epidemiological evidence linking poor air quality to substantial numbers of premature deaths and cases of acute illness (for example, Schwartz 1994a; Pope et al. 1995). The second stems from the emergence of economic evidence indicating the high value individuals place on reducing risks of morbidity and premature mortality (for example, Viscusi 1993; Johnson et al. 1997). These two factors combine to produce high estimates of the (health) cost associated with air pollution, particularly in urban areas, and the consequent high estimates of the value of air pollution control programmes (for example, Pearce and Crowards 1996; Ostro 1994).

In this chapter, we present results from one of the first economic studies of the health costs of air pollution in Spain. This uses the results of a survey, conducted in the city of Vigo, in which people are asked about the value of preventing respiratory illness. This survey employs a design specifically intended to make the results compatible with existing epidemiological 'endpoints' for air pollution-related morbidity. We show how the survey results can be combined with data on current air pollution levels in Vigo, and a selection of epidemiological 'exposure-response' relationships, to produce estimates of the morbidity costs of air pollution. It is thus possible to estimate the potential benefits from air pollution control in Vigo. We conclude by highlighting the strengths and weaknesses of the work.

* The support of the European Commission DGXII (project number ENV4-CT96-0234) is gratefully acknowledged.

AIR QUALITY AND AIR POLLUTION IN VIGO

Vigo is the most populated city in the region of Galicia, an area located on the north-west coast of Spain. The metropolitan area of the city extends over 3500 km^2, with nearly 400 000 inhabitants. The population density in the city centre is well above the European Union average, at over 2400 inhabitants/ km^2. Perhaps the most remarkable feature of Vigo has been its rate of population growth over the last 150 years – the population size has increased from 8214 people in 1857 to about 400 000 people in the 1990s.

Fast rates of industrial and economic development and population growth have resulted in serious air quality problems, mainly relating to particulate matter (PM_{10}). The main sources of the high PM_{10} concentrations are heavy industrial traffic around the harbour and commuter traffic from the outskirts to the city centre. The geographic location of Vigo, on a hillside down to the sea, inhibits the dispersal of pollution. This is compounded by an infrastructure system which restricts traffic circulation and leads to congestion in the city centre.

The Local Network for Atmospheric Pollution Monitoring and Control publishes annual figures of PM_{10} concentrations in Vigo. Figure 3.1 shows annual daily concentrations of PM_{10} ($\mu g/m^3$) measured at seven monitoring stations located around the city. Over the 1990–97 period, there has been a slight downward trend in average concentrations from just above 100 mg/m^3 at the start of the period to about 75 $\mu g/m^3$ in 1997. The highest overall mean concentration was recorded in the first two years of the period, coinciding with the years of lowest rainfall. However, this overall picture masks the situation at individual stations. In particular, station E2 shows no significant decline over the period and remains the location with the highest mean concentration (137 $\mu g/m^3$ over the period). Station E1 began the period with equally high readings, but these seem to have fallen quite significantly over the seven years. Both of these stations are located in the city centre, and record some of the highest traffic densities in the city. On the other hand, station E5, which records some of the lowest PM_{10} concentrations, has higher traffic density than either of these two stations. This indicates the importance of local geography in determining the extent to which pollution can be dispersed.

The US Environmental Protection Agency's guideline for annual mean daily concentrations of total suspended particulates (TSP) is 75 $\mu g/m^3$. Pearce and Crowards (1996) state a conversion factor of $PM_{10} = 0.55$TSP. Hence, the EPA standard translates into a PM_{10} figure of 41.25 $\mu g/m^3$. Thus, according to this standard, it appears that particulate pollution was very high in Vigo at the beginning of the decade. Though it has since declined, at the majority of locations concentrations remain far in excess of the US guideline.

There are fewer data available on the levels of other pollutants in Vigo.

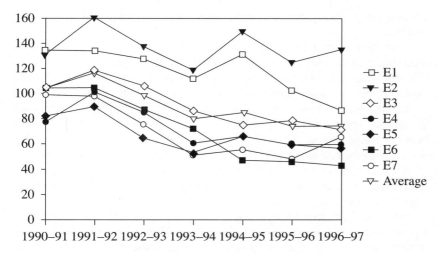

Figure 3.1   Annual daily mean concentrations of PM_{10} ($\mu g/m^3$)

Ozone monitoring has commenced only very recently (January 1998) and as yet no data are available. This is unfortunate since many of the respiratory illnesses that have been linked to air pollution have been linked to ozone in particular (see below). Although there is information on the levels of nitrogen oxides (which can be related to ozone formation), this is insufficient to predict ozone levels. Therefore, in this study we will concentrate on estimating the number and costs of illness which can be attributed to PM_{10}.

THE MORBIDITY EFFECTS OF AIR POLLUTION – CLINICAL AND EPIDEMIOLOGICAL EVIDENCE

The potential effects of air pollution on human health have long been recognized – particularly in the light of serious acute pollution events such as the London smog of 1952, when an estimated 4000 fatalities occurred in the space of just a few days. However, it is only with the arrival of relatively recent epidemiological evidence (supported by clinical experiments) that the full range of possible health impacts of air pollution has been appreciated. The role of air pollution in provoking bronchitis (Sunyer et al. 1993; Schwartz 1994b) and asthma attacks (Cody et al. 1992; Schwartz et al. 1993) may be expected, but the idea that it might also play a role in minor illnesses such as colds, influenza and symptoms of coughing and eye irritation (Ostro 1987; Krupnick et al. 1990) might be more surprising. Particulate matter, ozone and sulphur dioxide have all been implicated, whether due to their effects as irritants, or because they penetrate deep into the lung and affect lung function.

Some indication of the current respiratory health situation in Vigo can be ascertained from two sources: the Spanish Health Service register of those illnesses which it is compulsory to report; and the Hospital Morbidity Survey published by the National Institute of Statistics. The latter contains statistics for the province of Pontevedra (in Galicia), of which Vigo is the main city. Pontevedra appears to have a much higher incidence of respiratory illnesses than the rest of Galicia (8.5 per 1000 people compared with an average of 6.0 per 1000 for the rest of Galicia). The incidence of pneumonia is 1.26 per 1000 in Pontevedra compared with 0.84 per 1000 elsewhere. The corresponding figures for acute and chronic bronchitis and asthma combined are 1.1 and 1.0, respectively (all figures for 1993).

The register of illness, which it is compulsory for clinics (not hospitals) to report, reveals the importance of respiratory illnesses relative to the total number of reported illnesses. Of about 100 000 reported illnesses in 1996, two-thirds were acute respiratory infections[1] and a further fifth were cases of influenza. Moreover, clinics located in the urban centre report a much higher number of respiratory illnesses than those located further away from the most-polluted areas. For example, a clinic located about 50 metres from monitoring station E2 (one of the pollution black spots) reported 16 596 acute respiratory infections – over 25 per cent of the total number of acute respiratory infections reported in the Vigo area.

In this study, we are mainly concerned with acute morbidity impacts that have been examined in a number of previous epidemiological studies. These were selected for a number of different reasons – in particular, because they relate to those relationships which are well established and potentially significant from both a health and an economic perspective. They span the range of endpoints, from the very serious (hospital admission for respiratory illness) to the relatively mild (daily symptoms of sneezing or coughing). They also represent relationships which can be 'monetized' for use in integrated assessments of air pollution damage and control. Table 3.1 summarizes the endpoints selected and the associated relationships. The coefficients given for each endpoint represent the number of expected cases occurring for each $\mu g/m^3$ of PM_{10} in a population of 100 000 (column 4). Thus, the study by Schwartz (1994b) estimated that between 0.124 and 0.251 hospital admissions for respiratory infection would occur in a population of 100 000 for each $\mu g/m^3$ of PM_{10} concentration. We can see from Table 3.1 that although hospital admissions may be the most serious of the endpoints under consideration, 'restricted activity days' are by far the most common.

As indicated in the previous section, air pollution data are only available for PM_{10}. Thus calculations of the number and costs of respiratory illnesses can be

Table 3.1   Epidemiological endpoints selected for the study

Endpoint	Study	Coefficient	Per	Translation[a]
Hospital admission	Schwartz (1994b)			'Hospital' – '3 days in hospital, 5 days in bed'
Respiratory infection		0.124–0.251	100 000	
Chronic obstructive pulmonary disease		0.161–0.293	100 000	
Emergency room visit	Sunyer et al. (1993)	0.58–0.86	100 000	'Casualty' – '4 hours in hospital, 5 days in bed'
Restricted activity day	Ostro (1987)	3100.8–7800.3	100 000	'Bed' – '3 days in bed'; 'Cough' – '1 day of coughing'; 'Eye' – '1 day of eye irritation'

Note: [a]Health state description used in the contingent valuation survey (see below).

made for this pollutant only. The epidemiological studies in Table 3.1 were selected for use in the European Commission ExternE study of the social costs of fuel cycles (ExternE 1995, 1998). They relate entirely to health impacts associated with PM_{10} exposure. The coefficients are low and high estimates of the relationship between PM_{10} concentrations (in $\mu g/m^3$) and the predicted number of cases of each illness. Space precludes a detailed assessment of the quality and validity of these epidemiology studies.

THE VALUE OF PREVENTING ACUTE MORBIDITY – A SIMPLE ECONOMIC MODEL

An expression for the value of preventing respiratory illness episodes can be derived from a simple economic model of utility and health formation (see, for example, Berger et al. 1994). We shall briefly examine a simple model in which there are only two states: perfect health and certain morbidity changes. This simplification is appropriate for a number of reasons. First, it greatly simplifies the form of any contingent valuation survey used to value morbidity impacts. Second, it is very similar to the model which allows for risk, if we assume constant marginal utility of income across states of health. Third, this treatment is consistent with the way in which epidemiological exposure-response functions for respiratory morbidity are presented in the literature, that is, in terms of illness outcomes (for example, the number of cases) rather than individual risk exposure.

In this model, assume a person's utility (U) depends on consumption (C) and the state of health, represented by a vector of health characteristics (H):

$$U = U(C, H). \tag{3.1}$$

We assume that health is merely the presence or absence of a morbidity condition, and that the probability of good health is a function of defensive activities/expenditures (X) and environmental factors such as air quality (E):

$$H = H(X, E). \tag{3.2}$$

Then the problem for the individual is to maximize expected utility, which is simply the probability-weighted average of utility when ill (U_1) and in full health (U_0):

$$\max E(U) = U_0(1 - H) + U_1 H \tag{3.3}$$

(where $U_0 = U(M - X, 0)$ and $U_1 = U(M - X - Z, 1)$, subject to the income constraint:

$$M = C + X + Z \tag{3.4}$$

that is, income (M) is the sum of consumption expenditures (C), defensive expenditures (X), and the costs of illness (Z) – lost wages, treatment costs and so on. Costs of illness only arise when the individual is actually ill (that is, $Z = 0$ in the expression for U_0). We can derive an expression for the willingness to pay (WTP) to prevent illness, by maximizing the expected utility function and solving for the income change that would keep expected utility constant in the face of a change in the risk of illness (for example, because of a change in environmental quality, E):

$$-dM/dE = -[(U_0 - U_1)/m^*].dH/dE - \{1+[(U_0 - U_1)/m^*].fH/fX\}.dX/dE \tag{3.5}$$

where m^* is the probability-weighted average marginal utility of income (that is, the expected marginal utility of income). The model is further explained in

Tolley et al. (1994). Substituting the first-order condition (that is, expression (3.3) into (3.5) and rearranging gives us:

$$-dM / dE = -[(U_0 - U_1) / m^*].fH / fE - dX / dE. \qquad (3.6)$$

Thus, WTP to avoid a small increase in pollution can be stated as follows: the expected difference in utility when healthy and ill multiplied by the change in the probability of illness (resulting from a change in environmental or other exogenous factors) plus the change in defensive expenditures resulting from the same environmental change. When we are concerned with certain changes in morbidity, expected consumer surplus from preventing illness is the difference between 'healthy' and 'sick' utility expressed in money terms. In this case, m is the actual (rather than expected) marginal utility of income. Thus, if we can assume that the marginal utility of income is the same in the healthy and ill states, then consumer surplus represents a baseline approximation to true WTP for morbidity changes. This is the basis for most of the morbidity valuation studies conducted previously, and it is the basis for the valuation study reported in this chapter.

DESIGN OF THE VALUATION SURVEY

There are a number of different approaches to the valuation of health impacts. Often these are based on observed behaviour in real markets – for example, labour markets, where health risks are traded against wage rates; product markets, where consumers buy products to improve their health directly. However, the questionnaire-based contingent valuation method (see, for example, Mitchell and Carson 1989) was employed in this study. This is because we are interested in the valuation of complex episodes of ill health which could well be difficult to trade (separately) in existing markets. Some types of episode may be unfamiliar to many people. Moreover, it is necessary to ensure that the 'valued' episodes are compatible with the endpoints employed in the epidemiological studies examined above. The contingent valuation method is the only technique which permits the necessary information to be provided to respondents.

The 'translation problem' is rarely addressed explicitly in economic valuation studies. It occurs in this context because epidemiological studies of health impacts consider the relationship between air quality and measurable clinical outcomes. However, individuals value illness prevention because illness may imply pain, inconvenience and restrictions on ability to carry out normal activities. The epidemiological coefficients presented in Table 3.1 are obtained from a statistical analysis relating the number of cases of a particular illness (as reported in hospital records or in daily diaries kept by study participants) to changes in the measured concentrations of particular pollutants, controlling for factors such as an individual's health status, whether or not he/she is a smoker and so on. To make economic valuation and epidemiological studies compatible, the epidemiological endpoints must be 'translated' into characterizations of the associated illness which individuals find meaningful and useful. In this study, in cooperation with primary care specialists, brief descriptions of the illness episodes were prepared. These descriptions give details of the likely symptoms, restrictions and duration of a representative case of each of the epidemiological endpoints. This is the primary source of information provided to respondents in the contingent valuation survey. Table 3.1 contains a brief version of these descriptions, giving the principal component events only.

The valuation scenario employed in the questionnaire requires respondents to imagine that in the few weeks following the interview they would experience each of the illness episodes considered in the study (independently and one at a time). They are then asked to estimate how much they would be willing to pay to prevent each episode from occurring. No information is given about the cause of the illness episodes, that is, no explicit mention of the possible role of air pollution or the mechanism by which the episode could be prevented. The disadvantages of such a hypothetical scenario are offset by the ability to consider illnesses which respondents may not have experienced before. It also permits the survey to form part of a structured experiment to estimate the effect of contextual information on estimated WTP to prevent illness (see Vázquez 1998) and to estimate the international 'transferability' of illness values, as part of a larger European research effort (Day et al. 1998).

Respondents are asked to consider only the symptoms, restrictions and duration of each illness, and not any illness costs such as treatment costs, lost wages and so on. Therefore, expressions of WTP are only partial estimates of the total value of preventing illness. To account for possible 'imprecision' in respondents' preferences for unusual goods (Dubourg et al. 1994, 1997), the elicitation procedure employs a payment ladder on which respondents are asked to tick (✓) those amounts they are 'almost certain' they would pay to prevent the episode, and to cross (✗) those amounts they are almost certain they would not pay. 'Almost certain' is defined as 'about 95 per cent certain'. When the respondent is less than 95 per cent certain, they are asked to leave the amount box blank.

Prior to the valuation questions, there is an illness episode ranking exercise in the questionnaire. This has two main functions: to present the illness episode information in a way that can be easily assimilated; and to provide a check on internal consistency of responses. Finally, the questionnaire collects information about respondents' current health status and previous health experience, health-related activities (for example, diet, smoking and exercise) and attitudes to health and illness. This is in addition to the usual information on socio-economic characteristics (income, education and so on).

RESULTS OF THE CONTINGENT VALUATION SURVEY

Six professional psychologists with extensive interviewing experience administered the contingent valuation survey to a sample of the urban population of Vigo in October 1997, and 448 interviews were successfully completed. This is in line with Arkin and Colton's (1962) recommendation of a sample size of 400 to obtain a 9 per cent confidence level with a target population above 100 000. The mean duration of the interviews was 23 minutes.

Table 3.2 summarizes the socio-economic characteristics of the sample. Of the 448 individuals, 54 per cent are female and the average age is just over 43. The majority of respondents are married (62) and the average household size is just under four. Forty-three per cent of respondents are educated only to primary level or less and less than 19 per cent are employed full time.

With regard to reported health status, 44 per cent of respondents consider themselves to have 'good health'; 23 per cent 'normal health'; and only 6 per cent 'very poor health'. The proportion suffering from relevant illnesses are as follows: 10 per cent from asthma; 9 per cent from chronic bronchitis; 27 per cent from an allergy; and 11 per cent from a respiratory allergy. A higher proportion know close friends or family suffering from these conditions.

Table 3.2 also presents data on the socio-economic characteristics of the urban population of Vigo over 16 years of age (214 460 individuals in the 1991 census). The sample and the urban population are broadly similar in the reported characteristics. One contrast is the higher proportion of the sample who are educated to degree or professional level (that is, 24.6 per cent compared with 6.3 per cent in the urban population). This might be partly due to over-reporting by university students. It might also arise from selection bias in the sample – if more highly educated individuals are more likely to participate in the survey. Information on personal and household income only exists for the extended metropolitan area (rather than the urban population of Vigo). This includes some rural areas with low agricultural incomes. This is likely to explain why the income figures for the population are lower than those reported for the sample.

Table 3.2   Socio-economic characteristics of the survey sample and the Vigo population

		Sample	Population
Total number of individuals over 16		448	214 460
Demographic breakdown			
Male:Female ratio		46:54	48:52
Age (years)		43.5	42.8
Marital status (%)	Single	28.4	30.6
	Married	61.8	59.7
	Divorced	3.6	8.4
	Widowed	6.3	1.3
Average household size		3.69	n/a
Education (%)	Secondary school or less	43.1	53.4
	High school	32.4	40.3
	University/Professional	24.6	6.3
Economic characteristics			
Monthly personal income (Pta)		121 955	
Monthly household income (Pta)		234 304	
Employment status (%)	Self-employed	14.5	5.9
	Full time	18.8	34.0
	Part time	5.6	n/a
	Homemaker	25.7	18.7
	Student	13.0	9.5
	Unemployed	9.4	11.2
	Retired	10.5	15.1

Note: See text for explanation of variable classifications and years.

64

SUMMARY STATISTICS ON WILLINGNESS TO PAY

Table 3.3 reports summary statistics on WTP to prevent each of the illness episodes. These are calculated after the exclusion of 28 individuals who were deemed to have stated zero as a 'protest' response.[2] We can see that the hospital admission episodes generate by far the highest mean and median value, at about Pta 75 000 and Pta 20 000, respectively (£1 = Pta 254 in April 1998). This is not surprising, given that this is the most serious of the 'episodes' described – both in clinical and in practical terms. The mean WTP value for casualty episodes and bed episodes are very close at Pta 19 458 and Pta 15 240, respectively. This may be due to similar descriptions for the two episodes – both require a three-day stay in bed. On the other hand, the casualty episode does involve extreme breathing difficulties and the administration of breathing assistance and drugs. Since the casualty description was not included in the prior ranking exercise, respondents may have had difficulty in assimilating this new information. The magnitudes of values for mean WTP for the two minor episodes, coughing and eye irritation, are both in the region of values estimated in previous studies for minor symptoms (for example, Navrud 1997 in Norway; Brien et al. 1994 in the United States). Finally, we can see that in all cases, mean values exceed median values by a considerable margin. This is a typical result in such surveys since WTP is effectively bounded from below at zero and may also be very influenced by a few individuals who bid large amounts.

Table 3.3   Summary statistics on WTP (pesetas) (£1 = Pta 254)

	Bed	Hospital	Cough	Casualty	Eye
Mean	15 240	74 558	1 832	19 458	4 292
Median	5 500	22 700	60	7 000	1 000
Min	0	0	0	0	0
Max	225 000	1 000 000	34 000	225 000	12 0000

n = 420

Even though the mean exceeds the median by a considerable margin for each episode, we still choose to use mean values. We would like the summary statistic used in our analysis to incorporate the high values reported by some individuals (exclusion of such values seems very arbitrary). Also mean WTP is the theoretically correct value for use in cost–benefit analysis, which is based on the Hicks–Kaldor 'potential compensation' criterion. Although using median measures might have a significant effect on the resulting benefits estimates, those estimates would then not be theoretically coherent. It would be informative to compare the standard deviation of our mean estimates with those reported in similar studies, to assess whether the estimates in this chapter are significantly greater and therefore potentially problematic. Unfortunately, this is outside of the scope of the current chapter.

REGRESSION ANALYSIS OF THE WTP RESPONSES

It is customary to use regression techniques to analyse responses to contingent valuation WTP questions. This allows validation of the results against the predictions of economic theory and also allows estimation of a WTP function which can be used to predict what WTP would be under differing circumstances. Table 3.4 presents results of the regression analysis in this study (reporting only significant coefficients). The methodology used is ordinary least squares, where the natural log of WTP is the dependent variable. All of the WTP responses are combined into a single data set with dummy variables used to identify the illness episode referred to in each response. The base (or excluded) category is the WTP to prevent a 'bed' episode. The estimated coefficients on the 'episode' dummies should be interpreted relative to the base category.

For the most part, results are in line with expectation. Most variables are significant at conventional levels (10 per cent for this type of statistical analysis) and have the expected signs. Personal income has a significant and positive effect on reported WTP, as one would expect. Age, marriage and household size are all positively related to WTP. Education and working status (not reported here) are not significant in the regression when we control for income. Excluding income, these variables become positive and significant.

WTP is positively associated with being bronchitic and knowing someone who has a respiratory illness. This suggests an 'information effect' – those with more experience of a respiratory illness might better appreciate its impacts and therefore have a higher WTP to avoid such an illness. This appears to conflict with the result that experience of 'cough days' and days in hospital in the previous year are negatively related to WTP. However, the size of the coefficient on these variables is very small.

The illness episode dummies are all highly significant and of the expected sign, indicating that individuals do respond rationally to illness severity in formulating their WTP. These results should be interpreted relative to the base category (that is, 'bed' episodes). Thus, relative to bed episodes, the hospital and casualty dummies have a positive impact on WTP. The coefficient on the

Table 3.4   Regression analysis of WTP responses

Variable	Coefficient	t statistic	Significance level (%)
Constant	7.326	31.153	<1
Age	7.876×10^{-3}	2.640	1
Personal income	4.109×10^{-6}	7.445	<1
Household size	6.660×10^{-2}	2.309	2
Marital status	0.109	1.643	10
Bronchitis dummy	0.537	3.764	<1
Respiratory-illness-in-family dummy	0.137	1.753	8
Days spent in hospital in last year	-4.040×10^{-3}	1.977	5
Cough episodes in last year	-4.390×10^{-3}	1.853	6
Sport dummy	0.352	4.626	<1
Interview duration	-1.770×10^{-2}	3.489	<1
Interviewer	0.148	5.702	<1
Cough dummy	-1.608	12.473	<1
Eye dummy	-1.112	9.122	<1
Casualty dummy	0.292	2.625	<1
Hospital dummy	1.426	12.896	<1
R^2	0.373		

casualty dummy is much lower, reflecting that WTP is affected in a similar way by 'casualty' and 'bed' episodes. Relative to the base category, the cough dummy (that is, one day of coughing) and the eye dummy (that is, one day of eye irritation) lower the estimated WTP.

Perhaps the least satisfactory result in Table 3.4 is the fact that the interviewer dummy is significant. This indicates that WTP results are significantly influenced by who is asking the question. The presence of such 'interviewer effects' is certainly not unknown and deserves further examination. Of course, the result could be spurious – the interviewer dummy might simply be reflecting the impact of an omitted variable (although tests for omitted variable bias do not support this possibility). Finally, interviews of longer duration are associated with lower WTP amounts. One interpretation is that respondents who take longer to complete an interview consider their answers more carefully and report more accurate and realistic WTP estimates. This is in accord with previous contingent valuation studies (for example, Whittington et al. 1992).

ESTIMATING THE MORBIDITY BENEFITS OF
AIR POLLUTION CONTROL IN VIGO

The next stage in estimating the morbidity benefits of reducing PM_{10} concentrations in Vigo involves combining our valuation figures with the selected epidemiological exposure-response functions and population numbers to produce 'monetized' damage functions. We can then apply air pollution data to these functions to estimate the value of reductions in pollution concentrations. We illustrate the procedure in this section.

Applying the WTP estimates derived above to the epidemiological exposure-response functions presented in Table 3.1 enables us to arrive at examples of what monetized 'air pollution health damage' functions might look like. These are presented in Table 3.5. Monetary estimates are calculated for the high and low coefficients reported in the epidemiology studies. The coefficients for 'restricted activity days' are calculated on the basis of a combination of the 'bed' and 'cough' WTP estimates from the contingent valuation survey. The former refers to an episode of three days confined to bed with respiratory symptoms. A restricted activity day does not always necessitate a stay in bed. Moreover, it is estimated that 80 per cent of restricted activity days occur in single day episodes (Ostro 1997). However, pilot-testing of the contingent valuation questionnaire suggested that individuals were generally sceptical of what would be a technically correct description of a restricted activity day and were much more receptive to a three-day episode description. Such a description was used in the final questionnaire. The 'cough' description did include some unspecified restrictions on activity, but is probably best seen as an example of a mild 'restricted activity day' – this seems to be how it was viewed by respondents. However, the 'eye' episode, although involving no restrictions, was seen as more serious, given the nature

Table 3.5   Monetized PM_{10} pollution health damage functions (all ages)

Endpoint	Physical coefficient (low/high)	Unit value (Pta)	Monetized coefficient (l/h)	Per μg/m³ per n population
Hospital admission				
Respiratory infection	0.124/0.251	74558	9245/18714	100000
Chronic obstructive pulmonary disease	0.161/0.293	74558	12004/21845	100000
Emergency room visit	0.58/0.86	19458	11286/16734	100000
Restricted activity day	31.8/78.3	3734	118741/292372	1000

of the symptoms. The true value for preventing a 'restricted activity day' is probably somewhere between the value reported for each of these.

The WTP figure used for a restricted activity day in this exercise is therefore constructed as follows. The WTP 'bed' estimate is divided by three to give an estimate of the value of preventing a 'bed day'. This assumes linearity in the WTP–episode duration relationship – perhaps not a demanding assumption given the relatively mild severity of the illnesses. We then take the average of this value and the values reported for 'cough' and 'eye'. This gives a value of Pta 3734 for preventing a 'restricted activity day'.

We combine the monetized damage functions with data on the size of the urban population in Vigo and average annual PM_{10} concentrations to arrive at first estimates of the health costs of PM_{10} pollution in Vigo. The simple average annual PM_{10} level for urban Vigo is 74.4 $\mu g/m^3$ in 1996–97 (from the data presented in Figure 3.1). The urban population of Vigo is approximately 214 460 (according to the 1991 census). The health cost of PM_{10} is then calculated by multiplying the monetary coefficient (that is, damage per unit of PM_{10}) by the average annual PM_{10} level for Vigo and the size of the population. Estimates are reported in Table 3.6. These estimates suggest that the monetary damage from PM_{10}-related respiratory illness in Vigo was at least Pta 1.9 billion (£7.5 million) in 1997, and could have been as high as Pta 4.7 billion (£18.4 million). Although unit value of a hospital admission episode is much higher than other episodes, by far the greatest proportion of the total health cost is accounted for by minor illnesses. This is due to the high frequency of

Table 3.6   Estimated morbidity costs of PM_{10} pollution in Vigo

Endpoint		Coefficient	PM_{10}	Population (Pta)	Monetary damage cases	Estimated physical cases
Hospital	*l*	9 245	74.4	214 460	1 475 116	20
admission (1)	*h*	18 714	74.4	214 460	2 985 973	40
Hospital	*l*	12 004	74.4	214 460	1 915 337	26
admission (2)	*h*	21 845	74.4	214 460	3 485 550	47
Emergency	*l*	11 286	74.4	214 460	1 800 774	93
room visit	*h*	16 734	74.4	214 460	2 670 048	137
Restricted	*l*	118 741	74.4	214 460	1 894 610 498	507 395
activity day	*h*	292 372	74.4	214 460	4 665 036 175	1 249 341
Total damage (low)					1 899 801 725	
Total damage (high)					4 674 177 746	

Note: Numbers may not compute exactly due to rounding.

minor illnesses. Most of the uncertainty in the total monetary cost is due to estimates of the number of 'restricted activity days' occurring at current PM_{10} levels. This ranges from one to six days per person per year. In contrast, PM_{10}-induced hospital admissions and casualty visits are predicted to be quite rare.

We can compare this number for 'restricted activity days' with numbers that have been reported elsewhere in the literature. For instance, Ostro (1987) reports that according to the US Health Interview Surveys for 1976–81, the average number of 'work-loss days' is about five per adult per year. This estimate is based on average PM_{10} levels of $20\mu g/m^3$ (Ostro and Rothschild 1989). From the same survey, Ostro and Rothschild report average figures for 'respiratory restricted activity days' and 'minor restricted activity days' of 3.06 and 7.8 per adult per year, respectively. Thus, it would appear that our estimates of the number of 'restricted activity days' experienced in Vigo as a result of PM_{10} exposure are not unreasonable.

Although a large proportion of PM_{10} emissions originates from road traffic, a significant proportion is naturally occurring – perhaps around 30 per cent (Pearce and Crowards 1996). Hence, rather than present the above results in terms of the overall cost of anthropogenic and 'natural' PM_{10}, it might make more sense to present results in terms of the potential benefits of PM_{10} control policies. For example, using these data, we can construct a first estimate of reducing PM_{10} levels in Vigo by 10 per cent from 1997 levels. The estimated monetary benefit of reducing the associated impact in morbidity is Pta 0.2–5 billion. Such figures can be used in a preliminary cost–benefit analysis of such a proposed policy.

DISCUSSION AND CONCLUSIONS

This chapter has presented preliminary estimates of the morbidity costs of PM_{10} pollution in Vigo, and hence of the potential benefits to be gained from PM_{10} control. There are a number of caveats with regard to the estimates.

First, they relate only to increases in morbidity, and not to mortality. The incomplete coverage of health impacts leads to an underestimate of the total health cost of PM_{10} pollution. Similarly, the unit monetary damage figures estimated in the contingent valuation survey cover the value of preventing 'pain and suffering' only and do not include the costs of treating illnesses or of lost production/wages as a result of loss of work time or reduced productivity while at work. Incorporating such effects may considerably increase damage estimates – especially for hospital admissions and casualty visits.

It is more difficult to assess the direction of the errors introduced because of other uncertainties in the calculations. For instance, the exposure-response functions assume that the illness burden is spread evenly across the whole population, whereas in practice certain individuals might be more susceptible to pollution-related illness than others. Thus, the exposure-response functions estimate overall illness burden rather than individual risk exposure. In practice this means that cases of a particular illness are unlikely to be spread evenly across the population. Certain subgroups are more likely to be affected (for example, old people). This could have an effect on the appropriate value to apply to illness prevention. It is not clear whether 50 individuals will value the prevention of a single illness episode more or less highly than one individual valuing 50 episodes. This uncertainty is compounded by the fact that the contingent valuation questionnaire asks individuals to value a single illness episode whereas, if susceptible, they may be more likely to experience frequent 'restricted activity days'.

Finally, it should be remembered that the analysis and calculations presented in this chapter are highly aggregated, and do not fully account for individual risk exposure, air pollution exposure, and individual preferences over these factors; or about the sources of PM_{10} pollution, variation over time and so on. As a result, the figures presented here should be regarded as tentative first estimates. Any actual cost–benefit analysis of PM_{10} control in Vigo should involve much more thorough modelling of the pollution, health and economic processes involved (for example, pollutant dispersal, air pollution exposure and full-cost pricing).

NOTES

1. 'Acute respiratory infections' include every respiratory illness that implies cough, chest infection and symptoms related to the upper respiratory tract, including light (acute) bronchitis. They do not include influenza, asthma or chronic bronchitis.
2. These were any zero responses for which the following reasons were given: 'The whole idea of paying money to avoid an episode of ill-health seems ridiculous to me', or 'I'm not used to making decisions like this and found it impossible to decide on a sensible answer to this question'.

REFERENCES

Arkin, H. and R.R. Colton (1962), *An Outline of Statistical Methods: As Applied to Economics, Business, Psychology, Education and Biology*, New York: Barnes & Noble.

Berger, M., G. Blomquist, D. Kenkel and G. Tolley (1994), 'Framework for valuing health risks', in Tolley et al. (eds), pp. 23–41.

Brien, M., D. Kenkel, A. Kelly and R. Fabian (1994), 'Empirical results from household personal interviews', in Tolley et al. (eds), pp. 165–87.

Cody, R.P., C.P. Wesel, G. Birnbaum and P.J. Lioy (1992), 'The effects of ozone associated with summertime photochemical smog on the frequency of asthma visits to hospital emergency departments', *Environmental Research*, **58**: 184–94.

Day, B.D., W.R. Dubourg, F. Machado, S. Mourato, S. Navrud, R.C. Ready, F. Spanninks and M.X. Vázquez (1998), 'Transferring context-free estimates of the benefits of avoiding pollution-related respiratory morbidity in Europe', Centre for Social and Economic Research on the Global Environment, University College London and University of East Anglia, mimeo, unpublished manuscript.

Dubourg, W.R., M.W. Jones-Lee and G. Loomes (1994), 'Imprecise preferences and the WTP/WTA disparity', *Journal of Risk and Uncertainty*, **9**: 115–34.

Dubourg, W.R., M.W. Jones-Lee and G. Loomes (1997), 'Imprecise preferences and questionnaire design in contingent valuation', *Economica*, **64**: 681–702.

ExternE (1995), *Externalities of Energy* (revised 1998), Luxembourg: European Commission.

Johnson, F.R., E.E. Fries and H.S. Banzhaf (1997), 'Valuing morbidity: an integration of the willingness-to-pay and health-status index literatures', *Journal of Health Economics*, **16**: 641–55.

Krupnick, A.J., W. Harrington and B. Ostro (1990), 'Ambient ozone and acute health effects', *Journal of Environmental Economics and Management*, **18**: 1–18.

Mitchell, R. and R.C. Carson (1989), *Using Surveys to Value Public Goods: The Contingent Valuation Method*, Washington, DC: Resources for the Future.

Navrud, S. (1997), 'Valuing health impacts from air pollution in Europe: new empirical evidence on morbidity', Department of Economics and Social Sciences, Agricultural University of Norway, mimeo.

Ostro, B.D. (1987), 'Air pollution and morbidity revisited: a specification test', *Journal of Environmental Economics and Management*, **10**: 371–82.

Ostro, B.D. (1994), 'Estimating the health effects of air pollution: a method with an application to Jakarta', Working Paper 1301, Policy Research Department, Washington, DC: World Bank.

Ostro, B.D. (1997), Personal communication to Richard Dubourg.

Ostro, B.D. and S. Rothschild (1989), 'Air pollution and acute respiratory morbidity: an observational study of multiple pollutants', *Environmental Research*, **50**: 238–47.

Pearce, D. and T. Crowards (1996), 'Particulate matter and human health in the United Kingdom', *Energy Policy*, **7**: 609–19.

Pope III, C.A., M.J. Thun, M. Namboordi, D.W. Dockery, J.D. Evans, F. Speizer and C.W. Health Jr. (1995), 'Particulate air pollution as a predictor of mortality in a prospective study of US adults', *American Journal of Respiratory and Critical Care Medicine*, **151**: 669–74.

Schwartz, J. (1994a), 'Air pollution and daily mortality: a review and meta-analysis', *Environmental Research*, **64**: 36–52.

Schwartz, J. (1994b), 'Air pollution and hospital admissions for the elderly in Detroit, Michigan', *American Journal of Respiratory and Critical Care Medicine*, **150**: 648–55.

Schwartz, J., D. Slater, T.V. Larson, W.E. Pierson and J.Q. Koenig (1993), 'Particulate air pollution and hospital emergency room visits for asthma in Seattle', *American Review of Respiratory Disease*, **147**: 826–31.

Sunyer, J., M. Saez, C. Murill, J. Castellsague, F. Martinez and J.M. Anto (1993), 'Air pollution and emergency room admissions for chronic obstructive pulmonary disease: a 5-year study', *American Journal of Epidemiology*, **137**: 701–5.

Tolley, G., D. Kenkel and R. Fabian (eds) (1994), *Valuing Health for Policy: An Economic Approach*, Chicago: University of Chicago Press.

Vázquez, M.X. (1998), 'The effect of contextual information on the willingness to pay to prevent respiratory morbidity: evidence from a contingent valuation experiment in Spain', University of Vigo, mimeo, forthcoming.

Viscusi, W.K. (1993), 'The values of risks to life and health', *Journal of Economic Literature*, **31**: 1912–46.

Whittington, D., V.K. Smith, A. Okorafor, A. Okore, J.L. Liu and A. McPhail (1992), 'Giving respondents time to think in contingent valuation studies: a developing-country application', *Journal of Environmental Economics and Management*, **22**: 205–25.

4. Air pollution and agricultural crop damage: can Europe learn from the United States?

Clive L. Spash*

INTRODUCTION

Air pollution plays an important role in altering the environment in which agricultural crops must be grown. A range of air pollutants are now recognized as likely causes of economic loss. These range from local ozone smog due to traffic emissions, regional acidic deposition from nitrogen oxide and sulphur dioxide, through to global climate change due to carbon dioxide, chlorofluorocarbons, methane and nitrous oxide. Economic assessments of the agricultural impact of air pollutants received most interest in the 1980s in the United States, boosted by government-funded research projects. Research into the economic impacts of air pollution in relationship to agricultural crops has been conducted for tropospheric ozone, acidic deposition and global climate change (or more specifically increased temperature or reduced soil moisture with/without carbon dioxide fertilization (Adams et al. 1988). As discussed in this review, European research has lagged sorely behind in this area.

   Economic assessments of crop losses related to air pollution are sometimes associated with an interest in forest declines. However, forestry is a multiple output production system and the assessment of impacts on forestry raises much wider issues of non-market valuation than agricultural crop loss (such as biodiversity, aesthetics and recreation). As a result, forest damages are poorly represented in purely market-related models as applied to agricultural crop loss. For example, Carrier and Kripple (1990) report on the economic losses in European forests due to sulphur dioxide, nitrogen oxide and ammonia, a study by the International Institute for Applied Systems Analysis (IIASA). They categorize the type of economic damages as (i) commercial wood harvest; (ii) value added in the wood-processing industry; and (iii) non-timber social benefits (for example, tourism, recreation, wildlife habitat, protection of

* This chapter was first published in *Journal of Economic Surveys*, Vol. 11, No. 1, March 1997, pp. 47–70.

soil and water). The crop assessment methods reported here concern only category (i), while (ii) and (iii) would normally be assumed constant. There is no simple relationship between timber loss and biodiversity or recreation which would allow a straightforward extension to category (iii). Despite this, some of the problems posed by attempts at non-market valuation in forestry are similar to those raised by demand-side benefit assessment due to changes in crop quality, discussed in the final section of this chapter. More generally, concern for wider ecosystem impacts shows how economic analysis is limited to assessing certain benefits and cannot measure the value of ecological structure and function, genetic diversity or cultural values (Tingey et al. 1990). Instead of trying to cover all these issues, the focus here is upon the literature as it relates to agricultural crops (those interested in forestry are referred to Mackenzie and El-Ashry 1989).

This chapter outlines the requirements for an economic assessment of crop loss, moving from scientific monitoring through to economic modelling. The next section briefly outlines the history of research into crop loss due to air pollution, describes the nature of major air pollutants affecting crops and reflects upon the different regulatory approaches which have developed. The third section introduces some of the problems with defining an adequate and consistent measure of air pollution concentrations with regard to crop damages. The fourth section relates how given measured concentrations are then reflected in crop losses. The fifth section reviews several different approaches which agricultural economists have adopted to assess the importance of air pollution for crop losses at the regional level, and gives examples of applications to ozone. The sixth section presents studies of crop loss due to acidic deposition and identifies problems for benefit assessment of this pollutant by comparison with ozone. The final section draws conclusions, and suggests how future studies of air pollution impacts on agriculture could be improved.

AIR POLLUTION AND PLANT GROWTH

European scientists began research into plant growth under atmospheric pollutants over 140 years ago (DuBay et al. 1985). Thomas (1951) cites work in Germany on vegetation damage due to residential fires published in the 1880s (Shröder and Reuss 1883). Early work in the twentieth century examined visible injury due to sulphur dioxide (Zimmerman and Crocker 1934; Thomas and Hill 1935) and injuries due to emissions from coal burning and the smelting of ores (Swain 1949). Other gaseous byproducts of industry were soon studied including nitrogen oxides, hydrogen fluoride and chlorine. However, the most extensive work in recent years has been conducted on ozone in the lower atmosphere (the troposphere).

Injury to plants from photochemical smog was first noted in 1944 when stippling and glazing or bronzing of the leaves of vegetables was discovered in the Los Angeles basin, California. Tropospheric ozone concentrations alone or in combination with sulphur dioxide and nitrogen dioxide have since been claimed to be the major source of crop losses caused by air pollution in the United States (Heck et al. 1982). Chameides et al. (1994) estimate 9–35 per cent of the world's cereal crops are presently exposed to ozone concentrations of 0.05 to 0.07 parts per million (ppm) seasonal mean, at which level yields start to fall by 5–10 per cent. The scientific evidence is growing that both ozone and acidic deposition are causing extensive damage to vegetation in both Europe and the US. However, the role of acidic deposition at ambient levels on commercial crops remains unclear (MacKenzie and El-Ashry 1989, p. 15). Research so far seems to suggest most commercial crop yields are relatively insensitive to acidic deposition on its own (Segerson 1991, p. 352). As the economic methodology employed to assess impacts of crop losses is common to all air pollutants, this chapter uses the example of tropospheric ozone to characterize the benefit assessment techniques. Studies related to acidic deposition are then discussed in the section following the review of ozone.

Ozone is formed in the lower atmosphere from precursor emissions: non-methane hydrocarbons, nitrogen dioxide and nitric oxide. The transportation sector is normally the primary source of anthropogenic ozone precursors. In Europe, ozone itself is uncontrolled. This might imply that ozone is either below levels at which damages occur or that current controls of precursor emissions are sufficient. However, the persistence of ozone smog in cities such as Athens suggests otherwise. There is also clear evidence of high ozone concentrations due to the cumulative loading of precursors on areas downwind of the London plume (Varey et al. 1988), while in north-west England, where levels are lower, concentrations frequently exceed 0.08 ppm daily maximum per hour (Colbeck 1988). Annual exceedance of 0.07 ppm maximum has occurred for 60 to 150 hours in rural UK areas, for 150 to 300 hours in central Germany, and at high latitudes in southern Germany for more than 350 hours (Wilson and Sinfield 1988, p. 516). In general, there has been an upward trend in background ozone in Europe with concentrations at least twice those of one hundred years ago (Grennfelt 1992, pp. 26–7). The increased frequency and duration of hot dry weather implied by global warming will increase the concentration of tropospheric ozone from available precursors. In addition, European precursor emissions will increase with the volume of traffic, which is rising with both population and car ownership per capita, as well as with sales to the previously unexploited market of the former Eastern bloc. Thus, ozone control is a policy issue of increasing importance across Europe.

European regulation has adopted the concept of critical loads for acidic deposition and critical levels for ozone. These were initially based upon US experimental data, raising questions over the extent to which crop response data is 'transferable'. The critical levels set for ozone in 1988 (United Nations Economic Commission for Europe (ECE), Bad Harzburg, Germany) have since been reviewed to take into account European experience, and are now considered more comprehensive than those in the US, being based upon three measures of dose instead of one. Ozone critical levels for agricultural crops are 0.075 ppm one-hour, 0.030 ppm eight-hour, and 0.025 ppm seven-hour seasonal mean. Grennfelt (1992) reports data from European monitoring stations for 1985 to 1987. Out of the 80 observations summarizing annual exceedance, he reports the frequency of exceedance of critical levels for ozone as 64 times for the one-hour mean, 80 times for the eight-hour mean, and 79 times for the seasonal mean.

As discussed in the next section, whether one or all of the selected measures of dose for ozone should be binding as the aim of control policy is undecided, and this is complicated by variations in the pattern of exceedances in different regions. At the UN ECE 1992 workshop (Egham, UK) cumulative dose was suggested as a better measure than the three mentioned above. Cumulative dose for ozone sums concentrations above 0.04 ppm during daylight hours with a critical level of 0.03 ppm was reported by Ashmore (1993).

The critical load of SO_2 for indirect effects on agricultural crops is 30 Fg m^{-3} with agricultural crops generally less sensitive than natural vegetation and forests (and similarly, in the case of NH_3 and NO_x). The critical load for direct effects on crops is equivalent to an annual mean pH of 3.0, and is unlikely to be exceeded anywhere in Europe (Ashmore 1993, p. 109). However, the extent to which crops are susceptible to multiple damage and synergistic effects is unclear. Greater consideration should be given to research on the sequential (rather than simultaneous) interaction of ozone with acidic precipitation and fog (Preston and Tingey 1988, p. 57). Critical loads for soil and freshwater acidification can be estimated from knowledge of systems buffering capacities, but there is no alternative to using dose-response functions to estimate critical levels for ozone. This requires experimental work on ozone and other pollutants to determine likely impacts. In this regard both the European (EOTCP) and US (NCLAN) data only address annual crops, which neglects economically important sectors such as permanent pasture and fruit trees (Ashmore 1993).

The critical load/level approach implies that a threshold exists above which damages occur and below which there are no damages. The idea of defining a critical level is then to protect the most sensitive receptor, ignoring considerations of control costs versus benefits. The European Open-Top Chamber Programme (EOTCP) was run from 1986 to 1991 to study mechanisms and interactions rather than attempt a qualitative assessment of crop losses due to air pollution in Europe (Mathy 1988; Unsworth and Geissler 1993). This approach is in direct contrast to the extensive project on crop damage due to ozone conducted by the National Crop Loss Assessment Network (NCLAN) of the United States Environmental Protection Agency (EPA) 1980 to 1987 (see Heck et al. 1991 for a review; or Heck et al. 1988). NCLAN was explicitly concerned to provide dose-response information for use in economic assessments of pollution damages, and stimulated much research in this area, as reported in sections below. According to Wilson and Sinfield (1988), UK research, which had a lead role in EOTCP, was to have assessed the potential economic losses of crops in the UK due to air pollutants, but no such research has yet appeared. The lack of European research into economic losses is inevitably due to an emphasis on critical levels which are set by scientific research. However, evidence that critical levels in sensitive areas are very low, but that reduction to such levels is impractical, has forced discussion of an acceptable level of damage, called target load (Kamari et al. 1992). Policy makers faced with the prospect of severe restrictions on fossil fuel combustion for trivial economic benefits will undoubtedly exceed the critical levels. Thus, the costs of control play a large role in actual attempts at attaining critical levels and will be evaluated in terms of their implied benefits, about which knowledge is seriously lacking for Europe.

The approach to air quality regulation in the US also consists of defining critical levels, with a primary standard designed to protect human health, and a secondary standard to protect other aspects of human welfare (for example, materials, crops, visibility). The primary standard aims to protect the health of even the most sensitive members of the public with a safety margin. The initial US national ambient air quality standard for ozone was set in 1971 at 0.08 ppm for both standards, allowing concentrations to exceed this for no more than one hour per year. Review of the standards in 1979 relaxed both to 0.12 ppm, with the standard to be exceeded no more than an average of three days over three consecutive years. While economic information had no role in setting these standards, economists have attempted to measure the social costs of pollution to assess whether a particular standard should be supported. In this respect the relaxation of the ozone standard from 0.08 ppm to 0.12 ppm led to several studies of the economic implications for crop production. In addition, there is good reason to have different primary and secondary standards and to adopt alternative measures of concentration for each, given the different damages society is trying to prevent in each case.

DEFINING DOSE

The effects of air pollution on vegetation are influenced by biotic, climatic and edaphic (that is, soil) variables. Inherent genetic resistance has been cited as probably the most important factor influencing plant response to air pollutants. Plant response to ozone varies among species of a given genus (for example, potato) and varieties or cultivars within a given species (Linzon et al. 1984).

Ozone, as with other air pollutants, damages a plant after entering the stomatal leaf opening (Holdgate 1979). Thus, factors affecting stomatal size and opening determine pollutant uptake and the potential for damage. For example, reduced moisture or increased temperature can cause reduced stomatal apertures and higher resistance to air pollution. Plants under no such stresses, growing under favourable conditions, may therefore be more susceptible to damage. In general, plants are better able to cope with exposure to ozone at night (because stomata are closed), and at lower temperatures and relative humidity; they are more susceptible to ozone damage when the leaves are mature, due to the increase in cell gaps (Medeiros and Moscowitz 1983).

Farm practices may also alter plant response to air pollution. For example, attempts to improve growing conditions (for example, irrigation) and reduce plant stress could increase ozone susceptibility. The mixture of production inputs is a factor often ignored in the derivation of dose-response functions under experimental conditions (Adams and Crocker 1984). Cultural and input variations between regions make dose-response functions, which have been derived in one area, inappropriate for use in another area. Even when the same inputs and cultivars are used in two different regions, all the other factors would have to concur before a dose-response function derived in one region could be used accurately to predict the yield loss in the second region. This problem is an important criticism of current dose-response methods.

The ambient ozone concentration, the length of time a particular concentration persists and the frequency of occurrences combine to form a measure of the dose of an air pollutant to which a plant is exposed: the 'exposure dose'. Other characteristics of plant exposure may also be important determinants of the nature and magnitude of the effects of ozone on plants: the length of time between exposures, the time of day of exposure, their sequence and pattern, and the total flux of ozone to the plant as it is affected by canopy characteristics and leaf boundary layers. However, in analysing 23 ozone studies into crop productivity, Jacobson (1982, p. 298) found exposure dose was defined in terms of concentration by 23, duration by 18, frequency by 16, time between exposures by 13, time of day by six, fluctuation of concentrations by three, and no considered patterns (sequence) or flux. NCLAN employed a seasonal seven-hour/day mean ozone concentration exposure statistic in all its published dose-response functions. This mean is calculated upon the seven hours judged to be the most susceptible for plants; that is, between 0900 and 1600 hours. The daily means for the seven-hour period are then averaged over the entire growing season, that is, the period of pollution concentrations relevant to the object being damaged.

The seasonal seven-hour mean statistic combines a large number of ozone concentration observations. Yet, as Heck et al. (1984) have pointed out, there is no consensus over the best exposure statistic over a growing season. Difficulties arise because the degree of plant response is affected more by differences in concentration than by differences in duration of exposure. For example, a given seasonal mean concentration with many high ozone concentrations could cause more damage than the same mean that includes only a few high ozone concentrations. The implication is that high ozone concentrations may be lost in the statistic but could be an important explanation of crop loss and therefore need to be taken into account. Thus, NCLAN discussed the use of alternative exposure statistics such as the peak (maximum) daily seven-hour mean ozone concentration occurring during the growing season; the seasonal mean of the daily maximum one-hour mean ozone concentrations; and the peak (maximum) one-hour mean ozone concentration occurring during the season. Thus, as Heck et al. conclude, no single exposure statistic may be adequate for all crops under all environmental conditions.

The measure of dose used must be compatible with ambient air quality data to enable the development of useful predictive models (Heck et al. 1980). Typically, ozone standards are set where the primary concern is with the threshold for acute damage to human health, and may therefore be inappropriate for crop dose-response studies. In order to use a different exposure statistic for a standard and a response model, the distribution of ozone in the ambient air needs to provide a basis for using one statistic as a surrogate for another. For example, assume that a seasonal mean concentration is discovered at which there is no crop loss, and that this seasonal mean is *never* exceeded when a certain hourly peak ozone concentration is not exceeded. Under these circumstances the analyst can reasonably assume that crops are protected when the hourly peak is not exceeded. Unfortunately, the seasonal mean can vary widely, while the peak value remains constant and is unlikely to *always* remain at or below a certain value. The implication for air pollution standards is that they should employ concentration measures which relate to chronic, as well as acute, damage.

FROM DOSE TO DAMAGE

There are three main approaches for deriving the influence of air quality on plants (dose-response relationships): (i) foliar injury models, (ii) secondary response data and (iii) experimentation. Response functions derived using these three approaches have been applied in economic assessments of ozone damage to agricultural crops. Early work in this area depended upon trained field observers using their judgement to estimate crop damage from visible symptoms (US EPA 1974). These subjective estimates (often arbitrarily converted into monetary values) were replaced by foliar injury models. In turn, foliar injury models have been found deficient in several aspects, and response functions derived from scientific field experimentation are now commonly applied in economic assessments.

Early studies assumed a threshold below which no damage was presumed to occur and related this to visible, normally foliar, injury. These foliar injury models can be misleading as signs of yield loss because tubers, roots and dry weight, among other factors, can be affected without visible damage. Conversely foliar injury may overestimate damage because some plants can suffer severe leaf damage without loss of photosynthetic ability, and recovery from visible injury can be quick (Leung et al. 1978). Generally, three types of response to air pollution can be defined: visible injury symptoms, growth responses and quality changes. Foliar injury models ignore 'hidden injury' which may occur with the latter two responses. Hidden injury includes reduced photosynthetic activity, accumulation of a pollutant within a leaf, an unhealthy appearance without necrotic lesions, reduced growth or yield, and increased susceptibility to disease, particularly insect invasion (Medeiros and Moscowitz 1983, p. 506). Studies with soybeans, tomatoes, annual rye grass, spinach, wheat, lettuce and potatoes have demonstrated that foliar-symptom production is an unreliable index of ozone effects on plant growth or yield (Jacobson 1982).

The use of secondary response data is the next method of deriving dose-response functions. Cross-sectional analysis of crop yield data is used to obtain dose-response functions via regression techniques. Information is required on the existing outdoor variations in air pollution, actual crop yields and other environmental factors. Such an approach can save time and money compared to the use of chamber studies under the experimental approach, discussed below. Leung et al. (1982) obtained statistically significant results for nine crops using this technique; however, the results were sometimes inconsistent when compared to experimental chamber studies, and ozone levels in the study region were high. Rowe and Chestnut (1985) attempted to derive dose-response functions for ten crops but could obtain significant results for only four of these. They found that the success of the approach was generally dependent upon the effort made to measure and incorporate non-air pollution variables in the yield functions. Generally, their results suggested that ozone was causing yield losses, but the secondary data regression approach captured the effects for only the most sensitive crops, that is, those which experienced high rates of damage at low ozone levels such as dry beans, cotton, grapes and potatoes.

The third approach is to use experimentation. Several experimental approaches have been developed in studies of ozone effects on crops; these include the use of greenhouses, field chambers (open-top or closed-top), unenclosed field plots and the pollution gradient approach. Each approach varies in design or exposure system but, for use in economic assessments, the environmental and exposure conditions occurring on actual farms should be replicated, with only air pollution concentration being modified (Unsworth 1982). While general responses to air pollution of plants grown in different environments may be similar, the quantitative relationships between dose and response are clearly affected by environmental conditions.

Table 4.1 shows that out of 18 economic studies of ozone, conducted since 1982, 11 have relied upon NCLAN response data, derived from field experiments, as their main source. Of six studies carried out at the national level, for the US, all used NCLAN data. At the regional level a mixture of data sources are often used. For example, the two studies using secondary data, discussed above, also made use of experimental data for some crops. NCLAN data are a primary source of response information but have so far been restricted to major US agricultural crops. In Europe the EOTCP could potentially supply dose-response functions for economic assessments but, unlike NCLAN, no integration with agricultural or environmental economists was considered, making NCLAN data a more useful source despite obvious variations in environmental conditions.

While the derivation of response functions used in economic assessments has improved, the application of the functions has sometimes been both technically and economically deficient. Serious errors can arise from extrapolating from a limited database. For example, the Organization for Economic Cooperation and Development (OECD 1981) performed a cost–benefit analysis of sulphur oxide which included the benefits expected from crop loss reductions under various scenarios. A dose–yield relationship was developed from information on the response to sulphur dioxide of rye grass (*Lolium perenne*) and applied to all crops throughout Europe. Barnes et al. (1983) have made the following major criticisms of this study:

Table 4.1   Main source(s) of response functions used in 18 economic studies of ozone effects on agriculture

Source of dose-response data	Number of publications
Experimentation	
NCLAN	11
Other	6
Secondary	2
Foliar injury	1
Field observation	0

1. It ignored crop and cultivar sensitivities: rye grass is one of the crops most sensitive to sulphur dioxide, resulting in overestimation of damages.
2. It ignored differences in soil sulphur content: the rye grass studies used gave the plant nutritionally adequate supplies, again leading to over-estimation of damage because nutrient-deficient soils actually benefit from sulphur deposition.
3. Overestimation was created by extended extrapolation beyond plant threshold and background pollutant levels, thus creating the illusion of damages when they would be absent or irrelevant to the control of anthropogenic sources.
4. The research into rye grass used was mostly from laboratory or greenhouse experiments. This can give results varying widely from plant response to sulphur oxide under field conditions.

This kind of extrapolation and use of response functions ignores the limits of the database. The application of one set of results to other crops, cultivars, regions or countries abstracts from variations in plant sensitivity and environmental conditions. However, a certain amount of extrapolation can be justified and would be required in Europe where economically useful dose-response data is limited. In the case of ozone, data are unavailable for many regionally important crops and cultivars; so far, experimental results are largely derived for the major crop-growing regions of the US. In the absence of alternative data, 'surrogate' response functions have been used for crops judged to be of similar sensitivity. For example, Howitt et al. (1984) studied the economic effects of ozone on 13 crops. They used NCLAN data for seven crops and derived five 'surrogate' response functions. Such use of response data relies upon the judgement of researchers and implicitly involves the subjective estimation of uncertainty. This type of probabilistic estimation requires explicit explanation of the areas of uncertainty so that the accuracy of, and possible bias in, the final results are clear.

REGIONAL ECONOMIC ASSESSMENTS OF CROP LOSS

In this section, studies using four assessment methods are described: the traditional model, linear and quadratic programming approaches, econometric approaches, and duality models. The majority of economic assessments of ozone damage to crops have been at the regional level, applying a range of economic modelling techniques. Those readers interested in national-level studies are referred to reviews in Adams et al. (1984), Kopp et al. (1985) and Adams and Crocker (1991). The national level study by Adams et al. (1984) was updated as part of the final reporting on the NCLAN programme and results appear in Adams et al. (1989), giving a regional breakdown of changes in producers' surplus for ozone control scenarios. The work done in this area before circa 1982 was scientifically orientated and concentrated upon the accuracy of physical estimates of ozone damage to crops. Where monetary values of damages were given, the traditional model was employed without regard for the overestimation this technique can cause. Published studies have concentrated on two main regions of the US; namely, the Corn Belt (Illinois, Indiana, Iowa, Ohio and Missouri) and California. These areas have a good supply of data on crop response and air quality, and are nationally important crop-growing regions.

An example of the traditional model is the work of Linzon et al. (1984) who analysed 15 crops grown in two regions of Ontario, Canada. Yield reductions were estimated for each crop using the experimental results of other researchers. No damage was assumed to occur at ozone levels of 0.03 ppm or lower (seven-hour seasonal mean). The traditional model was used to calculate monetary equivalents of the approximated crop losses. Increased yields, due to pollutant reduction, were multiplied by the current market price to give a producer benefit estimate equal to total revenue; extra production costs were deemed too small for subtraction. The constancy of price assumption was justified (i) by the small magnitude of crop production from the region relative to total market production, and (ii) by the existence of supply management and marketing boards. The fact that aggregate supply curves are normally positively sloped was ignored by Linzon et al.; thus the disjointed function of the traditional model was implicitly accepted. The traditional model seems certain to grossly overestimate the gain to producers from ozone reductions. This study estimated the average gain to producers of reducing ozone from current levels (the highest regional category being 0.05 ppm, seven-hour seasonal mean) to 0.03 ppm as $15 million per annum, with a range of $9–23 million (1980 dollars). Five crops accounted for over 80 per cent of the estimate due to their sensitivity to ozone – namely, potatoes, soybeans, tobacco, wheat and white beans. Other examples of the traditional approach are Forster (1984) and Pearson (1982), and the approach is shown to cause considerable overestimation by comparison with a quadratic programming model in Howitt and Goodman (1988).

Quadratic programming approaches have been applied in five economic regional studies, of ozone crop losses, published since 1982. Four of these were based on the agricultural crop-growing regions of California and employed similar models (Adams et al. 1982; Howitt et al. 1984; Rowe and Chestnut 1985; Howitt and Goodman 1988). The fifth study generated welfare estimates via a micro–macro model, using farm models to derive the effects of regional production changes on national markets (Adams and McCarl 1985). Two examples of linear programming models exist in the published literature.

Brown and Smith (1984) employ a linear programming model to look at cross-crop substitution for corn, soybeans and wheat grown in Indiana in response to reducing ambient ozone levels. More recently, a linear programming model has been used to analyse ozone impacts on seven crops in the Swiss Central Plateau using NCLAN and surrogate data along with results from Swiss open-top chamber experiments (Näf 1991; Näf and Fuhrer 1993).

Adams et al. (1982) studied 14 field crops in four regions of southern California. The dose-response functions are a major weakness of the study, being calculated from foliar injury models which have been converted to reflect yield loss. This approach showed broccoli, cantaloupes, carrots, cauliflower and lettuce to be ozone resistant, with little or no damage occurring. Lettuce in particular seems to be incorrectly classified, with evidence existing which states it to be an ozone sensitive crop. The optimal crop mix after ozone concentrations were reduced showed a very significant decrease in the production of these air pollution tolerant crops, due to their substantially reduced profitability relative to crops that were more sensitive to ozone.

Linear inverse demand functions were assumed for each crop, that is, price as a function of quantities. The supply functions for all production inputs were assumed to be perfectly price elastic. The Willig approximation conditions were invoked so that any differences between ordinary and compensated consumer surplus were assumed to be trivial. This invocation was justified because neither income elasticities nor expenditures as a percentage of income seemed likely to be large for the crops being studied.

The model (calibrated to 1976) was set up to maximize the sum of producer and consumer surpluses. Reducing ozone levels to 0.08 ppm, the state standard, would have increased 1976 producer quasi-rents by $35.1 million and consumer surplus by $10.1 million. Production changes induced by altering ozone concentrations were assumed to leave the input mix constant. Changes in ozone concentrations from 1976 levels were reflected by changes in the optimal mix of outputs. Due to the variety of demand price elasticities across crops, the distribution of benefits was a function of the mix of demand curves and resultant crop proportions in the solution. For example, the removal of cotton from the study caused the balance between consumer and producer surpluses to be reversed. Cotton has an elastic demand curve, so that the benefits from ozone reduction were largely in terms of a producer surplus. The exclusion of cotton reduced the producer gain to $9 million and left the consumer gain almost unchanged at $10 million.

Although mitigation was allowed for by cross-crop substitution, the authors felt that the use of fixed 1976 production coefficients and resource levels potentially constrained the possible producer mitigative adjustments on the input side. Thus, they warned that the subsequent programming results and welfare effects might be overestimated. They also suggested, among other things, that improvements could be made by allowing for non-zero cross-price elasticities, widening the scope to include effects in other regions and markets and studying a greater variety of crops.

Howitt et al. (1984) studied 13 crops, also in the state of California. They employed the NCLAN experimental results to derive dose-response functions for seven of the crops and other experimental results for one other crop. The remaining five crops were given 'surrogate' response functions. The California Agriculture Resources Model (CARM) was used to calculate consumer and producer surpluses. This quadratic programming model allowed for constrained cross-crop substitution and included 27 other crops which were assumed unaffected by ozone concentrations. The model was similar to that used by Adams et al. (1982) above but was calibrated to 1978 instead of 1976.

Three ozone scenarios were compared with a base case for 1978. The total welfare gain from a reduction in ambient ozone of approximately 25 per cent (to 0.04 ppm, seasonal seven-hour mean) was $35.8 million per annum, and the welfare loss from an increase in ozone levels by approximately 33 per cent (to 0.08 ppm, seasonal seven-hour mean) was $157.3 million. (These percentage estimates are given in Adams et al. (1984, p. 10).) Reductions in ozone concentrations cause a 'downward shift' of the supply function, which is shown graphically as a rotation, that is, the price intercept remains the same.

Rowe and Chestnut (1985) used the CARM, as utilized by Howitt et al. (1984), to study 16 crops in the San Joaquin Valley, California. Although 33 crops were included in the economic model, only 16 were judged to be affected by ozone or could be supplied with dose-response functions. The study analysed the use of field data regression to derive dose-response functions, but obtained statistically significant results for only four crops: dry beans, cotton, grapes and potatoes. As a result, NCLAN functions were used for six other crops, while a further six were derived from other sources and by the use of 'surrogate' functions. Three ozone scenarios were studied (0.12, 0.10 and 0.08 ppm seasonal hourly maximum) and results were given for both consumers and producers. Sulphur dioxide was also included in the study, but over 98 per cent of the economic value of the agricultural damages was attributed to ozone. If an ozone standard at which little or no crop damage was expected (defined as 0.08 ppm seasonal hourly maximum) had been met in 1978, the estimated gain to consumers would have been $30.3 million and the gain to producers $87.1 million.

Adams and McCarl (1985) studied three crops in the Corn Belt region of the US (Illinois, Indiana, Iowa, Missouri and Ohio) with a quadratic-programming model calibrated to 1980. The dose-response functions were taken from NCLAN results for 1980–82 and were Illinois specific (but also compared with pre-NCLAN response information). The model analysed the changes occurring throughout the agricultural sector at the national level as a result of the adjustments in Corn Belt output, *ceteris paribus*. This was achieved by characterizing regional agricultural production using 12 representative farm models. These representative farms were then used to generate supply adjustments in the national level model. Consumer and producer surpluses were calculated under two scenarios. An improvement in air quality of 25 per cent (a reduction of ozone from 0.12 ppm to 0.08 ppm one-hour seasonal mean) gave net benefits of $688 million (1980), a loss to producers of $1411 million and a gain to consumers of $2079 million. The other scenario took a 50 per cent degradation in air quality (an increase in ozone from 0.12 ppm to 0.16 ppm one-hour seasonal mean) and gave a net loss of benefits of $2225 million, a reduction of consumer surplus by $4986 million and an increase of producer surplus by $2761 million. Increases in crop supply were found to favour consumers while reductions in crop supply favoured producers. These distributional consequences are a result of supply shifts in the face of a price inelastic demand curve. That is, output increases but farmers lose out as the price falls by a relatively large amount.

Several econometric approaches of varying sophistication have been applied to the assessment of crop damage due to ozone pollution (Benson et al. 1982; Leung et al. 1982; Page et al. 1982; Spash 1987; Adomait et al. 1987). An example of an econometric model, which analyses producer surplus changes, is presented and then the dual approach is discussed and referenced separately. Published research shows variation between models, for example concerning assumptions about the nature of agricultural crop supply curves and production responses.

Benson et al. (1982) studied four crops in Minnesota. Originally, six crops were to have been studied but since dose-response functions could not be calculated for soybeans and oats, they were dropped. Dose response for the four remaining crops was calculated using experimental data reported by other researchers. The dose-response functions allowed for episodic (as opposed to chronic or acute) exposure by breaking the exposure into multiple time periods over the growing season. The functions were applied to Minnesota using actual or simulated county-level ozone data. This was used to derive a range of yield losses under different ozone concentrations.

The economic analysis, using a comprehensive econometric model of US agriculture, was carried out under two separate conditions: (i) crop loss was restricted to Minnesota alone, and Minnesota and US production levels were estimated; (ii) the same rate of loss as occurred in Minnesota was assumed to occur over the entire US, and again Minnesota and national production levels were estimated. A range of producer welfare estimates was derived, with the worst-case ozone level (0.12 ppm hourly concentration with ten occurrences per week) causing a *loss* of $30 366 409 under assumption (i) compared to

1980 production. The worst-case estimate under assumption (ii) gave a *gain* to producers of $67 540 745 compared to 1980 production.

The explanation for the gain under (ii) is that price rises as output is restricted and the 'price effect' dominates, whereas under (i) the 'production effect' dominates. The increase in the total value of production as ozone increases is due to the price-inelastic nature of demand for the commodities studied. This 'gain' to producers is in fact misleading for a couple of reasons. First, costs have risen due to ozone pollution, and so a loss of comparative advantage is suffered by all affected farmers (the gain is at best a short-run phenomenon as competition from other sources would drive high-cost producers out of the industry; as the authors note, scenario (i) is more likely in the long run). Second, focusing on the 'gain' to producers ignores the dynamics of consumer and producer welfare. Benson et al. do not calculate consumer surplus; therefore the net change in societal welfare and the distribution of welfare changes are unknown. In addition, scenario (ii) is highly dubious because of the assumption that regional dose-response/ozone estimates can be extrapolated to the national level.

Although a detailed national-level model was used, Benson's economic analysis is similar to that of the traditional model. A comprehensive econometric model of the US agricultural sector (calibrated to 1980) was used to capture crop supply and demand across multiple domestic and foreign markets. Despite accounting for national-level changes, the regional model remains simplistic in that quantity is being multiplied by price in order to estimate the 'value' of production (namely producer quasi-rents). Also, cross-crop substitution is ignored as a mitigative strategy.

The final method which has been used in economic assessment of crop losses is the duality approach. The first published example appears in several versions (Mjelde et al. 1984; Dixon et al. 1985; Garcia et al. 1986); all minor variations of the same model originally reported in Dixon et al. (1984). More recently another dual application has appeared in the literature with Young and Aidun (1993) studying ozone impacts on wheat in Alberta, Canada, estimating profit and cost functions.

The Dixon et al. (1984) model employed the neo-classical econometric model with a profit function. Duality models are not dependent on an explicit dose-response function to estimate the welfare changes from a change in crop yield. However, experimental data are required to frame the initial hypothesis and to cross-check the resulting estimates. The profit function, which includes ordinary economic variables and environmental variables (as fixed inputs), shows the effects of varying ozone concentrations on farm profits.

Pollution, which is deleterious to the production process, will exert an exogenous force upon producer decisions. Producers may respond by varying input mixes, even if they are unaware of the phenomenon causing the observed effects. Dixon et al. (1985, p. 404) note the advantage of a dual approach is that a profit function that has air quality as an input can be used directly to determine losses in a producer's profit and assess how inputs are adjusted in response to a change in air quality. A dose-response function cannot provide this latter type of information while under the dual approach the farmer's response incorporates adjustments triggered by price yield effects. However, part of this theoretical advantage may be lost in the case of ozone as producer adjustments should exclude a change of input mix. In order to compare the results of a dual study with experimental results, such as those of NCLAN, the mix of variable inputs is assumed constant. Although producers may be allowed to adjust their output mix under the dual approach, they are prevented from doing so in this study.

The Dixon et al. study, as reported in Mjelde et al. (1984), analysed three crops in Illinois. Detailed farm-level cost and production information was made available by the Illinois Association of Farm Business Farm Management, which provided a rich source of individual farm data unavailable in many other states. The study found that increased ozone levels depressed output and reduced the marginal productivity of variable inputs so that less was used. Ozone resulted in an aggregate loss in profits to Illinois farmers of approximately $50 million (1980). The assumption of a constant price ignores consumer surplus and may be unjustified because Illinois is a major grain producer. Also, if ozone reduction improved crop yields throughout the Corn Belt, both consumers and producers would be expected to benefit. The authors do recommend extreme caution in the use of their results (Mjelde et al. 1984, p. 361). In particular they note concern over the assumption that price remains constant because such an assumption is invalid if ambient ozone levels increase in other grain-producing regions. As a result the supply curve of feed grains would shift to the left, and (given a typically inelastic short-run demand curve) the corresponding price rise may leave producers better off than before the ozone increase, while consumers would be worse off.

ACIDIC DEPOSITION

Investigations of the effects of acidic precipitation on vegetation started in the 1970s but with regard to field crops mostly concerned soybeans until the US National Acid Precipitation Programme (NAPAP) in the mid-1980s (DuBay et al. 1985). Crops may be affected by foliage or above-ground exposure (direct effects) and by changes in soil chemistry due to additions of sulphur and nitrogen (indirect effects). These could potentially neutralize each other if the indirect effect of passive fertilization is strong enough, although this is dependent on edaphic factors and crop cultivar. There has been some debate concerning which crops are susceptible enough to be economically significant (see Adams et al. 1986a and the comment on this by Forster 1987) with corn and soybean appearing as most affected commercial crops. Adams et al. (1986a) give evidence for impacts on some soybean cultivars for large changes in acidity, a 50 per cent increase in acidity causing a 1–7 per cent yield loss. In the US, soybeans have been the only major, commercially important crop showing a consistently negative response to wet deposition (Irving 1983) with the majority of crops showing no response under experimental conditions (Huckabee 1983).

Forster (1984) pointed to evidence showing that corn was also susceptible to acidic deposition and claimed this could be important for Eastern Canada. However, using the traditional model, he calculated relatively small welfare losses of $105 million and a gain from passive fertilization of $2.6 million, for Ontario. In 1980, Crocker gave evidence to the US Congress that agricultural damages due to acidic deposition were $1 billion for the US (Crocker 1985; Crocker and Regens 1985). This loss was calculated using ozone pollution as a surrogate and was stated to be highly tentative. A study of SO_2 impacts on US corn, soybeans and cotton (Manuel et al. 1981) is reported in Brown and Smith (1984) but without citing the welfare changes. Adams et al. (1986a) used the quadratic programming model of Adams et al. (1984, 1986b) to calculate damages to US agriculture of $140 million (1980 dollars) for then current acidic deposition levels, but also calculated that passive fertilization could increase welfare by $50 million. Forster (1987) criticized this work, which focused solely on soybeans, and defended his own estimates which the authors had brought into question. Much seemed to depend upon which plant science evidence was trusted and use of the US NAPAP data reduced Forster's own estimates of losses for Ontario from $105 million to $2.4 million.

Ludlow and Smit (1987) conducted a far more comprehensive and defensible study of acidic deposition damages in Ontario. They estimated net crop losses of $43 million using a multiregional analysis (based at the county level) and employing a linear programming model for 17 crops and fruits. They used both available experimental evidence and surrogate dose-response functions. These functions give negative yield responses at ambient acidity levels for corn, potatoes, soybeans, apples, grapes, peaches and sweet corn, and positive yield responses for field beans, hay, tobacco, green peas and tomatoes. However, corn was by far the most important crop in welfare terms, with a change in farm value of $47 million.

The economic impacts estimated for the US are small compared to both other effects of acidic deposition (for example, on forests, aquatic resources and materials) and to crop losses from ozone (Segerson 1991). The NAPAP results show a $20–152 million loss (1984 dollars) for a 10–50 per cent increase in acidity (Callaway et al. 1986), which compares with a $2.4 billion loss estimated for a 25 per cent increase in ozone (Adams et al. 1984). This NAPAP study employed the same quadratic programming model as the ozone study to calculate these economic losses.

Segerson (1987) has identified several respects in which acidic deposition is a different issue from ozone, which have implications for its economic analysis with regard to impacts upon agricultural crops. First, acidic deposition is recognized to affect a wide range of non-market goods while ozone research has concentrated upon agricultural crops. Second, acidic deposition is a dynamic pollutant with effects accumulating over time, while ozone is episodic. Thus, ozone models can be based on short-term analyses in contrast to acidic deposition which should be based upon assessing accumulated impacts over time, for example, soil buffering capacity, heavy metals increase. Third, there is far greater uncertainty over acidic deposition impacts on crops than for ozone. Fourth, ozone pollution has been a regional/national problem while acidic deposition is an inter-regional/ international externality. However, concern is increasing over the threat of global smog, with evidence showing a rise in Northern Hemisphere background concentrations of 1–2 per cent per year over the last two decades (Fishman 1991).

In general, the economic interest in crop losses due to acidic deposition has probably been very low due to the relatively small size of the losses reported in published studies, despite potentially important regional impacts. Interestingly, some of the literature which at first appears to be concerned with acidic deposition is in fact misleadingly titled and actually devoted solely to tropospheric ozone with regards to crop loss (Phillips and Forster 1987; Adams and Crocker 1984).

CONCLUSIONS

In performing an economic assessment of crop loss due to air pollution, the response changes of interest are those related to both the costs of production and the marketability of a product (Adams et al. 1985; Adams and Crocker 1988). That is, there are two routes via which pollution-induced crop damage can influence the welfare of consumers and producers. First, a reduction in crop damage, expressed as an increase in yield, will reduce costs and therefore reduce the minimum price the producer must receive to supply a given quantity. Second, altered levels of air pollution may affect the attributes of a crop, thus changing the consumer's willingness to pay and the welfare derived from the consumption of a given quantity of a crop. The change in cost implies a supply response, while the change in quality a demand response.

Studies conducted on air pollution crop damage have tended to concentrate upon yield, and therefore are only relevant to the supply response. These supply responses have often ignored farmers' reactions in terms of changing the input mix and cross-crop substitution. Research into potential crop quality changes has received even less emphasis with only one study to date (Shortle et al. 1988 with regards to US soybean production). Yet there is evidence that such quality changes do result from air pollution. Examples of quality changes due to ozone are shrivelling in kernels of corn, reduction in the size of tomatoes, and alterations in chemical composition that affect cooking quality of potatoes and nutritional values of alfalfa (Jacobson 1982). Table 4.2 clearly shows a wide range of possible crop responses to ozone. Research is required to estimate the importance of these responses. This may be a difficult problem to resolve where consumer tastes are concerned, requiring objective characteristics to be associated with economic attributes in order to allow the derivation of dose-response functions appropriate for economic benefit assessments. However, without work in this area, economic assessments cannot be made of the full range of possible economic impacts caused by air pollution.

Crop damage is a function of the pollutant dose, crop species and cultivar, and biological, climatic, edaphic, production and other factors. The interaction of these variables makes accurate crop loss assessment, especially over large areas, an error-prone task. Results from field experiments, especially those of NCLAN, have increased the accuracy with which the economic consequences of plant damage caused by ozone can be estimated. Where crop or region-specific information is lacking, qualified approximations to actual responses can be made using surrogate functions. Current economic assessments of crop loss from ozone are restricted by a lack of information as to the importance of crop quality responses and must therefore concentrate upon supply response alone.

Table 4.2   Processes and characteristics of crop plants that may be affected by ozone

Growth	Development	Yield	Quality
Rate	Fruit set and development	Number	Appearance: size, shape, colour
Pattern	Branching Flowering	Mass	Storage life Texture/cooking quality Nutrient content Viability of seeds

Source: Jacobson (1982a), p. 296, Table 14.1.

Several methodologies are available for crop loss assessment and have been applied to the analysis of welfare changes due to alterations in air pollution levels. Among these the microtheoretic econometric models provide a theoretically rigorous structure and have become a common approach to studying the agricultural sector in general. In conceptualizing agricultural crop production changes, neutral factor productivity enhancement is unanimously accepted (that is, no input is favoured or harmed more than any other by ozone concentrations), while output substitution will depend upon particular circumstances. Demand functions must be estimated if credible welfare measures are to be obtained. Finally, the supply function characteristics used in recent studies have not been fully explained and may cause unjustified bias in benefit estimates.

A more general issue raised by the current methodology for economic assessment of air pollution impacts on agricultural crops is the dependence upon scientific research. Adams et al. (1985) have criticized the replicative approach to dose-response estimation due to the common abstraction from field conditions in the experimental approach and, more generally, the excessive use of scarce research resources for small returns in terms of accuracy. The number of observations being produced upon a single cultivar is excessive when prior information is employed in a Bayesian approach. Also, too much research is conducted into dose-response functions in terms of their application for economic benefit assessment because economic factors tend to be insensitive to minor changes in physical parameters. Ashmore (1993) points out that many published scientific studies use ozone concentrations far in excess of field conditions, that glasshouse and laboratory experiments affect plant response, and fumigation is only for a few weeks out of the plant's life rather than for the growing season. The European research of EOTCP tried to avoid these failures but neglected economic assessment (see the balance of research in Jäger et al. 1993), and persisted with open-top chambers compared to NCLAN field experiments.

However, even given field experiments, the cultivar by cultivar, single pollutant approach used to develop dose-response functions can appear unrealistically abstract from agricultural realities. Economic assessment is concerned with a multitude of crops and cultivars, and their exposure to a range of pollutants and environmental stresses. Interestingly, much attention has been paid to corn and soybeans in the regional economic assessments of ozone (Page et al. 1982; Adams and McCarl 1985; Brown and Smith 1984; Kopp et al. 1985; Mjelde et al. 1984; Shortle et al. 1988) and both crops have been indicated as susceptible to acidic deposition. Thus, the NCLAN finding of no significant decrease in crop yields from SO_2 or SO_2/O_3 interactions (Heck et al. 1991) is an important indicator that economic and scientific assessments have not failed by concentrating on ozone. Yet the tendency has been to perfect scientific data ignoring the potential for such interactions rather than starting out by showing that they are unimportant. In the field, crops are rarely exposed simultaneously to two or more pollutants, but rather go through a sequence of exposures in which the frequency and timing are important determinants of response. Preston and Tingey (1988) suggest ranking the importance of various factors on the basis of current knowledge or conducting principal component analysis to obtain a short list for further study. Adams and Crocker (1991) have argued that a basic understanding of the sign and magnitude of biological response under field conditions can be sufficient for economic implications of policy alternatives to be estimated. Developing such information might save research time and costs, but would require a level of communication between the economic and plant science disciplines which has so far been excluded by the European approach.

REFERENCES

Adams, R.M., J.M. Callaway and B.A. McCarl (1986a), 'Pollution, agriculture and social welfare: the case of acid deposition', *Canadian Journal of Agricultural Economics*, **34** (March): 3–19.

Adams, R.M. and T.D. Crocker (1984), 'Economically relevant response estimation and the value of information: acid deposition, in Crocker (ed.), pp. 35–64.

Adams, R.M. and T.D. Crocker (1988), 'Model requirements for economic evaluations of pollution impacts upon agriculture', in Heck et al. (eds), pp. 463–72.

Adams, R.M. and T.D. Crocker (1991), 'The economic impact of air pollution on agriculture: an assessment and review', in M.D. Young (ed.), *Towards Sustainable Agricultural Development*, London: Belhaven Press, Ch. 10, pp. 295–319.

Adams, R.M., T.D. Crocker and R.W. Katz (1985), 'Yield response data in benefit–cost analyses of pollution-induced vegetation damage', in W.E. Winner, H.A. Mooney and R.A. Goldstein (eds), *Sulphur Dioxide and Vegetation: Physiology, Ecology and Policy Issues*, Stanford, CA: Stanford University Press, pp. 56–72.

Adams, R.M., T.D. Crocker and N. Thanavibulchai (1982), 'An economic assessment of air pollution damages to selected annual crops in Southern California', *Journal of Environmental Economics and Management*, **9**: 42–58.

Adams, R.M., J.D. Glyer, S.L. Johnson and B.A. McCarl (1989), 'A reassessment of the economic effects of ozone on United States agriculture', *Journal of the Air and Waste Management Association*, **39**(7): 960–68.

Adams, R.M., S.A. Hamilton and B.A. McCarl (1984), 'The economic effects of ozone on agriculture', Corvallis, OR: Environmental Research Laboratory, US Environmental Protection Agency.

Adams, R.M., S.A. Hamilton and B.A. McCarl (1986b), 'The benefits of pollution control: the case of ozone and U.S. agriculture', *American Journal of Agricultural Economics*, **68**(4): 886–93.

Adams, R.M. and B.A. McCarl (1985), 'Assessing the benefits of alternative ozone standards on agriculture: the role of response information', *Journal of Environmental Economics and Management*, **12**: 264–76.

Adams, R.M., B.A. McCarl, D.J. Dudek and J.D. Glyer (1988), 'Implications of global climate change for western agriculture', *Western Journal of Agricultural Economics*, **13**(2): 348–56.

Adomait, E.J., J. Ensing and G. Hofstra (1987), 'A dose-response function for the impact of O₃ on Ontario grown white bean and an estimate of economic loss', *Canadian Journal of Plant Science*, **67**: 131–6.

Ashmore, M.R. (1993), 'Critical levels and agriculture in Europe', in Jäger et al. (eds), pp. 105–29.

Barnes, R.A., G.S. Parkinson and A.E. Smith (1983), 'The costs and benefits of sulphur oxide control', *Journal of Air Pollution Control Association*, **33**: 737–41.

Benson, E.J., S. Krupa, P.S. Teng and P.E. Welsch (1982), 'Economic assessment of air pollution damages to agricultural and silvicultural crops', final report to Minnesota Pollution Control Agency.

Brown, D. and M. Smith (1984), 'Crop substitution in the estimation of the economic benefits due to ozone reduction', *Journal of Environmental Economics and Management*, **11**(4): 347–62.

Callaway, J.M., R.F. Darwin and R.J. Nesse (1986), 'Economic valuation of acidic deposition damages: preliminary results from the 1985 NAPAP assessment', *Water Air and Soil Pollution*, **31**(3–4): 1021–36.

Carrier, J.-G. and E. Kripple (1990), 'Comprehensive study of European forests assesses damage and economic losses from air pollution', *Environmental Conservation*, **17**(4): 365–6.

Chameides, W.L., P.S. Kasibhatla, J. Yienger and H. Levy (1994), 'Growth of continental-scale metro-agro-plexes, regional ozone pollution, and world food production', *Science*, 264 (April): 74–7.

Colbeck, I. (1988), 'The occurrence of nocturnal ozone maxima at a rural site in northwest England', *Environmental Technology Letters*, **9**(1): 75–80.

Crocker, T.D. (ed.) (1984), *Economic Perspectives on Acid Deposition Control*, London: Butterworth.

Crocker, T.D. (1985), 'Estimates of acid deposition control benefits: a Bayesian perspective', in Mandelbaum (ed.), pp. 77–94.

Crocker, T.D and J.L. Regens (1985), 'Acid deposition control: a benefit–cost analysis', *Environmental Science and Technology*, **19**: 112–15.

Dixon, B.L., P. Garcia and J.W. Mjelde (1985), 'Primal versus dual methods measuring the impacts of ozone on cash grain farms', *American Journal of Agricultural Economics*, **67**(2): 402–6.

Dixon, B.L., P. Garcia, J.W. Mjelde and R.M. Adams (1984), 'Estimation of the cost of ozone on Illinois cash grain farms: an application of duality', Urbana, IL: Agricultural Economics Staff Paper No. 84 E-276, University of Illinois.

DuBay, D.T., R.I. Bruck, C.L. Campbell, J.D. Elson, R.E. Ferell, W.W. Heck and J.M. Stucky (1985), 'Acid deposition in North Carolina: effects on agricultural crops', Triangle Conference on Environmental Technology, Raleigh, North Carolina, 3–4 April.

Fishman, J. (1991), 'Global smog: a new environmental threat', in R.L. Berglund, D.R. Lawson and D.K. McKee (eds), *Tropospheric Ozone and the Environment: Papers from an International Conference*, Pittsburgh: Air and Waste Management Association, pp. 38–51.

Forster, B.A. (1984), 'An economic assessment of the significance of long-range transported air pollutants for agricultural in eastern Canada', *Canadian Journal of Agricultural Economics*, **32**(3): 498–525.

Forster, B.A. (1987), 'Agricultural impacts of acid deposition: some issues to consider', *Canadian Journal of Agricultural Economics*, **35**(1): 241-7.

Garcia, P., B.L. Dixon, J.W. Mjelde and R.M. Adams (1986), 'Measuring the benefits of environmental change using a duality approach: the case of ozone and Illinois cash grain farms', *Journal of Environmental Economics and Management*, **13**(1): 69-80.

Grennfelt, P. (1992), 'The critical levels for ozone and the necessary reductions of the emissions of ozone precursors', in C. Agre and P. Elvingson, *Critical Loads for Air Pollutants*, Göteborg: Swedish NGO Secretariat on Acid Rain, pp. 24-8.

Heck, W.W., W.W. Cure, J.O. Rawlings, L.J. Zaragoza, A.S. Heagle, H.E. Heggestad, R.J. Kohut, L.W. Kress and P.J. Temple (1984), 'Assessing impacts of ozone on agricultural crops: I', *Journal of Air Pollution Control Association*, **34**(7): 729-35.

Heck, W.W., R.I. Larsen and A.S. Heagle (1980), 'Measuring the acute dose-response of plants to ozone', paper presented at E.C. Stakman Commemorative Symposium, University of Minnesota, Minneapolis.

Heck, W.W., A.S. Heagle, J.E. Miller and J.O. Rawlings (1991), 'A national program (NCLAN) to assess the impact of ozone on agricultural resources', in R.L. Berglund, D.R. Lawson and D.K. McKee (eds), *Tropospheric Ozone and the Environment: Papers from an International Conference*, Pittsburgh: Air and Waste Management Association, pp. 225-54.

Heck, W.W., O.C. Taylor, R. Adams, G. Bingham, J. Miller, E. Preston and L. Weinstein (1982), 'Assessment of crop loss from ozone', *Journal of Air Pollution Control Association*, **32**(4): 353-61.

Heck, W.W., O.C. Taylor and D.T. Tingey (eds) (1988), *Assessment of Crop Loss from Air Pollutants*, London: Elsevier Science.

Holdgate, M.W. (1979), *A Perspective of Environmental Pollution*, Cambridge: Cambridge University Press.

Howitt, R.E. and C. Goodman (1988), 'Economic impacts of regional ozone standards on agricultural crops', *Environmental Pollution*, **53**: 387-95.

Howitt, R.E., Gossard T.E. and Adams R.M. (1984), 'Effects of alternative ozone levels and response data on economic assessments: the case of California crops', *Journal of Air Pollution Control Association*, **34**(11): 1122-7.

Huckabee, J. (1983), 'Effects of acidic deposition on agricultural crops', *Electric Power Research Institute*, July–August: 51-3.

Irving, P.M. (1983), 'Acidic precipitation effects on crops: a review and analysis of research', *Journal of Environmental Quality*, **12**: 442-53.

Jacobson, J.S. (1982), 'Ozone and the growth and productivity of agricultural crops', in M.H. Unsworth and D.P. Ormond (eds), *Effects of Gaseous Air Pollutants in Agriculture and Horticulture*, London: Butterworths.

Jäger, H.J., M. Unsworth, L. de Temmerman and P. Mathy (1993), *Effects of Air Pollution on Agricultural Crops in Europe*, Brussels: Commission of the European Communities.

Kamari, J., M. Amann, Y. Brodin, M.J. Chadwick, A. Henriksen, J.P. Heltelingh, J. Kuylenstierna, M. Posch and H. Sverdrup (1992), 'The use of critical loads for the assessment of future alternatives to acidification', *Ambio*, **21**(5): 377-86.

Kopp, R.J., W.J. Vaughan, M. Hazilla and R. Carson (1985), 'Implications of environmental policy for United States agriculture: the case of ambient ozone standards', *Journal of Environmental Management*, **20**(4): 321-31.

Leung, S.K., W. Reed, S. Cauchois and R. Howitt (1978), 'Methodologies for valuation of agricultural crop yield changes: a review', Sacramento, CA: Eureka Laboratories, Corvallis, OR: US, EPA, EPA/600/5-78/018, NTIS/PB-288.

Leung, S.K., W. Reed and S. Geng (1982), 'Estimation of ozone damage to selected crops grown in Southern California', *Journal of Air Pollution Control Association*, **32**: 160–64.

Linzon, S.N., R.G. Pearson, J.A. Donnan and F.N. Durham (1984), 'Ozone effects on crops in Ontario and related monetary values', Ontario: Ministry of Environment.

Ludlow, L. and B. Smit (1987), 'Assessing the implications of environmental change for agricultural production: the case of acid rain in Ontario, Canada', *Journal of Environmental Management*, **25**: 27–44.

MacKenzie, J.J. and M.T. El-Ashry (1989), *Air Pollution's Toll on Forests and Crops*, New Haven, CT: Yale University Press.

Mandelbaum, P. (ed.) (1985), *Acid Rain: Economic Assessment*, New York: Plenum Press.

Manuel, E.H., R.L. Hoist, K.M. Brennan, W.N. Lansen, M.C. Duff and J.K. Tapiero (1981), *Benefits Analysis of Alternative Secondary National Ambient Air Quality Standards for Sulphur Dioxide and Total Suspended Particulates*, Vol. IV, EPA-68-02-3392, Office of Air Quality Planning and Standards, EPA Washington, DC.

Mathy, P. (1988), 'The European open-top chambers programme: objectives and implementation', in Heck et al. (eds), pp. 505-13.

Medeiros, W.H. and P.D. Moscowitz (1983), 'Quantifying effects of oxidant air pollutants on agricultural crops', *Environment International*, **9**: 505-13.

Mjelde, J.W., R.M. Adams, B.L. Dixon and P. Garcia (1984), 'Using farmers' actions to measure crop loss due to air pollution', *Journal of Air Pollution Control Association*, **31**: 360-64.

Näf, W. (1991), 'Economic consequences of air pollution by ozone for arable farming of Switzerland', *Landwirtschaft Schweiz Band*, **4**(9): 501-6 (in German with English abstract).

Näf, W. and J. Fuhrer (1993), 'Modelling economic effects of ozone: a case study in Switzerland', in Jäger et al. (eds), pp. 297-306.

Organization for Economic Cooperation and Development (1981), *The Costs and Benefits of Sulphur Oxide Control*, Paris: OECD.

Page, W.P., G. Arbogast, R.G. Fabian and J. Ciecka (1982), 'Estimation of economic losses to the agricultural sector from airborne residuals in the Ohio River Basin region', *Journal of Air Pollution Control Association*, **32**: 151-4.

Pearson, R.G. (1982), 'Oxidant effects on agricultural crops in Ontario', unpublished, Ontario Ministry of the Environment, Toronto, Canada.

Phillips, T. and B.A. Forster (1987), 'Economic impacts of acid rain on forest, aquatic, and agricultural ecosystems in Canada', *American Journal of Agricultural Economics*, **69**(5): 963-9.

Preston, E.M. and D.T. Tingey (1988), 'The NCLAN program for crop loss assessment', in Heck et al. (eds), pp. 45-62.

Rowe, R.D. and L.G. Chestnut (1985), 'Economic assessment of the effects of air pollution on agricultural crops in the San Joaquin Valley', *Journal of Air Pollution Control Association*, **35**: 728-34.

Segerson, K. (1987), 'Economic impacts of ozone and acid rain: discussion', *American Journal of Agricultural Economics*, December: 970-71.

Segerson, K. (1991), 'Air pollution and agriculture: a review and evaluation of policy interactions', in R.E. Just and N. Bockstael (eds), *Commodity and Resource Policies in Agricultural Systems*, Berlin: Springer-Verlag, Ch. 18, pp. 349–67.

Shortle, J.S., M. Phillips and J.W. Dunn (1988), 'Economic assessment of crop damages due to air pollution: the role of quality effects', *Environmental Pollution*, 53(1–4): 377–85.

Shröder, J. and C. Reuss (1883), *Die Beschädigung der Vegetation durch Rauch und die Oberharzer Hüttenrauchschäden*, Berlin: P. Parey.

Spash, C.L. (1987), 'Measuring the tangible benefits of environmental improvement: an economic appraisal of regional crop damages due to ozone', unpublished MSc dissertation, University of British Columbia, Canada.

Swain, R.E. (1949), 'Smoke and fume investigations: a historical review', *Industrial and Engineering Chemistry*, 41(11): 2384–8.

Thomas, M.D. (1951), 'Gas damage to plants', *Annual Review of Plant Physiology*, 2: 293–322.

Thomas, M.D. and G.R. Hill (1935), 'Absorption of sulphur dioxide by alfalfa and its relation to leaf injury', *Plant Physiology*, 10: 291–307.

Tingey, D.T., W.E. Hodsett and S. Henderson (1990), 'Definition of adverse effects for the purpose of establishing secondary national ambient air quality standards', *Journal of Environmental Quality*, 19(4): 635–9.

United States, Environmental Research Centre, Environmental Protection Agency (1974), 'The economic damages of air pollution', EPA-600/5-74-012.

Unsworth, M.H. (1982), 'Exposure to gaseous pollutants and uptake by plants', in M.H. Unsworth and D.P. Ormond (eds), *Effects of Gaseous Air Pollutants in Agriculture and Horticulture*, London: Butterworths, pp. 38–54.

Unsworth, M.H. and P. Geissler (1993), 'Results and achievements of the European open-top chamber network', in Jäger et al. (eds), pp. 9–22.

Varey, R.H., D.J. Ball, A.J. Crane, P.H. Laxen and F.J. Sandalls (1988), 'Ozone formation in the London plume', *Atmospheric Environment*, 22(7): 1335–46.

Wilson, R.B. and A.C. Sinfield (1988), 'Policy implications for crop loss assessment research: a United Kingdom perspective', in Heck et al. (eds), pp. 515–19.

Young, D. and S. Aidun (1993), 'Ozone and wheat farming in Alberta: a micro-study of the effects of environmental change', *Canadian Journal of Agricultural Economics*, 41: 27–43.

Zimmerman, P.W. and W. Crocker (1934), 'Toxicity of air containing sulphur dioxide gas', *Contributions from Boyce Thompson Institute*, 6: 455–70.

5. Monetary valuation of the toxic impacts due to acidic deposition in Scotland

Douglas Macmillan*

INTRODUCTION

Emissions of sulphur dioxide (SO_2) have resulted in the acidification of relatively undisturbed ecosystems in remote areas of North America and northern Europe. Although economic activity is limited in these areas, they are important spawning areas for commercially important fish species, especially salmon (*Salmo salar*) and for nature conservation. In the United Kingdom, for example, a recent survey of Sites of Special Scientific Interest (SSSI) by English Nature (Rimes 1992) has revealed acidification damage in almost one-quarter of the total area classified as an SSSI.

Under the EC's Large Combustion Plant Directive (88/609/EEC), the UK is committed to reducing emissions of SO_2 (which contribute approximately two-thirds of all acidic inputs) by 60 per cent in year 2003, with further cuts agreed under the Second Sulphur Protocol of the United Nations Economic Commission for Europe (UNECE). Although the cost of meeting these pollution targets is expected to be over £600 million per year (Sliggers and Klaassen 1994), there have been few attempts to quantify the benefits of SO_2 abatement.

Individuals are expected to value recovery in the natural environment for a number of reasons: (i) anglers will benefit directly from healthier fish populations; (ii) other individuals will obtain indirect benefits from recovery (for example, by reading or watching TV programmes); and (iii) all individuals could derive non-use benefits. Monetary valuation of the environmental benefits of recovery from acidification must overcome three major problems. First, the relationship between SO_2 emissions and environmental damage is complex and reliable dose-response functions are difficult to establish. Second, recovery from acidification will take many years

* The research was funded by the Scottish Office Agriculture, Environment and Fisheries Department.

and economic models must accommodate this long timescale. Third, as non-use benefit values cannot be measured using market data, hypothetical market measures are required.

This chapter describes the application of two different monetary valuation techniques to estimate the economic benefits of recovery from acidification in Scotland. In the first case study, the hedonic price model (HPM) is used to estimate the direct use benefits to anglers, by linking future changes to water chemistry and recovery in fish populations to the market value of salmon fishing. The second case study involves the application of the contingent valuation method (CVM) to estimate the non-use benefits arising from an improvement in the biodiversity of polluted areas. The chapter concludes with a discussion regarding the reliability of the benefit estimates and their relevance to policy decisions.

THE HEDONIC PRICE MODEL (HPM)

The HPM has been widely used by economists to estimate the benefits of environmental improvements in capital markets, particularly for residential properties (Willis and Garrod 1991; Brookshire et al. 1982). It derives from Lancaster's (1966) theory of value, which proposes that each commodity can be described by a combination of its characteristics, one or more of which may be linked to environmental quality.

In Scotland the rights to fish for salmon on rivers using rod and line (angling) are privately owned by individuals, local angling clubs, or commercial enterprises such as hotels and time shares. As average salmon catch is an important determinant of the market value of a beat, it should be possible to use the HPM to estimate the economic value of recovery in salmon catch following abatement, through enhanced capital values for salmon beats.[1]

The HPM is applied in the uplands of the Galloway region in south-west Scotland. Due to a combination of acid-sensitive soils and highly acidic deposition this region has become increasingly acidified over the last 100 years. A wide range of flora and fauna has been affected, with fish populations particularly sensitive to acidification. For example, the upper reaches of six major salmon rivers (Cree and Fleet, Doon, Bladnoch, Dee, Girvan and Stinchar) are thought to have suffered a 50 per cent decline in the average salmon and sea trout catch during the period from 1972 to 1981 (Waters and Kay 1988).

In order to predict the economic value of recovery in the Galloway salmon fishery it is necessary: (i) to predict the effect of reduced acidic deposition on water quality and fish population status; (ii) to link changes in fish population status to fish catch; and (iii) to predict the effect of higher catch on the market value of the salmon fishery. Each stage is briefly described below (full details in Macmillan and Ferrier 1994).

Changes in Water Quality and Fish Populations

The effect of reducing SO_2 emissions on soil and water processes and fish health in Galloway was predicted using the MAGIC model. MAGIC (*M*odel of *A*cidification of *G*roundwaters *I*n *C*atchments) is a process-orientated, intermediate-complexity model which has been widely used in the UK and North America for predicting future water chemistry at the catchment level (Cosby et al. 1990). The MAGIC model was run for the Galloway region using data gathered from a sample of over 30 individual upland catchments that were located in areas considered to be vulnerable to acidification. In the absence of detailed information on the extent of acidification damage in Galloway, the boundary of the affected area was identified from the Scottish critical load map for soils (Figure 5.1).[2]

Predictions of fish population status depend upon water chemistry variables such as pH, alkalinity, and acid neutralizing capacity (ANC). Population status is described in terms of the probability that the fish population will fall into three distinct categories (Wright et al. 1994): (i) healthy (a vigorous population unaffected by acidic deposition), (ii) marginal (a sparse population, either historically thin or damaged by acidic deposition), and (iii) extinct (population lost).

Three SO_2 abatement scenarios were modelled: (i) status quo (emission levels remain constant at 1988 levels); (ii) emissions reduced by 60 per cent from 1980 levels by 1993 (equivalent to the UK's commitment to reduce acidification under the Large Combustion Plant Directive of the EC); and (iii) emissions reduced by 30 per cent in 1993; 60 per cent by 2003 and 90 per cent by 2008 (similar to the Second UNECE Sulphur Protocol). Values for fish population status (H, M, E) and water quality variables were predicted over a 50-year period at five-yearly intervals.

Salmon Catch

It was expected that average salmon catch would be directly related to changes in water quality and fish population status. Reliable data on water quality and fish catch (per unit of effort) is difficult to obtain and a quantitative relationship between fish catch and water quality in the context of acidification has not been established. Fortunately detailed catch data (per boat trip) between the period 1945 and 1970 for Loch Reicawr (one of the catchments sampled in the Galloway application of MAGIC) was obtained

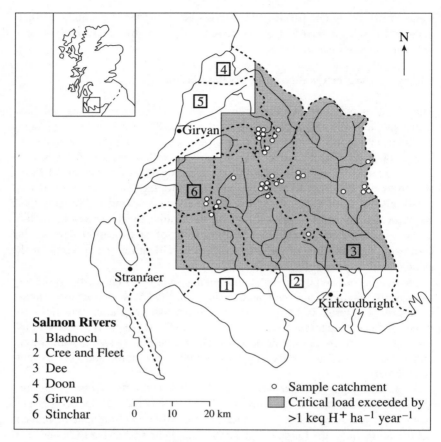

Figure 5.1   Location of sample catchments in the Galloway fishery

from the Balloch Fishing Club and this allowed the relationship between various water quality parameters and fish catch over time to be explored.

Average catch per boat trip (C) was estimated for each year and regressed against a range of water chemistry and fish health parameters that have been predicted for Loch Reicawr from a hindcast projection by MAGIC. The highest correlation was found to be between C and H (the percentage probability of there being a healthy fish population):

$$C = 24.2 - 0.974\,H \tag{5.1}$$

where C = average fish catch per boat trip.

Since data on fish catch per unit effort were not available for other catchments, it was necessary to assume that this relationship accurately reflected the catch response to changes in H for all waters affected by acidification in the fishery. For those catchments unaffected by acidification, the fish population was assumed healthy (that is, a value of 100 per cent for the H parameter). The overall regional values for H were derived from the average predicted catchment value weighted by catchment area. Regional changes in salmon catch (C) over the 50-year period were then predicted at five-yearly intervals from equation (5.1).

Market Value of Salmon Catch

The market value of a salmon beat is influenced by a number of characteristics including average salmon catch, number of holding pools, access, location, and prestige 'value' of the beat. By linking the market value to catch level using the HPM, it should be possible to estimate the net benefits of SO_2 abatement to the Galloway salmon fishery.

Unfortunately, as salmon beats are only infrequently traded in the open market, there are relatively few data from which to develop an HPM for the Galloway fishery. Hence, it was decided to adapt a model developed by Radford et al. (1991) for all UK salmon fisheries (equation (5.2)):

$$lnPb = 1.550 + 0.547lnCb + 0.423lnNb + 0.337Db \qquad (5.2)$$

where

lnPb = log sale value of the salmon beat b
lnCb = log salmon average catch for each beat
lnNb = log number of named pools for each beat
Db   = double bank dummy variable for each beat.

It is expected that the value of the salmon beat will increase with the catch – but at a decreasing rate. Hence, the marginal value of an additional salmon caught depends on the overall level of the catch. In equation (5.2), a log-linear specification of this relationship is presented. Differentiating equation (5.2) with respect to lnC (the log of average salmon) yields the implicit price of a unit increase in salmon catch. The value obtained is 0.547 which indicates that a 10 per cent increase in salmon catch will lead to a 5.47 per cent increase in the market value of the fishery.

Changes in the market value of the entire Galloway fishery were estimated at five-year intervals using equation (5.2) (see Figure 5.2). The baseline market value and salmon catch were estimated from Scottish Office data (SOAFD 1988). Under the status quo, the market value of the fishery declines gradually from £12.6 million in 1988 to £11.8 million in 2033. In contrast, 60 per cent and 90 per cent reductions in SO$_2$ levels initiate a rapid recovery in market value. Over the 50-year period, a 60 per cent reduction in emissions leads to a rise in the market value of the fishery, peaking at £14.4 million in 2028, before falling back to £14.2 million by the end of the forecast period. This represents a 14 per cent increase over the estimated 1988 value and a net gain over the status quo of £2.44 million (21 per cent). A 90 per cent reduction in SO$_2$ levels leads to a peak in market value of £14.8 million in 2023. The final value of £14.7 million represents an increase of 17 per cent over the initial market value in 1988 and a 25 per cent increase over the status quo value in 2038.

Comparing the present value of the 'emission reduction' scenarios with a scenario based on the status quo, a 60 per cent reduction increases the market value by £1.13 million whereas a 90 per cent reduction increases the market value by £1.21 million. This assumes a discount rate of 6 per cent. Hence, the estimated value of increasing the percentage reduction in SO$_2$ emission levels from 60 per cent to 90 per cent is £0.08 million.

Although the Galloway salmon fishery is the most acidified fishery in Scotland, it is only one of a number of fisheries thought to have suffered fish population loss as a result of acid deposition. Estimating the aggregate benefits of recovery in all Scottish salmon fisheries using the HPM would require *de novo* application of the MAGIC model to all affected catchments. Since MAGIC is catchment based, this exercise would require the model to be

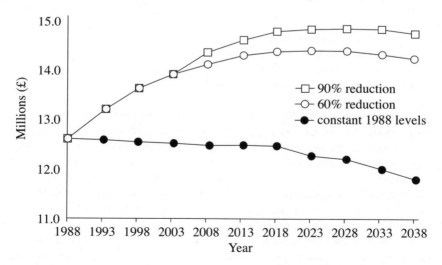

Figure 5.2   Predicted market value (£m) of the Galloway salmon fishery under alternative abatement scenarios

recalibrated with environmental data which are not currently available. It was therefore decided to estimate aggregate benefits by transferring the percentage change predicted for the Galloway fishery to all other affected fisheries. Using this approach, aggregate benefits were estimated to range from £7.8 million under 60 per cent abatement to £8.9 million under 90 per cent abatement (further details in Macmillan 1996).

VALUING NON-USE BENEFITS USING CONTINGENT VALUATION

The impacts of acidic deposition on the natural environment are pervasive. Although salmon is the main commercial species affected, wide-ranging damage to other species has been observed. These non-market effects are a cause for concern among scientists and the general public. The contingent valuation method (CVM) was applied in this study to estimate the non-market benefits arising from an improvement in biodiversity, following recovery from acidification.

The basic objective of a CVM questionnaire is to create a hypothetical, but realistic market where individuals are given the opportunity to express a monetary preference for non-market environmental goods. Although CVM is now fairly widely used for measuring non-market benefits, its application to the biodiversity impact provides three major methodological challenges. First, there are difficulties with presenting pervasive, complex and subtle changes in environmental quality to the general public. Second, the rate and extent of recovery (following abatement) and damage (if abatement does not occur) are uncertain. Third, the survey instrument must overcome a considerable degree of unfamiliarity among the general public. For example, a national survey found that less than 10 per cent of Scottish residents 'knew a great deal' about acid rain and its effects (Government Statistical Service 1991).

The next subsection briefly summarizes the impacts of acidification on biodiversity in Scotland, and the prospects for recovery following SO_2 abatement. The second subsection covers the design and implementation of the CV survey, with the results given in the final subsection.

Biodiversity Impacts

Changes in the chemical status of soil and freshwaters during acidification have resulted in a wide range of impacts on the diversity and abundance of flora and fauna in the natural areas of Scotland. These impacts operate at a number of temporal and spatial scales. Some organisms, such as fish and invertebrates, can be killed by severe, and relatively transient acidic conditions following rainfall events. In the longer term, changes in species composition induced by acidification also trigger disturbance to the delicate process of competition. For example, certain species of sphagnum, which can survive acid conditions, are very efficient scavengers of the available nutrient pool and as lakes become progressively more oligotrophic, many other micro and macro plant species can be lost (Friberg et al. 1980).

Recovery processes following SO_2 abatement are also likely to be complex and our current understanding of the dynamics of recolonization of acidified environments is partial. Some species have exhibited a fairly rapid recovery towards pre-acidification levels, but the general recovery pattern is unclear. Some floral and invertebrate assemblages may show a marked delay in response to improved water quality and, indeed, it is possible that some acidified areas will be unable to recover to pristine conditions due to local extinctions and other irreversible changes (Weatherly and Ormerod 1991).

Development of CV Questionnaire

As considerable scientific uncertainty surrounds the future recovery of biodiversity in acidified environments under policy-on, and potential future biodiversity damage levels under policy-off (no abatement), it was decided to investigate the sensitivity of willingness to pay (WTP) to six alternative scenarios relative to 1990 levels of biodiversity. These involved three distinct recovery levels (A: pristine; B: intermediate; C: no recovery); and two levels of damage under policy-off (D: low and E: high). As the timing of recovery is also not known at present, the rate of recovery was also investigated by replicating each of the six recovery/damage scenarios for two recovery periods (20 years and 120 years). WTP was therefore estimated for 12 separate scenarios, each involving a specified recovery level, damage level and timescale.

Given the complexity of the environmental impacts of acidification, considerable effort was spent on developing an information set which would convey the nature of the environmental damage and recovery path from acidification in a simple, but accurate fashion. Following focus group work it was decided to use pictorial information (species boxes) to convey changes in species composition and population levels in a quantitative, yet interesting and stimulating way (Figure 5.3).

The WTP question was framed in terms of a specified rise in prices on an annual basis.[3] The discrete choice (DC) payment format was used because it is incentive compatible and presents the respondent with an easy and familiar purchase decision. As recommended by the NOAA Panel (1993), a 'don't know' option was introduced so that respondents who are unsure (either of their preference or about the questionnaire) are not 'forced' to declare a

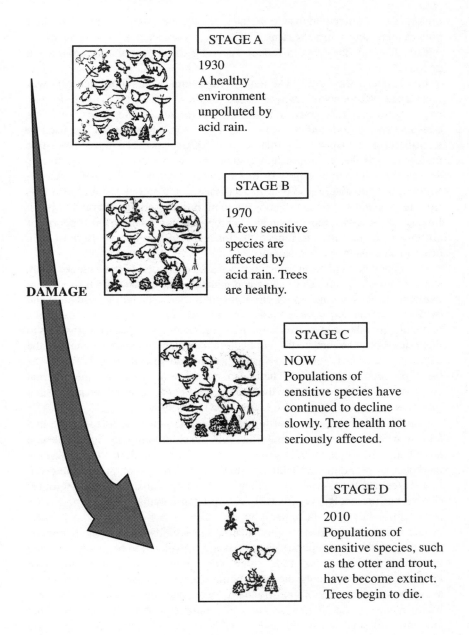

STAGE A

1930
A healthy
environment
unpolluted by
acid rain.

STAGE B

1970
A few sensitive
species are
affected by
acid rain. Trees
are healthy.

DAMAGE

STAGE C

NOW
Populations of
sensitive species have
continued to decline
slowly. Tree health not
seriously affected.

STAGE D

2010
Populations of
sensitive species, such
as the otter and trout,
have become extinct.
Trees begin to die.

Figure 5.3   Description of environmental change (with certainty): option B

preference. In order to enhance realism, respondents were reminded of their budget constraint (Burness et al. 1983), and were asked to specify in which budget category they would reduce spending to pay for the environmental good.

Immediately prior to the DC payment question, a screening question was introduced. Respondents where asked if they would be willing to pay anything, even a very small amount, towards reducing acid deposition. This question was introduced for a number of reasons. First, it can be used to identify protest responses – that is, individuals who may have a positive preference for the environmental change, but who are not prepared to pay anything because they object to one or more aspects of the questionnaire. Second, for statistical reasons, it is necessary to screen out genuine zero bids from respondents who would pay something but refused the offered bid level. Finally, as it gives the respondent an opportunity to register support for abatement, it may help to reduce the incentive to accept the offered bid in order to show support (yea-saying).

A number of validation questions were incorporated. These ranged from standard questions on income, age and education, to questions which attempt to identify levels of concern for environmental issues (including acid rain) and evidence for an altruistic attitude towards the environment (for example, recycling, membership of environmental organizations and so on). Answers to these questions can then be used to explore the extent to which response to the payment question is related to variables expected to influence WTP on the basis of economic theory. They also enable assessment of the internal consistency of responses so that some confidence can be acquired that 'answers corresponded to some reality' (NOAA 1993).

Considerable time was spent testing the questionnaire so as to ensure that all respondents (even those unfamiliar with the commodity and inexperienced at valuation in a hypothetical situation) could formulate their WTP given the market context and the available information set. The testing process involved five stages: (i) discussions with scientists to verify realism; (ii) focus groups; (iii) verbal protocols; (iv) a small-scale pilot involving students; and (v) a mailed pilot survey of the general public.

The sample was drawn from residential households listed in the telephone directory. Although telephone directories are considered to be incomplete and therefore biased (for example some very poor families may not have telephones), it is probably the most comprehensive national listing publicly available. A total of 3000 questionnaires were sent out – distributed evenly between each of the 15 scenarios in a split-sample design. The number of bid amounts (m), the actual bid level values ($b_1 \ldots b_m$), and the sample size corresponding to each bid value ($n_i \ldots n_m$) were determined using Cooper's (1993) optimal bid design method.

Results

Out of 3000 questionnaires mailed out to households in Scotland, a total of 1820 were returned. Disregarding questionnaires that were not delivered to the intended household, this represents an overall response rate of 67 per cent. Protestors and incomplete forms accounted for 8 per cent of all returned questionnaires.

A step-wise logistic regression procedure was used to identify the covariates that significantly influenced the probability of a 'yes' response $E(y)$ to the payment question. Twenty-nine covariates were initially included – such as the transformed value for bid (*transbid*) and ordinal variables for future recovery level, future damage level, the rate of recovery, and socio-economic variables such as income and membership of environmental charities. Protestors and those respondents who replied 'don't know' to the bid question were excluded from the analysis because their preferences for recovery from acidification were not revealed.

The covariates of the fitted model are listed in Table 5.1, together with their parameter estimates, standard errors and *t*-values. As expected, the probability of a 'yes' response decreases with bid level and increases with *income*. A greater understanding about acid rain (*understand*),[4] and whether the respondent is a member of an environmental charity (*member*) also increases the probability of a 'yes' response. People who believe the government has an important role in protecting the environment (*govt*), who ranked pollution (*pollu*) higher in order of importance among six social issues (for example, employment, education and so on) and who returned their questionnaire earlier (*return*) were also more likely to say 'yes'. Respondents particularly concerned about environmental issues outside the UK are also more likely to accept the offered bid level. This is slightly surprising in that the survey deals only with damage in Scotland, but perhaps suggests that altruistic concern for big environmental problems underpins WTP.

In relation to the scope of the environmental change, future damage level (*dam*) was the only variable that significantly influenced WTP, with a high damage level associated with a higher probability of saying 'yes' to the payment question. Future recovery level and rate of recovery did not significantly influence the bid response.

Mean WTP for each scenario was estimated by integration using the method described in Buckland et al. (1998). Respondents who stated that they would be unwilling to pay anything (even a very small amount) were not included in the integration procedure. Accounting for 17 per cent of all valid responses, this group presents several difficulties for modelling the bid function. First, since the logistic curve is continuous, there should not be a discrete 'lump' of probability anywhere along the bid function.

Table 5.1   Estimates of regression coefficients included in the final logistic regression model

Covariate	Estimate	Std error	Student's *t*
Constant	1.079	0.699	1.54
transbid	−0.004	0.001	−8.72
income	0.419	0.048	8.70
govt	−0.427	0.147	−2.91
return	−0.406	0.122	−3.34
understand	−0.372	0.129	−2.89
member	0.371	0.146	2.55
pollu	−0.173	0.075	−2.31
dam	0.306	0.153	2.01
abroad	0.132	0.066	2.01

Second, logistic regression requires that there should be a bid that everyone would accept. Failure to identify and screen out non-payers would have meant that the upper asymptote of the curve would not approach unity. However, respondents unwilling to pay anything were not ignored as mean WTP derived by integration was weighted by multiplying by the proportion of non-zero payers.

The calculated mean household WTP per annum for each scenario is presented in Table 5.2. As suggested by the logistic regression, there is no clear evidence that either recovery level or recovery time affected mean WTP. On the other hand, WTP is consistently higher for the high-damage scenario across all recovery levels. Aggregate CVM benefits for the Scottish population range from £772 million per annum (high damage) to £551 million (low damage).

Table 5.2   Mean WTP ($£annum^{-1}household^{-1}$) for alternative recovery/ damage scenarios

Recovery time	Damage level	Recovery level		
		Low	Moderate	High
20 years	low (x)	189	360	301
	high (y)	420	378	515
120 years	low (x)	267	290	320
	high (y)	435	419	365

COMPARING CVM AND HPM

The annual non-use benefits from the CVM exercise are substantially greater than the predicted market benefits to the Scottish salmon fishery. Table 5.3 shows the aggregate net present value of the benefits of abatement predicted over a 50-year period. Non-use benefits range from £8–12 billion, compared to under £4 million for salmon angling. Ignoring non-use benefit estimates in a cost–benefit analysis of abatement policy would therefore significantly under-represent the benefits of recovery in the semi-natural environment.

Table 5.3   Present value of aggregate economic benefits of SO_2 abatement (£m)

	Salmon fishery	Non-use biodiversity benefits	
		Low damage	High damage
Present value	3.7	8 684.7	12 167.8

Although CV studies are now relatively commonplace, non-use values would appear to have played little role in the formulation of policy on SO_2 or environmental policy in general. Non-use values which dwarf market benefits and hence dominate the estimated economic value presents the policy makers with a dilemma. Although large values *per se* may be welcomed by policy makers anxious to justify environmental programmes,[5] there is an obvious concern that the benefit figures are simply too big and thus cannot possibly represent a true economic commitment (Diamond and Hausman 1994). Indeed, there is considerable evidence from studies comparing hypothetical and actual payments that CV-derived estimates of WTP exceed actual WTP by a factor of between two and ten (Dickie et al. 1987; Kealy et al. 1990; Seip and Strand 1992; Duffield and Patterson 1993; Neill et al. 1994; Navrud and Viesten 1996).

Furthermore, CV studies which produce high values for non-use benefits and which are relatively insensitive to the scope of the environmental change arguably do little to inform the debate about how much SO_2 emissions should be reduced by. In this study, all projected scenarios would comfortably pass the cost–benefit test based on non-use values alone. Therefore, when it comes to making actual decisions on abatement levels, policy makers may prefer to rely on other decision-support techniques such as cost-effectiveness analysis or multicriteria analysis.

The large values generated by CVM tend to support, rather than conflict with ethical and environmental demands for more environmental investment.

Somewhat surprisingly perhaps, when viewed in this context, CVM has attracted considerable opposition from environmental groups (Bowers 1992). Rather than grasping the opportunities CVM offers in influencing economic analysis and policy, environmentalists have been outspoken in their criticism. There may be several reasons for this position. First, some environmentalists appear to oppose fundamentally any form of economic analysis of environmental issues, believing that environmental concerns transcend economics. Second, CVM results, derived from the views of an uninformed public, cannot substitute for expert environmental judgement (particularly in the eyes of those experts!). Third, CVM may be considered by some to be prone to manipulation in order to achieve the 'desired answer'.

Opposition from environmentalists and scepticism about the hypothetical nature of WTP estimates are perhaps two of the most important reasons why the results of CVM studies have not been more fully incorporated into abatement decisions. In contrast, the HPM which generates 'real money' estimates, may be more appealing to policy makers as it provides tangible evidence of market benefits to offset substantial costs imposed on manufacturing industry. An increased salmon catch will not only benefit the owners of riparian angling rights, it is also likely to support employment and expenditure by anglers in economically fragile rural areas.[6] Non-use benefits on the other hand, will have little or no impact on employment or profitability of local businesses.

By taking a more scientific approach, for example by incorporating MAGIC to model a fairly complex environmental process, the hedonic price approach is perhaps also more intuitively appealing to scientists. The government's scientific advisors have played an important role in the development of policy for controlling acidic deposition, and just as one would expect 'real' money to weigh more heavily than 'hypothetical' money with politicians, the more scientific approach of the HPM is also likely to find favour with scientists. CVM estimates, based as they are on a simplified information set, and the personal preferences of the general public, are less likely to impress!

However, the HPM approach also has some limitations in terms of policy development, particularly in relation to aggregation. MAGIC is a catchment specific model hence it would be necessary to recalibrate the model for each acidified catchment in Scotland in order to estimate aggregate fishery benefits. The data for such an exercise are not currently available, hence a crude benefit transfer approach had to be adopted. As more extensive national environmental datasets become available and with the increasing deployment of Geographic Information Systems (GIS) in economic research, this constraint on the applicability of sophisticated dose-response models to policy issues may recede.

Appropriate market data for HPMs are also very difficult to obtain for various reasons, including market confidentiality or market distortions caused by government intervention (for example, in the case of agricultural subsidies and land markets). In order to overcome the lack of appropriate market data, this study used a model which was based on 'expected' sale value provided by the current owner. As these estimates may be biased, it follows that the implicit price relationship may not reflect the true value of a marginal change in environmental quality. However, Freeman (1979) reports that studies based on expected value are broadly consistent with those based on actual transactions and suggests that the error introduced by self-reporting is generally small and random.

A second limitation of the model was that it used cross-sectional rather than time-series data. Cross-sectional data does not capture the dynamic relationship between value and future catch level: with cross-sectional data the implicit price represents the value of a marginal change in environmental quality, where that level is assumed to hold across all future time periods. As Abelson and Markandya (1985) establish, the implicit price should capture the capitalized value placed on anticipated future changes in environmental quality. In the case of salmon fisheries recovering from acidification damage, where salmon catch is expected to increase steadily over time, the implicit price based on cross-sectional data will be underestimated.[7]

CONCLUSIONS

The annual non-use benefits estimated by CVM are substantially greater than the predicted market benefits to the Scottish salmon fishery. Ignoring non-use benefit estimates in a cost–benefit analysis of abatement policy would therefore significantly under-represent the benefits of recovery in the natural environment. However, CVM estimates of non-use benefits appear to lack credibility among policy makers due to the hypothetical nature of the approach and the scepticism of most scientists and environmental groups. In comparison the hedonic price estimates are likely to be more influential in the decision-making process as it is regarded as more scientific, and is concerned with more tangible economic benefits to rural areas.

NOTES

1. The rights to fish in major Scottish salmon rivers are divided into a number of short stretches known as salmon beats. Each beat differs with respect to those characteristics which influence market value such as salmon catch, accessibility and amenity.
2. Critical load maps perhaps provide the most soundly-based scientific assessment of the extent of acidification damage in Europe. The approach identifies a damage that would be expected to rise following stricter pollution control.
3. Higher prices on a wide range of commonly purchased consumer items (for example,

electricity, cars and central heating) was considered to be the most realistic payment vehicles as prices *understand* were ranked as 4.

4. The coefficient on *understand* is negative because respondents who had greatest *understanding* about the acid rain issue were ranked 1, while respondents who had no understanding threshold for the response of ecosystems to acidic deposition: the critical load is the 'highest deposition load that will not cause chemical changes leading to long-term harmful effects on ecosystem structure and function' (Sverdrup et al. 1990).

5. In the UK most CV government-funded studies have been carried out for existing programmes and used to justify previous investment decisions, rather than as part of an *ex ante* appraisal of possible policy options.

6. Currently salmon angling in Scotland generates over 3000 jobs and injects £50 million into the rural economy (Mackay 1989).

7. More detailed comparisons of HPM and CVM can be found in a number of texts, including Hanley and Spash (1993).

REFERENCES

Abelson, P.W. and A. Markandya (1985), 'The interpretation of capitalised hedonic prices in a dynamic environment', *Journal of Environmental Economics and Management*, **12**: 195–206.

Bowers, J. (1992), *Economics of the Environment: The Conservationists' Response to the Pearce Report*, Telford: British Association of Nature Conservationists.

Brookshire, D.S., M.A. Thayer, W.D. Schulze and R.C. d'Arge (1982), 'Valuing public goods: a comparison of survey and hedonic approaches', *American Economic Review*, **72**: 165–76.

Buckland, S.T., D.C. Macmillan, E.I. Duff and N. Hanley (1998), 'Estimating willingness to pay from dichotomous choice contingent valuation studies', *Statistician*, **48**(1): 109–24.

Burness, H.S., R.G. Cummings, A.F. Mehr and M.S. Walbert (1983), 'Valuing policies which reduce environmental risk', *Natural Resources Journal*, **23**: 675–82.

Cooper, J.C. (1993), 'Optimal bid selection for dichotomous choice contingent valuation surveys', *Journal of Environmental Economics and Management*, **24**: 25–40.

Cosby, B.J., A. Jenkins, R.C. Ferrier, J.D. Miller and T.A.B. Walker (1990), 'Modelling stream acidification in afforested catchments: long-term reconstructions at two sites in central Scotland', *Journal of Hydrology*, **120**: 143–62.

Diamond, P.A. and J. Hausman (1994), 'Contingent valuation: is some number better than no number?', *Journal of Economic Perspectives*, **8**(4): 24–42.

Dickie, M., S. Gerking, D.S. Brookshire, D.L. Coursey, W.D. Schulze, A. Coulson and D. Tashkin (1987), 'Reconciling averting behaviour and contingent valuation benefit estimates of reduced symptoms of ozone exposure', in *Improving Accuracy and Reducing Costs of Environmental Benefit Assessments*, Washington, DC: US EPA, pp. 61–5.

Duffield, J.W. and D.A. Patterson (1993), 'Field testing the existence values: an instream flow trust fund for Montana rivers', University of Montana (mimeo).

Freeman, A.M. (1979), *The Benefits of Environmental Improvement: Theory and Practice*, Baltimore, MD: Johns Hopkins University Press.

Friberg, F., C. Otto and B. Svensson (1980), 'Effects of acidification on the dynamics of allochthonous leaf material and benthic invertebrate communities in running water', in D. Drablos and A. Tollan (eds), *Ecological Impact of Acid Precipitation*, Sandefjord, Norway: University of Oslo, pp. 304–5.

Government Statistical Service (1991), *The Scottish Environment Statistics*, Edinburgh: Scottish Office.

Hanley, N. and C. Spash (1993), *Cost–Benefit Analysis and the Environment*, Aldershot: Edward Elgar.

Kealy, M.J., M. Montgomery and J.F. Dovidio (1990), 'Reliability and predictive validity of contingent values: does the nature of the good matter?', *Journal of Environmental Economics and Management*, **19**: 244–63.

Lancaster, K. (1966), 'A new approach to consumer theory', *Journal of Political Economy*, **74**: 132–57.

Mackay, D. (1989), *Economic Importance of Salmon Fishing and Netting in Scotland*, Inverness: Highlands and Islands Development Board/Scottish Tourist Board.

Macmillan, D.C. (1996), 'Valuing the environmental benefits of reduced acid deposition in the semi-natural environment', PhD Thesis, University of Stirling.

Macmillan, D.C. and R.C. Ferrier (1994), 'A bioeconomic model for estimating the benefits of acid rain abatement to salmon fishing: a case study in South-West Scotland', *Journal of Environmental Planning and Management*, **37**(2): 131–44.

National Oceanic and Atmospheric Administration (NOAA) (1993), 'Natural resource damage assessments: proposed rules', *Federal Register*, **59**(5): 1062–191.

Navrud, S.K. and K. Veisten (1996), 'Validity of non-use values in contingent valuation: an empirical test with real payments', paper presented to the 7th European Association of Environmental and Resource Economists (EAERE) Conference, Lisbon.

Neill, H.R., R.G. Cummings, P.T. Ganderton, G.W. Harrison and T. McGuckin (1994), 'Hypothetical surveys and real economic commitments', *Land Economics*, **70**(2): 145–254.

Radford, A.F., A.C. Hatcher and D.J. Whitmarsh (1991), *An Economic Evaluation of Salmon Fisheries in Great Britain: Summary Report,* Centre for Marine Resource Economics, Portsmouth Polytechnic.

Rimes, C. (1992), *Freshwater Acidification of SSSIs in Great Britain I: Overview*, Peterborough: English Nature.

Seip, K.J. and J. Strand (1992), 'Willingness to pay for environmental goods in Norway', *Environmental and Resource Economics*, **2**: 91–106.

Sliggers, J.G. and G. Klaassen (1994), 'Cost sharing for the abatement of sulphur in Europe: the missing link in the new sulphur protocol', *European Environment*, **4**(1): 5–11.

SOAFD (1988), 'Scottish salmon/trout catches 1987', Statistical Bulletin Series, Edinburgh: Scottish Office.

Sverdrup, H., W. de Vries and A. Henrikson (1990), *Mapping Critical Load*, Copenhagen: Nordic Council of Ministers.

Waters, D. and D. Kay (1988), 'Trends in salmon catches – a critical evaluation of the United Kingdom Acid Waters Review Group interpretation', *Area*, **19**(3): 223–35.

Weatherly, N.S. and S.J. Ormerod (1991), 'The importance of acid episodes in determining faunal distributions in Welsh streams', *Freshwater Biology*, **25**: 71–84.

Willis, K.G. and G. Garrod (1991), 'The hedonic price method and the valuation of countryside characteristics', Countryside Change Centre Working Paper 14, University of Newcastle upon Tyne.

Wright, R.F., B.J. Cosby, R.C. Ferrier, A. Jenkins, A.J. Bulger and R. Harriman (1994), 'Changes in acidification of lochs in Galloway, southwestern Scotland, 1979–1988', *Journal of Hydrology*, **124**: 24–37.

6. Linking physical and economic indicators of environmental damages: acidic deposition in Norway

Ståle Navrud*

INTRODUCTION

There are two distinct ways of introducing the sustainability concept in decision making, either as an exogenous variable in the form of physical indicators or as an endogenous variable in economic models, that is, economic indicators. These two approaches are termed here 'strong sustainability' and 'weak sustainability', respectively. This chapter is an attempt to provide links between these two concepts, by using the strong sustainability indicator of critical loads to describe the environmental change to be valued in a contingent valuation (CV) survey. The CV survey produces monetary values, which are the unit of measure for the weak sustainability indicators. Since the strong sustainability approach is advocated mainly by ecologists and the weak sustainability approach by economists, this study is also an attempt at linking these two often divergent views of sustainable development.

The next section reviews definitions of the concept of sustainability and identifies alternative approaches to sustainability, ranging from very weak to very strong. The third section describes the methodology used to link the strong sustainability indicator of critical loads of sulphur (S) and nitrogen (N) for acidification and impacts on fish stocks, with environmental valuation techniques like the CV method. The goal is to try to integrate the sustainability dimension in the damage function approach of environmental and resource

* The contingent valuation study reported here is part of the LEVE project ('Air pollution, effects and values'), of the Norwegian Pollution Control Authority (SFT), which also provided financial support for the survey. I would like to thank project leader Eivind Selvig, head of section Audun Rosland, and all members of the reference group of the LEVE project for valuable comments on the survey instrument and results. Dr Arne Henriksen of the Norwegian Institute of Water Research (NIVA) deserves special thanks for designing the critical load and fish damage maps. The work on linking strong sustainability indicators and economic valuation is part of the ExternE (External Costs of Fuel Cycles) project of the European Comission, DG XII, which provided financial support for writing this chapter.

economics. The fourth section reports the results of a CV survey that aims at estimating the willingness to pay (WTP) of the Norwegian population for the increased freshwater fish stocks from reduced exceedance of critical loads for sulphur. The fifth section reports a combined weak sustainability–strong sustainability indicator of economic value per tonne of critical load sulphur, and discusses the potential of transfer of this value from Norway to other European countries. The final section concludes.

WEAK AND STRONG SUSTAINABILITY

In scholarly usage the term sustainability originally referred to harvesting regimen for specific reproducible natural resources that could be maintained over time (for example, sustained-yield fishing). That meaning has been considerably broadened by ecologists in order to express concerns about preserving the status and function of entire ecological systems. Economists, on the other hand, usually have emphasized the maintenance and improvement of human living standards, in which natural resources and the environment may be important but represent only part of the story. Other disciplines, notably geography and anthropology, bring in concerns about the condition of the social and cultural systems (for example, preservation of aboriginal knowledge and skills).

Even between economists there are significant differences in the interpretation of this concept. Some treat sustainability as not much more than another way of espousing economic efficiency in the management of services derived from nature (Dasgupta and Mäler 1991), which in itself would be no small accomplishment given the current inefficiencies of resource use throughout the world. Others claim that conventional economic efficiency criteria are inadequate for addressing sustainability concerns (Norgaard 1988; Daly and Cobb 1989; and a number of essays in Constanza 1991). Meanwhile, Solow (1993a, 1993b) acknowledges the significance of intergenerational equity in sustainability, but largely emphasizes conventional efficiency criteria.

Despite the lack of 'textbook' definitions of sustainability which command widespread acceptance, two issues are agreed to be central: (i) intergenerational equity and (ii) resource substitutability. The first issue reflects a concern for the well-being of future generations in the face of the growing pressure on the natural environment to provide a range of services (extractable materials, waste absorption, ecological system resilience, aesthetics and recreational opportunities). Hence, the definition of sustainable development presented in the report of the World Commission on Environment and Development (1987, p. 43) emphasizes: 'development that meets the need of the present without compromising the ability of future generations to meet their own needs'. The second key aspect of defining sustainable development, is the capacity of the economic system to substitute other man-made capital for natural capital in order to maintain the welfare of future generations constant. Natural capital is the total repository of service capacities from the natural environment, and man-made capital can be viewed as the sum of manufactured capital, cultural and human capital.

Thus, the substitutability between different forms of resources or capital is closely related to the question of the carrying capacity of natural ecosystems. Given potential non-substitutability between services derived from natural and man-made capital, a complete sustainability criterion must address the flow of natural capital services as well as intergenerational fairness. Concepts of defining and measuring sustainable development can broadly be placed in four categories, ranging from very weak to very strong sustainability (Klassen and Opschoor 1990).

Very Weak Sustainability

This sustainability rule merely requires that the overall stock of capital assets should remain constant over time. The rule is, however, consistent with any one asset being reduced as long as another capital asset is increased to compensate. This concept is based on mainstream neo-classical economic theory and assumes that natural and man-made capitals are close substitutes.

Weak Sustainability

Some UK-based environmental economists have modified the very weak sustainability approach by introducing an upper bound on the assimilative capacity assumption, as well as a lower bound on the level of natural capital stocks that can support sustainable development (Barbier and Markandya 1990; Pearce and Turner 1990). The concept of critical natural capital (for example, keystone species and processes) has also been introduced to account for non-substitutability of certain types of natural capital (for example, environmental support services) and man-made capital.

This implies a sustainability constraint which will restrict, to some degree, resource-using economic activities. The constraint will be required to maintain populations/resource stocks within bounds thought to be consistent with ecosystem stability and resilience. A set of physical indicators will be required in order to monitor and measure biodiversity and ecosystem resilience. As yet there is no scientific consensus on how biodiversity should be measured. For some commentators, sustainability constraints of this type represent expressions of the precautionary principle (O'Riordan 1992) and might be related to safe minimum standards as developed by Ciriacy-Wantrup (1952) and Bishop (1978).

Figure 6.1 illustrates the weak sustainability approach. The vertical line depicts the critical level of natural capital (K). Substitution between natural capital and man-made capital is possible only to the right of this line. To get increased economic growth (that is, increased man-made capital) natural capital must be reduced. The very weak sustainability approach, on the other hand, assumes there is no such critical level, and that substitution is possible over the whole range of natural and man-made capital. The World Commission on Environment and Development (1987) argues that the two forms of capital are complements, rather than substitutes. In Figure 6.1 this could be illustrated by a straight line drawn from origin to the upper right corner of the diagram. Substitution between natural capital and man-made capital is possible only to the right of K, which is the critical level of natural capital. The complementarity hypothesis implies that increased economic growth (that is, increased man-made capital) leads to an increase in natural capital, since poverty could lead to short-term planning and overutilization of natural resources. This hypothesis might describe the situation in developing countries, while the 'trade-off' (substitution) hypothesis in Figure 6.1 gives a better picture of developed countries. However, if developed countries have reduced their natural capital to the left of K, natural capital and man-made capital could be viewed as complementary (that is, an increase in natural capital would be necessary to get increased economic growth).

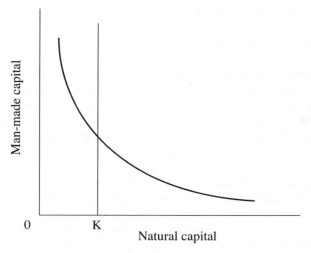

Figure 6.1   The weak sustainability view

Strong Sustainability

The weaker sustainability rules assume that monetary values can be attached to all parts of natural capital. Many ecosystem functions and services can be adequately valued in economic terms, but others may not be amenable to meaningful monetary valuation. Critics of conventional economics have argued that the full contribution of component species and the processes provided by ecosystems for life support are beyond capture in economic values (Ehrlich and Ehrlich 1992). This sustainability view, which might be termed the ecological economics approach, requires that natural capital is constant, and the rule be measured via physical indicators.

While akin to safe minimum standards, strong sustainability is different. Safe minimum standards say conserve unless the benefits forgone (social opportunity costs) are very large. Strong sustainability says, whatever the benefits forgone, some 'critical', natural capital losses are unacceptable. Strong sustainability need not imply a steady-state, stationary economy, but rather changing economic resource allocations over time which are insufficient to affect the overall ecosystem parameters significantly. A certain degree of economic growth should therefore be possible via investment in technical change, substitution of intermediate natural capital for natural capital, and environmental restoration.

In practice, the difference between weak sustainability and strong sustainability will probably be less clear-cut, becoming more a difference in motivation and psychology. Given the social, economic and scientific uncertainties, a safety margin mentality with respect to 'critical' and 'other' natural capital would be dominant.

Very Strong Sustainability

This criterion defines a stationary state sustainability. A steady-state economic system is based on thermodynamic limits and the constraints they impose on the overall scale of the macro-economy. Daly (1991) has defined the 'scale effect' as the scale of human impact relative to global carrying capacity. To Daly, the greenhouse effect, ozone layer depletion and acid rain all prove that we have already gone beyond a prudent 'Plimsoll line' for the scale of the macro-economy. Zero economic growth and zero population growth are required for a zero increase in the 'scale' of the macro-economy.

In practice, these various sustainability paradigms are less clearly defined and overlapping. However, to simplify, one could say that the weak sustainability criterion uses monetary indicators (that is, economic valuation of environmental impacts), while the strong criterion uses physical indicators (for example, critical loads of pollutants).

METHODOLOGY

Critical Loads

In an attempt to combine the weak sustainability and strong sustainability approaches empirically, we use the strong sustainability indicator of critical loads in the damage function approach. The damage function approach applied to the impact of air pollution on ecosystems has four main steps:

1. use air dispersion models to estimate how changes in emissions of a pollutant affect atmospheric concentrations;
2. calculate how changes in atmospheric concentration will affect deposition and concentration of the pollutant in the recipient (soil, water);
3. use dose-response functions to calculate the impacts on affected ecosystems (for example, fish stocks) from changed depositions; and
4. estimate damages (or benefits) by calculating the economic values of the impact. In the case of *reduced* emissions, the damage function approach should rather be termed the *benefit* function approach

The concepts of critical levels and critical loads were developed in the framework of the 1979 Convention on Long Range Transboundary Air Pollution (LTRAP) of the United Nations Economic Commission for Europe, and widely accepted as a basis for designing control strategies in the Second Sulphur Protocol signed in Oslo in June 1994 (UN-ECE 1996). Critical levels refer to the direct effect of pollutant concentrations while critical loads are derived for pollutant depositions, also taking into account accumulation effects in soil and water. For sulphur and nitrogen acidity, the critical load is defined as 'the highest deposition of acidifying compounds that will not cause chemical changes leading to harmful effects on ecosystem structure and function' (UN-ECE 1996). Thus, steps 2 and 3 in the damage function approach would consist of calculating changes in critical load exceedance and its impact on fish stocks.

Linking Changes in Emissions and Exceedance of Critical Loads

Critical loads for surface water are calculated from the concept that the annual acid deposition to a watershed should not exceed the amount of alkalinity (that is, buffer capacity) that is produced annually in the watershed and the lake. The buffering capacity is determined by the geology and soil characteristics of the watershed. The acid deposition should be less than the buffering capacity in order to leave a minimum level of buffer capacity which is necessary to avoid damages to aquatic organisms including fish. Thus, this critical biological value varies with the natural buffer capacity of surface water, measured as acid neutralizing capacity.

In Norway this limit has been set at 20 μeq/l (microequivalents per litre) which was found to be a realistic value for aquatic organisms (Lien et al. 1992). This value is based on the most common freshwater fish species in Norway, brown trout (*Salmo trutta L.*). In other countries other fish species are more abundant and a variable limit is necessary to protect most of the aquatic organisms. However, the natural acid neutralizing capacity of surface water in areas dominated by granite and gneiss and a thin soil layer can be 20 μeq/l or less, which would produce 'negative' critical loads. For these lakes the critical load is set to zero. In areas with little acid rain the probability of fish damage is small even if acid neutralizing capacity is close to zero, while in areas with much acid rain fish damage can occur even at this value. Therefore, the minimum buffering capacity was treated as a variable, that is, as a function of the acid deposition to the lakes, when the Norwegian Institute of Water Research (NIVA) used the steady state water chemistry model to calculate critical loads for surface water in Norway with respect to acidification (Henriksen et al. 1995a, b, 1998); see also Figure 6.2. The model is based on the assumption that sulphate is a completely mobile anion and that the sulphur deposition can be used to indicate the acidifying effect of sulphur. It further assumes that the only acidifying effect of nitrogen deposition is the part that is leached as nitrate in runoff. Figure 6.2 shows that most of the surface water area in Southern Norway and parts of Northern Norway have low critical loads, that is, below 50 μeq/m^2/year. This means that the annual deposition must be less than 0.80g sulphur/m^2/year to avoid exceeding the critical load. These two areas (light and mid grey in Figure 6.2) represent areas which are most sensitive to acidic deposition.

NIVA then used the critical load function (Posch et al. 1997) to calculate exceedance of critical loads for each of the geographical grid cells at the 1990 deposition level (that is, an average value for the 1988–92 period), and in year 2010 according to the commitments of the Second Sulphur Protocol. Deposition of nitrogen is assumed to be constant from 1990 to 2010. Figure 6.3 shows the estimated exceedance of critical loads for sulphur and nitrogen in surface water in Norway in 1990 and 2010. If we compare the map to the left in Figure 6.3 with Figure 6.2, we see the effect of acidic deposition. Note that the sensitive areas in Figure 6.2 are mostly the same areas where critical loads for sulphur are exceeded in Figure 6.3. These areas are mid and light grey, in order of increasing level of critical load exceedance. The map to the right shows the significant reduction in these areas that the Second Sulphur Protocol is expected to produce in 2010, while the left map shows the situation in 1990. The largest areas with the highest exceedance level (light grey) can be found in the south and western parts of Southern

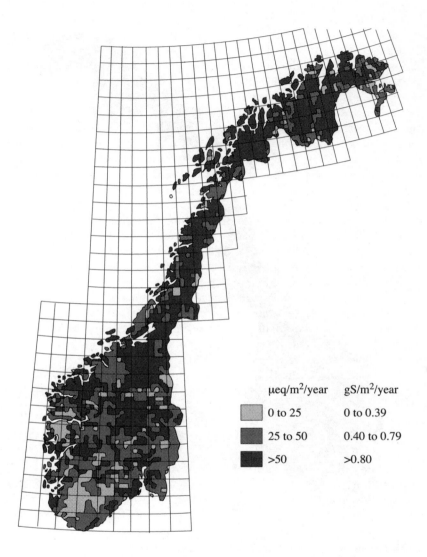

Note: In the original colour figure there were six classes, however, in order to produce the figure clearly in black and white, the classes have been reduced to three.

Source: Norwegian Institute of Water Research (NIVA).

Figure 6.2   Critical loads for surface water in Norway

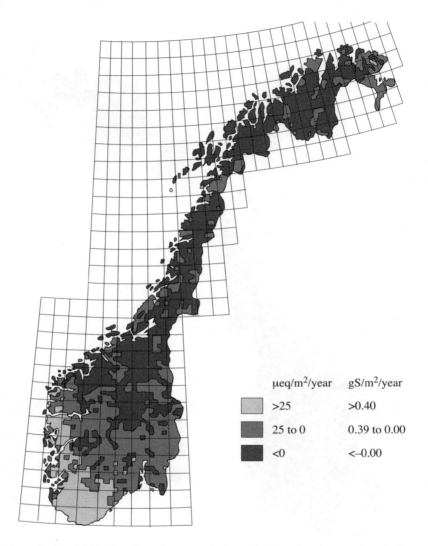

Note: In the original colour figure there were six classes, however, in order to produce the figure clearly in black and white, the classes have been reduced to three.
The predicted deposition of sulphur in 2010 is based on the fulfilment of the Second Sulphur Protocol. Deposition of nitrogen is assumed to be constant at the 1990 level.

Source: Norwegian Institute of Water Research (NIVA).

Figure 6.3   Exceedance of critical loads for sulphur and nitrogen in surface water in 1990 (left) and 2010 (right)

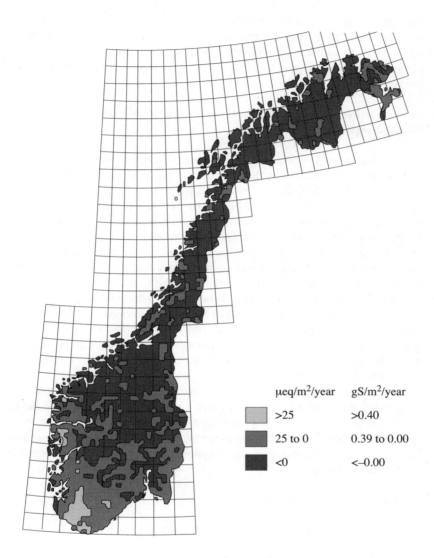

	µeq/m²/year	gS/m²/year
	>25	>0.40
	25 to 0	0.39 to 0.00
	<0	<–0.00

Norway, but the eastern part and the west coast of Southern Norway are also affected. The critical loads for surface water are also exceeded in the northern tip of Norway, which is caused mainly by sulphur emissions from industrial plants and coal-fired power plants in the neighbouring Kola Peninsula in Russia.

Dose-response Functions for Exceedance of Critical Loads and Fish Damage

A '1000 lake survey' collected data on water chemistry and status of the fish populations from 1005 lakes throughout Norway in 1986. Fish damage was then presented in the same grid system as the critical loads, that is, a system of grids of 0.5° latitude by 1° longitude divided into 16 subgrids. Additional data for areas poorly covered was collected in 1989 and 1990 (Henriksen et al. 1988, 1989, 1998). Water samples were collected from each lake and analysed. Status for all fish species (brown trout, arctic char, perch and pike) was recorded for each lake, based on interviews with representatives of the environmental authorities at the county level. The status of the fish society in each lake was classified using a fish damage index with three categories. Class 1 (unaffected) indicates no reduction in the fish populations, class 2 (reduced) indicates a reduction in the densities of one or more populations, and class 3 (extinct) indicates that all populations are extinct. Naturally thin populations were classified as unaffected. After excluding limed lakes, 697 lakes with acceptable fish information remained

Dose-response functions between exceedance of critical loads and fish status were then estimated for each class. Using a logistic regression model Henriksen et al. (1995b, 1998) calculated how exceedance of critical loads affects the probability for a fish population to be classified in each of the three damage classes. The estimated dose-response functions for the three damage classes were estimated as:

Damage class 1 (unaffected)

$$p\,(1) = 1/\,[1 + \exp(-1.395 + 0.006\ CL - E)] \qquad (6.1)$$

Damage class 2 (reduced)

$$p\,(2) = 1/\,[1 + \exp(-3.320 + 0.006\ CL - EX)] - p\,(1) \qquad (6.2)$$

Damage class 3 (extinct)

$$p\,(3) = 1 - 1/\,[1 + \exp(-1.320 + 0.006\ CL - EX)] \qquad (6.3)$$

where:

$p(i)$ = probability of acidification damage to fish populations in damage class i; 0 – 1 CL – EX = exceedance (EX) of critical load (CL); μeq/L.

These three dose-response functions are shown in Figure 6.4. The figure shows that when the critical load is not exceeded there is a very small probability of damage to the fish populations, that is, low probability of damage class 3 in the left-hand side of the diagram. When the critical load is exceeded the probability of fish damage increases with increasing exceedance, that is, increasing probability of damage class 3 as we move to the right-side of the diagram.

Figure 6.4 also shows that it is difficult to predict damage class 2, since the curves for damage class 1 and 3 are so close. The reason is that damage class 2 fails to represent a stable state, since the fish population will disappear (that is, class 3) without a large reduction in deposition. Predicting whether a lake has damages to its fish population or not (that is, damage class 3 or 1) at a given level of critical level exceedance is relatively easy. These three damage classes formed the basis for the contingent valuation survey performed in April 1996. However, in a reanalysis of the data with only two damage classes

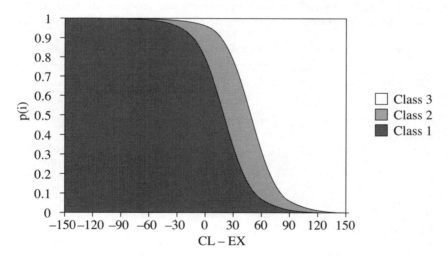

Note: p(i) (i = 1 – 3) probability of fish damage as a function of critical load exceedance (CL – EX).

Source: Henriksen et al. (1995a, figure 2).

Figure 6.4   Probability of fish damages by class

(damaged and undamaged), Henriksen et al. (1998) were able to identify dose-response functions which could correctly predict 83 per cent and 85 per cent of the undamaged and damaged fish populations, respectively.

Table 6.1 shows the number and percentage of correct and wrong predictions of damage class from the estimated dose-response functions as compared to the original data from the '1000 lake survey'. It confirms the difficulty of predicting the number of lakes in class 2, but that for classes 1 and 3 the results are satisfactory. At high exceedances there are still some lakes which are not damaged (damage class 1). Test fishing showed that interviews generally underestimate fish damages, especially by reporting extinct populations as reduced (Hesthagen et al. 1993). This could be due to the fact that there is a time lag from the lake reaching a critical chemical composition until the fish stocks are lost.

The geographical location of the lakes and rivers in the three damages classes is shown in Figure 6.5. The map to the left shows the situation as of 1990 and the map to the right estimates the state of the fish stocks after the fulfilment of the Second Sulphur Protocol in 2010.

Economic Valuation of Fish Damages

Since acid rain is one of the largest environmental problems in Norway, the entire Norwegian population was considered to be affected by this change in

Table 6.1   Correct and incorrect classification of fish damage by class

Predicted	Observed			
	Class 1	Class 2	Class 3	Total
Class 1				
N	**248**	49	15	312
%	**83.2**	30.4	6.3	100
Class 2				
N	30	**48**	36	114
%	10.1	**29.8**	15.1	100
Class 3				
N	20	64	**187**	271
%	6.7	39.8	**78.6**	100
Total	298	161	238	697

Note: Bold numbers indicate correct classifications.

Source: Henriksen et al. (1995a, 1998).

fish stocks, even though the largest impacts occur in Southern Norway. Thus, a nation-wide survey with in-person interviews of 1009 Norwegian households was carried out in April 1996.

We used the stated preference method of contingent valuation to estimate the economic value of the increased number of lakes with undamaged fish stocks. The maps in Figure 6.5, together with the following oral presentation, were used as the scenario description in the CV survey:

> Map A (map to the left in Figure 6.5) shows the areas in Norway with fish stocks damaged by acid rain. Acid rain is mainly due to long-range transported air pollutants from other European countries. International agreements will reduce emissions of sulphur dioxide and nitrogen oxides, which cause acidification. In spite of reduced emissions the acidification damages to fish stocks have increased over the last decade.
>
> While we wait for the reductions in emissions to become large enough to reduce the damages, the Norwegian government has started liming lakes and rivers. They are now considering a plan to increase the level of liming, which will reduce acidification damages to fish stock as shown in map B (map to the right in Figure 6.5). We will then get back viable fish stocks in the brown trout lakes and the salmon and sea trout rivers in areas where the stocks are currently reduced or extinct. These areas have changed from mid grey and light grey in map A to dark grey in map B. This new liming programme will cost each household in Norway X kroner annually. The government will issue a new tax earmarked for this liming programme.
>
> Is your household willing to pay X kroner annually to get the increment in areas with viable fish stocks as shown in map B? Remember that this means you have to use less money for other purposes.

This WTP question was part of a larger CV study of respiratory symptoms (from air pollution), acid rain damages to fish stocks and noise from road traffic. Thus, this WTP question came after WTP questions about avoiding symptoms like cough, bronchitis, itching eyes and headaches (Navrud 1997, 1998). This procedure should avoid the potential problem of respondents overstating their WTP for a particular environmental problem, when a CV survey focuses on only one topic.

Each respondent was asked to answer 'yes', 'no' or 'don't know' to only one amount, and the amount varied from 100 to 1000 Norwegian kroner (NOK) (1 NOK = 0.11 euros). This dichotomous choice WTP question was then followed by an open-ended WTP question:

> The liming costs are uncertain. What is the most your household is willing to pay annually to get to the situation shown in map B?

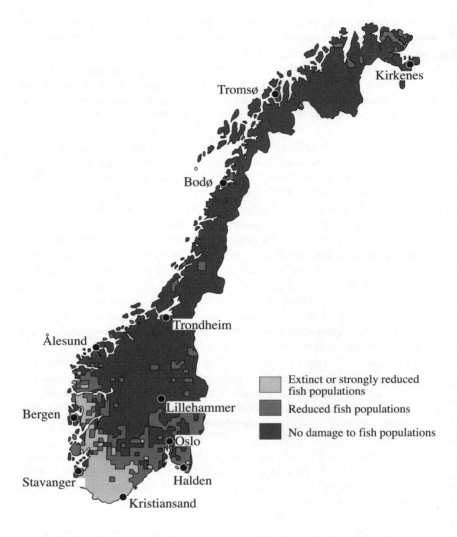

Note: The 2010 scenario is based on sulphur deposition in accordance with the Second Sulphur Protocol. Deposition of nitrogen is assumed to be constant at the 1990 level.

Source: Norwegian Institute of Water Research (NIVA).

Figure 6.5   Predicted damages to fish stocks from exceedance of critical loads for sulphur and nitrogen in surface water in Norway in 1990 (left) and 2010 (right)

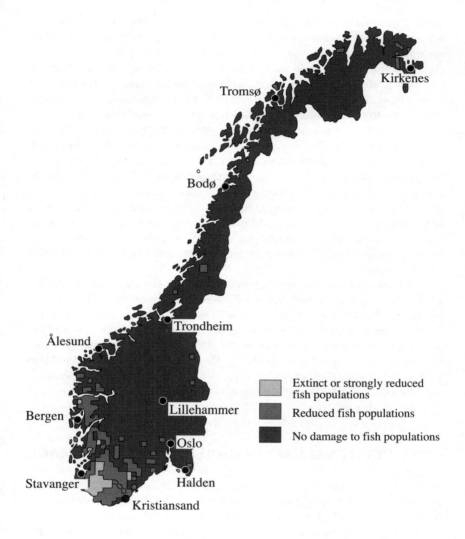

Thus, a national liming programme having the same impact as the Second Sulphur Protocol was used instead of ascribing the impacts to the international agreement. Pre-tests of the survey instrument showed that respondents protested against a scenario where they were asked to pay for increments in fish stocks which was the result of reduced sulphur emissions mainly from other European countries (Norway receives about 90 per cent of its sulphur depositions from other countries). Many respondents stated zero WTP because they thought that the countries causing the depositions should pay, rather than because they had no utility from increased fish stocks. Thus, these protest zero answers will lead to understatement of WTP and aggregated benefits to the Norwegian households of this environmental improvement. This clearly illustrates the problem of valuing transboundary pollution impacts. Even though the national liming programme scenario avoided much of this protest behaviour, it is impossible to avoid protesters completely since some people also find it unfair that they should pay for the liming even if their utility from the programme is positive. However, this type of protest behaviour is found in most CV studies.

A new tax earmarked for liming was accepted as a fair and realistic payment vehicle both in the pre-test and the final survey. Given the relatively high income tax level in Norway, an increase in general income taxes is known to create protest behaviour in CV surveys. Increased fishing licences would fail to capture the non-use value, and would also probably understate use value (mainly recreational value of angling). This is because the WTP could be anchored in current costs of fishing licences and express what the respondents thought was a 'fair' price of fishing licences rather than their welfare gain from increased fish stocks.

CONTINGENT VALUATION OF REDUCED FISH DAMAGE

In the dichotomous choice WTP question the proportion of yes answers decreases as the bid amount increase. Thus, 70, 66, 59, 51 and 43 per cent said 'yes' to paying 100, 200, 300, 500 and 1000 NOK, respectively. This is as expected, but there is a surprisingly large proportion of yes answers to the highest amount, that is, the distribution (survival curve) has a fat right tail. The amounts were selected based on the results from two pre-tests that used open-ended WTP questions. Several studies have found dichotomous choice to give higher mean WTP than that obtained using open-ended questions (Boyle et al. 1996; Brown et al. 1996; Ready et al. 1996). One reason for this discrepancy could be that the respondents use a lower certainty level of paying when answering dichotomous choice compared to open-ended questions. When the certainty level is specified (that is, asking questions like 'Are you 95 per cent sure you would pay X NOK?'), the open-ended and dichotomous choice results come together. Thus, we should expect different results from our dichotomous choice and open-ended questions where certainty levels are unspecified, which is the usual approach.

Table 6.2 reports the results from the dichotomous choice question. Household income and recreational fishing had a significant, positive effect on WTP while a low educational level had a significant, negative effect. The mean WTP calculated from the single and multiple logit models was 705 and 653 NOK/household/year, respectively.

Table 6.2   WTP for increased fish stocks

Variable or static	Model (1)	Model (2)
Bid	–0.001292**	–0.001272**
Household gross income (thousands)	–	0.001361**
Recreational fishing days last 12 months	–	0.052232**
Children (1) or not (0) in household	–	–0.19589
Highest education primary school	–	–0.54363
Highest education high school	–	–0.03472*
Intercept	0.9117**	0.82940**
Percent of correct predictions	62	62
Pesudo *R*-squared value (Maddala)	0.03	0.07
N	900	786
Mean WTP/household/year (NOK)	705	653

Notes
Dichotomous choice, NOKa 100, 200, 300, 500, 1000, logit models.
University education level is a hidden dummy.
* significant at the 5% level.
** significant at the 1% level.

The reported WTP from the open-ended question ranged from 0 to 10 000 NOK with mean and median values of 367 and 200 NOK/household/year, respectively (Std = 664). Thirty-one per cent of the respondents stated zero WTP. Table 6.3 shows that the two reasons stated most frequently are protest answers. These respondents state zero WTP because they think others should pay or take responsibility for reducing the damages. Thus, as many as 77 per cent of the zero WTP answers are at least partly protest answers (since respondents are allowed to state more than one reason for their zero answer). If all these answers are left out, that is, implicitly assuming that these respondents have a 'real' WTP of the average of the other respondents' mean WTP, increases by 35 per cent to 496 NOK.

Table 6.3   Reasons for zero WTP to open-ended survey

Reason	Percentage
1. Government must pay for liming	53
2. Other countries must reduce their acid emissions	24
3. Cannot afford it	24
4. It is more important to pay for other government tasks	16
5. Do not fish myself	14
6. Difficult to state an amount	1
7. Other answers	3

Note: Respondents were not given pre-specified alternatives when asked to state their reasons for zero WTP. They were allowed to state more than one reason. $N = 295$, that is 31% of the respondents.

Combining the open-ended and dichotomous choice results, the annual WTP per household seems to be in the range of 367–705 NOK. The annual aggregate benefits for all 1.98 million Norwegian households can then be calculated at 727–1396 million NOK, which is equivalent to 80.0–153.6 million euros. These benefits can be compared to the saved costs of liming these watercourses from fulfilment of the Second Sulphur Protocol of 211 million NOK/year (Henriksen and Hindar 1997, Table 4). Thus, the benefit–cost ratio of such a liming project would be 3.45–6.62.

THE POTENTIAL FOR BENEFIT TRANSFERS

There are at least two options in selecting a *unit of transfer* of this valuation estimate: (i) per tonne of reduced sulphur deposition, measured as critical load exceedance sulphur, and (ii) per square kilometre reduced land area of critical load exceedance. Both these options combine the weak and strong sustainability indicators of economic value and critical loads.

Looking at the weight-based unit first, we find that in 1990 145 000 tonnes of sulphur was deposited in Norway, which is 30 000 tonnes above the critical load. In 2010, with the fulfilment of the Second Sulphur Protocol, the annual deposition in Norway would be reduced to 69 000 tonnes, of which 10 000 tons exceeds the critical load. Thus, there is a reduction of 20 000 tonnes (66.7 per cent) in terms of 'critical load exceedance' by sulphur. If we assume a linear relationship between the reduced deposition and the economic value, we can calculate the annual economic value per tonne of 'critical load exceedance'of sulphur at 4000–7680 euros. The corresponding numbers on a per household basis is 2.0–3.9 meuros/tonne/year (1 meuro = 10^{-3} (0.001) euros). Since the impact caused by one tonne of sulphur varies from location to location due to differences in buffering capacity of the soils, and thus the critical loads, the economic value as ecu per reduced tonne of critical load exceedance of sulphur is a better measure than reduction in total sulphur deposition for transfer of these estimates to other locations in Europe.

The second area-based unit can be calculated in a similar way. Henriksen and Hindar (1997) found that the area where the critical load for sulphur was exceeded was 80 040 km^2 in 1990, that is, 25.0 per cent of the total area. They predict that this area will be 34 550 km^2 (10.8 per cent of total land area) with the Second Sulphur Protocol in 2010. This is a reduction in area with exceeded critical loads of 45 490 km^2 (56.8 per cent). Again assuming a linear relationship (that is, constant economic value per unit of reduced area with exceeded critical loads), we find an economic value of 15 982–30 688 euro/km^2/year. This is equivalent to 8.1–15.4 meuro/ km^2/year.

However, none of these approaches accounts for the difference in population density, and thus the number of users and non-users affected by the policy. This will greatly affect the aggregated damages or benefits of a policy. According to the UN (1998), Europe had 729 million inhabitants in 1997, 374 million lived within the European Union, and 4 million lived in Norway. The land area of Europe is 23 million km^2, of which the Union covers 3 million km^2, and Norway 0.3 million km^2. The population density of Europe, the Union and Norway is 31.65, 115.38 and 13.5 inhabitants per km^2, respectively. Norway is much more sparsely populated than the average for Europe. Thus, the number of people affected by a change in fish stocks and environmental quality in general is higher within the Union and Europe as a whole. Therefore, a direct transfer of the Norwegian damage estimate per tonne of sulphur would underestimate the damage costs to Europe. Differences in income level, other socio-economic variables, cultural preferences and institutions in different countries should also be taken into account.

There are three main approaches to benefit transfer:

1. Unit value transfer
   a. simple unit value transfer
   b. unit value transfer with adjustment for income differences.
2. Function transfer
   a. benefit function transfer
   b. meta-analysis.

In the first approach, the unit value at the study site (Norway) is assumed to be representative for the policy site (Europe); either without (a) or with (b) adjustment for differences in income levels between the two sites (by using GDP per capita or purchase power parity indices). In the second approach, a benefit function is estimated at the early study site and transferred to the policy site (a), or a benefit function is estimated from several study sites using meta-analysis (b), then values for the independent variables at the policy site are used in the function to calculate WTP at the policy site. A benefit function from a CV survey would be WTP as a function of site and good characteristics, and characteristics of the respondent. Meta-analysis would also include characteristics of the different studies as a variable, since estimated values could be affected by even small methodological differences.

Ready et al. (1999) was the first, and so far the only, study to test the reliability of benefit transfer across several countries. In five European countries, the Netherlands, Norway, Portugal, Spain and the UK, respondents in a CV study were asked their WTP to avoid six specific episodes of ill health (which correspond to endpoints in exposure – response functions between air and water pollution and ill health). We found that if the goal was to predict average WTP across a population, approaches 1(a),1(b) and 2(a) performed equally well. The transfer error was ±37–39 per cent, which should be assessed relative to a random sampling error within each country of 16 per cent. Thus, if the goal is to predict average WTP of the entire population of the target country, the simple unit value transfer method does this cheaply and with relatively low error. The question is then whether the error is acceptably low for policy used like benefit–cost analyses. To answer this question, the policy makers could compare the costs of doing a new study with the expected costs of making the wrong decision when using the benefit transfer estimates in a cost–benefit analysis. Statistical decision theory and Bayesian analysis would be ideal instruments for this purpose.

Whether the result from Ready et al. (1999) also applies to environmental goods like freshwater fish stocks, we do not know. However, it shows that benefit transfer across countries in Europe is possible, and could produce estimates reliable enough for cost–benefit analysis at considerable cost and time savings compared to conducting new valuation studies.

CONCLUSION

There is large uncertainty inherent in these estimates. The uncertainty stems both from the calculation of impacts (that is, uncertain dose-response functions) and the economic valuation procedure (that is, uncertainty of the contingent valuation surveys). To be able to use these estimates to calculate parts of the social benefits of second generation international agreements on emission reductions of SO_2 and NO_x based on critical load, we must assume that the marginal WTP is constant, that is, independent of the current level of acid deposition, and that Norwegians are representative of all Europeans when it comes to WTP for reducing fish damages. However, this study shows that it is possible to link the critical loads concept with economic valuation. Similar studies in other European countries should be performed to test the validity of these estimates. The possibility of applying this methodological framework to other potential impacts from sulphur and nitrogen depositions, for example, impacts on forest ecosystems, should be considered.

REFERENCES

Barbier, E.B. and A. Markandya (1990), 'The conditions for achieving environmentally sensitive development', *European Economic Review*, **34**: 659–69.

Bishop, R.C. (1978), 'Endangered species and uncertainty: the economics of a safe minimum standard', *American Journal of Agricultural Economics*, February: 10–18.

Boyle, K.J., F.R. Johnson, D.W. McCollum, W.H. Desvousges, R.M. Dunford and S.P. Hudson (1996), 'Valuing public goods: discrete versus continuous contingent-valuation responses', *Land Economics*, **72**(3): 381–96.

Brown, T.C., P.A. Champ, R.C. Bishop and D.W. McCollum (1996), 'Which response format reveals the truth about donations to a public good?', *Land Economics*, **72**(2): 152–66.

Ciriacy-Wantrup, S.V. (1952), *Resource Conservation: Economics and Policy*, Berkeley, CA: University of California Press.

Constanza, R. (ed.) (1991*), Ecological Economics: The Science and Management of Sustainability*, New York: Columbia University Press.

Daly, H. (1991), 'Towards an environmental macroeconomics', *Land Economics*, **67**: 255–9.

Daly, H. and J. Cobb (1989), *For the Common Good*, Boston, MA: Beacon Press.

Dasgupta, P.S. and K.-G. Mäler (1991), 'The environment and emerging development issues', in *Proceedings of the World Bank Annual Conference on Development Economics 1990*, Washington, DC: World Bank.

Ehrlich, P.R. and A.H. Ehrlich (1992), 'The value of biodiversity', *Ambio*, **21**: 219–26.

Henriksen, A., E. Fjeld and T. Hesthagen (1998), 'Critical load exceedance and damage to fish populations', 17 pp. Submitted to *Ambio*.

Henriksen, A., E. Fjeld and L. Lien (1995a), 'Exceedance of critical loads for acidification of slakes, rivers and the state of the ecosystems. Development of a damage function for impacts from acidification effects on fish stocks', Report 15 November, Norwegian Institute for Water Research (in Norwegian).

Henriksen, A. and A. Hindar (1997), 'Critical loads for acidification of surface water – a useful concept?', *Vann*, No. 2–97: 219–34 (in Norwegian).

Henriksen, A., L. Lien, B.O. Rosseland, T.S. Traaen and I.S. Sevaldrud (1989), 'Lake acidification in Norway – present and predicted fish status', *Ambio*, **18**: 314–21.

Henriksen, A., L. Lien, T.S. Traaen, I.S. Sevaldrud and D.F. Brakke (1988), 'Lake acidification in Norway – present and predicted chemical status', *Ambio*, **17**: 259–66

Henriksen, A., M. Posch, H. Hultberg and L. Lien (1995b), 'Critical loads of acidity for surface waters: can the ANC_{limit} be considered variable?', *Water, Air and Soil Pollution*, **85**: 2419–24.

Hesthagen, T., B.O. Rosseland, H.M. Berger and B.M. Larsen (1993), 'Fish community status in Norwegian lakes in relation to acidification: a comparison between interviews and actual catches by test-fishing', *Nordic Journal of Freshwater Research*, **86**: 34–41.

Klassen, G.K. and J.B. Opschoor (1990), 'Economics of sustainability or the sustainability of economics: different paradigms', *Ecological Economics*, **4**: 93–116.

Lien, L., G.G. Raddum and A. Fjellheim (1992), 'Critical loads for surface water – fish and vertebrates', Norwegian Institute for Water Research (NIVA), Report O-89185 (Naturens Tålegrenser, Fagrapport nr. 21, Miljøverndep.), 29 pp.

Navrud, S. (1997), 'Willingness-to-pay for health symptoms, increased fish populations due to reduced acidification and road traffic noise. Results from a Contingent Valuation study' (in Norwegian), Report 97:14, National Pollution Control Authority (SFT), Oslo, Norway.

Navrud, S. (1998), 'Valuing health impacts from air pollution in Europe. New empirical evidence on morbidity', submitted to *Environmental and Resource Economics*.

Norgaard, R.B. (1988), 'Sustainable development: a co-evolutionary view', *Futures*, **20**(6): 606–20.

O'Riordan, T. (1992), 'The precaution principle in environmental management', CSERGE GEC Working Paper 92–03, Centre for Social and Economic Research on the Global Environment (University College London and University of East Anglia, Norwich).

Pearce, D.W. and R.K. Turner (1990), *Economics of Natural Resources and the Environment*, Hemel Hempstead, Herts: Harvester Wheatsheaf.

Posch, M., J. Kamari, A. Henriksen, M. Forsius and A. Wilander (1997), 'Exceedance of critical loads for lakes in Finland, Norway and Sweden: reduction requirements for acidifying nitrogen and sulphur deposition', *Environmental Management*, **21**, 291–304.

Ready, R.C., J.C. Buzby and D. Hu (1996), 'Differences between continuous and discrete contingent value estimates', *Land Economics*, **72**(3): 396–411.

Ready, R.C., S. Navrud, B. Day, R. Dubourg, F. Machado, S. Mourato, F. Spanninks and M.X.V. Rodríguez (1999), 'Benefit transfer in Europe: are values consistent across countries?', paper presented at the EU Concerted Action of Environmental Values in Europe (EVE) Workshop on Benefit Transfer, Lillehammer, Norway, 14–16 October.

Solow, R.M. (1993a), 'An almost practical step towards sustainability', *Resource Policy*, **19**(3): 162–72

Solow, R.M. (1993b), 'Sustainability – an economist's perspective', in R. Dorfman and N. Dorfman (eds), *Selected Readings in Environmental Economics*, 3rd edn, New York: Norton.

United Nations (UN) (1998), 'Population and vital statistics report', Statistical Papers Series A, Vol. L No. 2, April, Department of Economic and Social Affairs, Statistics Division, New York: UN.

United Nations Economic Commission for Europe (UN-ECE) (1996), *1979 Convention on Long Range Transboundary Air Pollution and its Protocols*, New York: UN.

World Commission on Environment and Development (WCED) (1987), *Our Common Future*, New York: Oxford University Press.

7. Prioritizing toxic chemical clean-up in Hungary using monetary valuation

John Powell

INTRODUCTION

The Hungarian people are only now, nine years after the first freely elected government, beginning to realize the full extent of land contamination in their country. Some activities causing contamination, previously kept secret even from those potentially affected, have ceased, though their legacy remains and is proving difficult to remedy in a situation where environmental issues are far from the top of the political agenda. Other activities continue to cause land degradation in a context of poor waste management infrastructure and low levels of enforcement (Lehoczki 1993; Research Triangle Institute 1994). Even where potentially damaging sites have been identified, only a few have been decontaminated effectively because of the scale and complexity of the problems, and the fear that high costs are involved.

Little work has been carried out on the economics of contaminated land remediation in Hungary and there have been no attempts to estimate benefits. Even the estimated clean-up costs are often no more than an indication of the order of magnitude of likely costs. This has proved problematic for the government trying to implement a clean-up programme while operating with a very small annual budget. Government agencies involved in financing and regulating land remediation presently rely solely on a complex risk assessment procedure in deciding which sites should be attended to first. There is thus no indication of any returns on resources invested in land remediation. In order to rectify this situation and to ensure that benefits are included in decision making for site remediation, along with assessed risks, the Ministry of Environment and Regional Policy (MERP) has been investigating methods for benefits estimation. This chapter discusses one attempt to estimate the non-market, social and environmental, benefits resulting from decontamination of a site. The work reported here aimed to develop an improved decision-making process for ensuring effective use of the limited resources available for reducing toxic land throughout the country. How such environmental valuation information will be received and acted upon within the relevant ministries remains to be seen.

THE CONTAMINATED LAND DATABASE

The existence of many contaminated sites in Hungary is known but reliable information exists for only a small percentage of these sites. A study of the Sajo valley in the Borsod-Abauj-Zemplen region of north-eastern Hungary, for example, noted over 1000 waste disposal sites and 94 sites handling hazardous wastes (Regional Environment Centre 1994) in this area alone. A toxic land database which consists of approximately 173 sites (as of September 1998) has been developed by investigating reports from local government agencies, regional inspectorates and individual citizens, about sites over which they had some concern. Once alerted to a potential contaminated site, MERP personnel visit the area and collect a range of information concerning the site, its ownership, history of activities, and threats to the environment or public health.

The nature of sites varies widely in terms of source of contamination, size, and in risks posed to the environment and public health. The sites on the list range from large industrial areas contaminated by many sources (for example, the northern part of Csepel Island) to small isolated industrial sites (such as the individual electroplating plant in the village of Kallosemjen), and from large toxic waste sites where a variety of unknown toxic wastes have been dumped over the years (for example, Garé) to individual buildings used for temporary storage of hazardous waste (such as the storage of materials in old farm buildings outside Tatabanya). Some sites are located within residential areas (30 sites are within a town boundary and a further 32 less than 500 metres from a town boundary), some are in isolated rural areas, others are in karstic regions with thin soils where rapid transport of materials is a potential threat. A risk assessment was therefore developed by MERP to study the threat posed by sites to the various environmental media (soil, air, surface water, ground-water) and to public health. In some cases costs of decontaminating the site have been estimated. In 1996–97, actual clean-up started and only one site (Bekescsaba) has been decontaminated to date. In addition, various kinds of emergency action have been taken on approximately 50 other sites (though in some cases this is limited to merely covering waste piles with plastic sheeting).

Table 7.1 gives an indication of the range of contamination sources and some estimated clean-up costs for the sites listed on the database. These estimates should be treated with caution, as they are very preliminary. Estimated clean-up costs vary enormously from under 1 million Hungarian

Table 7.1   Estimated clean-up costs for a variety of contamination sources

Source of Contamination	Number of cases with cost data	Range of estimated clean-up costs (£000)
Municipal solid wastes	11	15–212
Industrial solid wastes	5	15–150
Toxic wastes	6	30–1000
Pesticides	4	6–100
Electroplating	12	1.5–250
Communal sewage	9	1.5–7500
Liquid wastes	3	30–40
Manure	4	24–60
Aluminium	3	12–600
Gas production	4	60–2100
Leather tanning	2	15–6000
Mining	4	113–1000
Oil storage	3	12–330
Oil derivatives	8	70–12 000

forints (HUF) (£3000), to over HUF 4 billion (£12 million). Twenty per cent of registered sites are estimated to cost less than £30 000 to decontaminate while 5 per cent of sites are estimated to cost over £3 million. However, there is no information regarding the costs of removing toxic waste and repairing the damage at over one-third of the sites.

Analysis of the available data reveals that the source of pollution is known in 81.5 per cent of the registered sites, and unknown in 2.5 per cent of cases. No data exists for the remaining 16 per cent about the pollution source. The most common sources of pollution are sewage wastes (from various sources but, in particular, pumped liquid waste and sludge from septic systems), municipal and industrial solid wastes, and waste materials from various manufacturing industries including electroplating works, pesticide manufacturers, leather tanning, coal gas production and aluminium production. There are also a significant number of sites indicated as containing oils, oil derivatives and other toxic wastes.

In some cases the source of pollution goes back many decades while others are very recent. Records indicate establishment of activities on one site in 1869 and on five other sites before 1930. In one-third of the sites, however, there is no indication of how long the polluting activities have been occurring.

Interestingly, a significant number of contaminated land sites have been caused by the establishment of activities during the 1990s. The interpretation of this development is complex. Some of these new sites may simply be caused by the movement and storage of hazardous materials at new locations, rather than actual contamination of land, while others may be due to the creation of new privatized companies that have taken on the liabilities of previously state-owned firms. However, this suggests that land contamination is an ongoing activity that needs to be addressed if the stock of contaminated sites is to be decreased.

Ownership of identified polluted sites varies but, as Table 7.2 shows, the majority are in private hands although local authorities are also significant owners. The state, owning 5 per cent of sites, appears to have minimized its liabilities in this area but there is no data for 25 per cent of the sites in the database. In a further 12 per cent of cases, information is uncertain or the owner unknown. Thus ownership is unclear for approximately 37 per cent of sites.

Table 7.2   Sites where ownership is known (n = *123*)

Owner	Percentage of sites owned
The state	5
Local government	28.5
Owned by private companies	52
Private individuals	9
Mixed ownership	5.5

THE REMEDIATION PROGRAMME AND RISK ASSESSMENT APPROACH

Creation of the Contaminated Land Remediation Programme

Contaminated land problems have clearly not been handled adequately during the main privatization period and remain a potential source of environmental harm (Paczi and Kaderjak 1997). Perhaps too much was expected from a process aimed at generating revenues for the government and for turning centrally controlled organizations into independent and efficient units of production. Contamination from past activities will not disappear and the problem continues to haunt successive governments. Only in 1996 did the government establish a land remediation programme as a result of some widely publicized cases and increasing public pressure concerning highly visible sites. This represents a second attempt, since in 1993 a Contaminated Land Programme was established which concentrated on cleaning up ex-Soviet military sites but the programme was closed down after only one year. Section 3 of Government Decree 2205/1996 states that a programme should be developed to handle remediation of sites with special regard to companies belonging to the state property agency, where contamination is connected to state property or is on state property, or where the state controls the contaminating activities. The concern here is for decontamination at sites which are the responsibility of state institutions. The decree also requires the programme to clarify that responsibility and develop a programme that details how to proceed with decontamination. The programme is the responsibility of MERP but should also include input from the ministries of Finance and Labour. Section 6 of the decree requires the development of a national environmental clean-up priority list using information gathered by the programme and from soil and groundwater monitoring programmes already in existence.

A further decree one year later (2304/1997) signalled the government's intention to accept a medium-term programme to clean up sites during the 1998–2002 period. MERP was ordered to carry out the programme subject to financial constraints. Section 4 of the decree required MERP to develop a methodology that would prevent sites from falling under state responsibility, thus limiting the financial burden on the state. Although, in some respects, this represents a belated attempt to prevent problems from falling back into state hands after privatization. The programme must also deal with cases that have failed to pass into the private sector.

The specific remit of the programme is to identify, appraise and clean up contaminated sites in Hungary. The programme budget is currently set at HUF 1 billion (£3.03 million) per year, sourced initially from privatization revenues (and later on, funding is to come from general revenues). The ministry has stated its intention is to decontaminate land only to the level of use for which the area is zoned. It sees its responsibilities as preventing immediate risks from occurring and after that to reduce risks to a 'safe' level.

The Remediation Programme

The remediation programme consists of six phases, illustrated in Figure 7.1. The process starts by collecting and recording information from agencies and individuals. In phase 1, ministry personnel conduct an initial appraisal of information and register the site. When the programme was initiated, all regional environmental inspectorates were asked to submit

information on sites of which they were aware. Various government
ministries were also asked to collect information on potentially contaminated
sites in their areas of responsibility. The result was the database discussed
above.

At the start of phase 2, an assessment of ownership is made and the
responsibilities of the state for site remediation are identified. Liability issues
are examined and the programme determines whether decontamination is the
responsibility of the state. In cases where a site is in private ownership an
assessment is made as to whether the state should give financial aid for
decontamination. Following this stage the site is placed on the national
environmental clean-up priority list and more detailed environmental appraisal
is carried out which may include the establishment of some monitoring.
Emergency actions to limit risks of damage are carried out if it judged
necessary. National Environmental Clean-up Priority List I contains all the

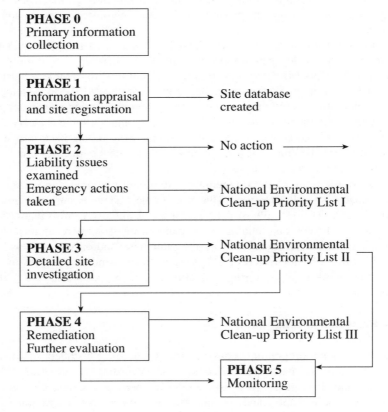

Figure 7.1　The contaminated land remediation programme

sites which have received initial appraisal and for which the state feels it is either directly responsible or should contribute financially.

As resources permit, more detailed site investigation occurs in phase 3, following which a decision is made whether or not to proceed with clean-up. If the decision is made to remediate, the site goes on to National Environmental Clean-up Priority List II. The third phase allows for a more considered evaluation of the site once any emergency actions have been taken. A detailed examination of the potential risks is undertaken, monitoring information is assessed and a decision made as to whether the site should go onto National Environmental Clean-up Priority List II. At this stage no further clean-up may also be recommended. If further action is felt unnecessary then there may still be some monitoring and future inspections of the site.

In phase 4 actual remediation work is carried out. Sites placed on the national priority list receive remediation treatment to be followed by future inspections and monitoring. Following initial remediation, sites will receive further evaluation and might be placed on National Environmental Clean-up Priority List III for further clean-up work. An evaluation at the end of phase 4 establishes whether the site is clean enough or should stay on the priority list and receive further treatment. The final phase is a monitoring stage to ensure sites pose no threat to the environment or public health.

Risk Assessment

The final result is a priority rating for sites using a scale which consists of a risk index for the site itself multiplied by a weighting factor purporting to represent the 'degree of protest against the pollution source'. How the values are derived and why they should be used as a weighting factor to rank sites that have been given a risk assessment score are both unclear. If anything, this weighting clouds the issue over which are the most dangerous sites in terms of public health and ecological impact. Unfortunately there is no attempt to categorize site priority ratings into some qualitative assessment to indicate where risks are negligible, of some importance, or extremely high. The result is an open-ended scale with no indication of the difference in magnitude of risk between numerical scores derived. The level of detail required to produce these risk scores would be better utilized during the final phase of a site risk assessment where it could provide input into designing the site-specific remediation plans. Risk assessment takes place during phases 2, 3 and 4. The present risk assessment procedure appears to be based on a 'source–pathway–receptor' approach. This is complex and difficult, requiring large amounts of data on, for example, distance to receptors, vulnerability of receptors to damage and assumptions regarding the level of public opinion and knowledge. The procedure examines impacts on soils, surface water and groundwater and air, taking into account the nature of the materials released, the amount of materials and any protection provided. Much of the risk assessment is additive in that risks from one aspect are added to others taking into account certain physical conditions in the surrounding area and on site. The underlying methodology is unclear and many of the calculations are convoluted making the final risk scores very difficult to understand or to utilize (Futaki 1997). Thus, the procedure, as it presently operates, is problematic.

Integrating Risk Assessment and Economic Benefit Information

While the 'source–pathway–receptor' relationship must be the basis for a risk assessment procedure that will determine the best remediation plans for a particular site, the management of a remediation programme requires a more qualitative and judgemental risk assessment procedure in order to allow for the most efficient allocation of limited financial resources and skilled personnel. This is a process that must also encompass a measure of expected benefits from site remediation in order to allow decision making on the ranking of sites for clean-up. Indicating a high-risk score is inadequate because sites will vary enormously in terms of clean-up costs, benefits to society and the distribution of benefits across society.

In order to improve the decision-making process, two changes to the present remediation programme should be implemented. First, phase 2 risk assessment should be simplified and risks categorized as 'low', 'medium' or 'high'. Second, phases 2 and 3 should include estimates of remediation benefits. Figure 7.2 illustrates the present situation where only the left half of the diagram is being addressed: sites are merely assigned a risk assessment score. Although this information can be utilized to rank contaminated sites based on the assessed risk, it says nothing about what benefits might accrue to these receptors (or beneficiaries) when the site is decontaminated (the right half of the diagram). Benefit measures are proposed in order to provide an indication of high, medium or low benefits. An integrated system that assesses both risks and benefits to 'receptors' would allow decision-makers to identify where both contamination risks and remediation benefits lie, allow them to focus on high-risk/high-benefit sites, and to understand who stands to lose or gain when remediation takes place. The aim therefore is to develop money measures of estimation for the full range of beneficiaries from contaminated land remediation and then integrate these estimates with the risk assessment process already in place. The next section describes an attempt to employ this approach at an actual site in Hungary.

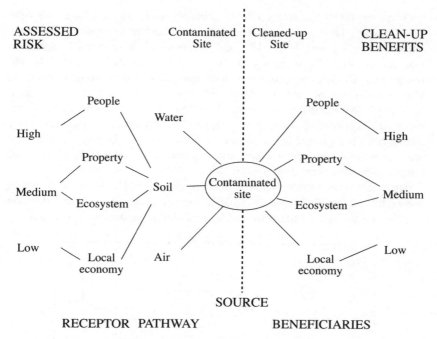

ASSESSED   Contaminated ┊ Cleaned-up   CLEAN-UP
RISK   Site   ┊   Site   BENEFITS

RECEPTOR PATHWAY   SOURCE   BENEFICIARIES

Figure 7.2   Integrating benefits with risk assessment

CASE STUDY: ESTIMATING REMEDIATION BENEFITS AT THE SZÍKGÁT SITE

The site selected for this study was Szíkgát, located on the south-west edge of the city of Debrecen in eastern Hungary. Immediately to the east of the site, and separated by a small stream (the Tocó), is the city's sewage treatment works. To the south is an area of both abandoned and active landfills which form the major landfill for the city. To the south-east is a former Soviet military air base and to the west is high-quality agricultural land. Many people live near the site, mostly in the large, panel-block housing estates of Tégláskert, Tócó Völgyi and Tócóskert. There are also some small settlements to the south and west of the site such as the village of Szepes.

Like many other contaminated sites in Hungary, Szíkgát has a complex history of both toxic waste disposal and ownership patterns. In the 1950s a municipal company collected liquid household wastes (septic tank wastes) from Debrecen and the surrounding region which were placed in a series of shallow, unlined lagoons created for de-watering liquid wastes (lagoons 1 to 5). Channels were created to remove water to a shallow lake in order to decrease the biological oxygen demand before releasing the effluent into the Tocó stream. During the same period, solid and liquid industrial wastes (deposited in lagoons 10 to 13), and pharmaceutical wastes (deposited in lagoons 14 and 15), were also brought to the site (see Figure 7.3). No information was kept regarding which companies were depositing waste at the site or the types of material deposited. These wastes are shown to have included heavy metals, acids, used oils, oil emulsions, phenols, cyanide and other materials deposited over a 40-year period. Concentrations of some heavy metals have been found in the sludge remaining on site, benzene and arsenic have been found in groundwater, and oils and oily sludge exists in several unlined lagoons (Temesvary 1998).

The site was originally owned by the municipality of Debrecen. The present ownership pattern is complex as in 1998 the operating company transformed itself into a limited company owned by nine municipalities (ownership being

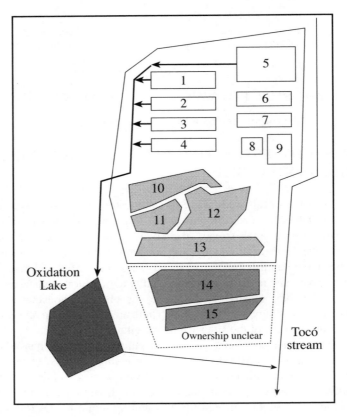

Figure 7.3   The Szíkgát site, Debrecen

determined by the percentage share of waste deposited on the site). The company now owns lagoons 1 to 13 but not the oxidation lake, which is owned by a state cooperative farm. Ownership of lagoons 14 and 15 is unclear though at one point they were owned by an Austrian company which entered into a joint venture with the city of Debrecen to operate the landfill. When MERP requested that the new Austrian owners decontaminate lagoons 14 and 15, they suddenly returned the site to the previous owner (KMI 1997). Apparently, a small fraction of this parcel has now been taken back by the municipality and the rest is in individual private ownership. The existing proposal put forward by MERP, however, is to decontaminate all 15 lagoons and the oxidation lake (although the farm manager has yet to be consulted about this proposal). Estimated clean-up costs are in the range HUF 350–400 million (£1–£1.2 million) or one-third of the annual MERP budget for land decontamination.

Szíkgát is representative of a multitude of small sites around the country. Ecological damage has been caused through deposition of various toxic materials, and discharges to surface water and groundwater. The source of contamination remains *in situ* and a large quantity of pollutants remain in the soil potentially threatening groundwater supplies and surface water bodies in the surrounding area. At the same time it is extremely difficult to apportion liability, as the sources of wastes are largely unknown and unprovable. Past and present ownership patterns are complex and the new owners lack the resources to engage in any form of remediation.

MEASURING THE BENEFITS OF SITE REMEDIATION

Three studies were attempted to capture the social and environmental benefits of cleaning up the site: a hedonic pricing (HP) study, a property owner valuation, and a contingent valuation method survey (CVM). Full details of the surveys conducted at the Szíkgát site can be found in Harvard Institute for International Development (1998). Unfortunately the HP study was unsuccessful and results were unusable. Data on 361 property sales were collected from estate agents in the Debrecen area for a two-year period prior to 1998, but much of the information required was missing and a large proportion of the data proved to be inadequate for statistical analysis. A reduced dataset did suggest that prices for apartments with similar characteristics were lower in Tócóskert and Tócó Völgyi (which are areas of panel-block buildings close to the site) but this difference could not be ascribed to the proximity of these areas to the Szíkgát toxic waste site. The application of an HP approach was thus rejected due to the difficulties of obtaining data, of sufficient quality, on property sales.

The Property Owner and Contingent Valuation Surveys

The aim of the property owner survey was to investigate perceived changes in the value of residential property in the Debrecen area resulting from the proposed clean-up of the hazardous waste site at Szíkgát. The idea behind the study was to offer an alternative measure of benefits for comparison with both CVM and HP models. Respondents were asked to predict the change in value of their own property resulting from clean-up of the Szíkgát site (that is, an improvement in environmental quality). The approach is based on the acknowledgement that the largest investment that many people make in their lives is in the house (or apartment) that they purchase. This is a serious investment decision and people investigate the property market carefully before their purchase. Property owners were therefore hypothesized to be highly sensitive to changes in local environmental quality which could have a detrimental or beneficial effect on the value of their investment, and be able to predict fairly accurately a percentage change in the value of their investment resulting from an environmental change such as remediation of a contaminated site.

The CVM survey was a more straightforward application. A dichotomous choice format was selected. This asked respondents to indicate whether or not they would be willing to pay a given amount for decontamination of the Szíkgát site over a ten-year period.

Sample Descriptions

Table 7.3 illustrates that in terms of the main socio-economic characteristics the two samples are quite similar. A major difference is in the mean age, with the property owner sample being ten years older. This may be a function of timing of respondent interviews, some of which were conducted during working hours and this may also account for the gender bias. In other respects the samples are similar. Interviews were conducted in July and August 1998, on random samples of residents from a range of locations at varying distances from the Szíkgát hazardous waste site (see Figure 7.4). Approximately three-quarters of the samples live in panel blocks and the remainder in detached houses, which reflects the actual situation in the area.

Very few households (less than 5 per cent) of either sample have a gross household income greater than HUF 200000 per month (£606) while two-thirds have monthly household incomes of below HUF 80000 (£240 per month). Average income for the CVM sample, for example, is HUF 62509 per household per month (£190) though this ranges from a low of HUF 10000 per household per month (£30) up to a high of HUF 225000 per household per month (£680). The mean monthly household income for the property owner

Table 7.3   Socio-economic characteristics of survey samples

Characteristic	Property owner survey	Contingent valuation survey
Date of survey	July 1998	August 1998
Sample size	560	583
Gender		
Male (%)	35	34
Female (%)	65	66
Per cent of sample living in panel block buildings	76	78
Median number of rooms	3	3
Household size of sample (%)		
3 or 4 people	56.5	61.4
>4 people	7.5	11.3
Mean age (years)	53.7	43.2
Mean monthly household income (HUF)	59 300	62 509
Education level (%)		
Primary	20	15
Secondary	53	61
Higher	27	24

sample is slightly lower than for the CVM sample although this may be due to the older mean age in the later sample. Although incomes appear to be low by western standards, these figures are supported by national statistics which indicate monthly gross earnings in the northern Alfold region of HUF 35 503 (£107) for females and HUF 43 744 (£132) for males (Statistical Yearbook of Hungary 1996). Accurate household income figures are always difficult to obtain because households usually have more than one wage earner and many people engage in more than one job but wish to hide these facts from officials. The majority of households have two to four persons in the household and only about one-tenth of the samples indicated households of more than four people. This is again in accordance with national statistics for 1996, which indicate an average of 2.57 persons per dwelling outside of Budapest and an average of 2.4 rooms per dwelling.

The Property Owner Survey

Respondents were asked a series of questions on the extent to which they felt certain changes in the local conditions would affect the value of their property. The aim was to see whether environmental improvements, and in particular

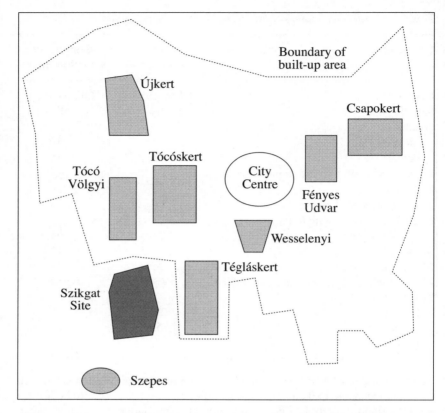

Figure 7.4   Location of Szíkgát to survey sampling sites in the Debrecen area

the cleaning up of a hazardous waste site in the area, would affect the respondents' perception of their own property value. Nearly three-quarters of the sample (72.7 per cent) indicated that decontaminating a hazardous waste site in the area would result in a moderate or significant increase in property values (this question was asked before any specific reference was made to Szíkgát).

Analysis of variance revealed statistically significant differences in predicted property value changes resulting from site remediation at various locations, but failed to signify whether these differences were attributed to distance from the site. Table 7.4 illustrates mean scores for a scale measuring perceived danger to self and family from the site (the Endanger scale) and the respondent's estimate of the price change effect on his/her property if the Szíkgát site was decontaminated. The table shows mean scores for each location with the distance to the toxic waste site indicated. The Endanger

Table 7.4 Perceived level of danger and estimated price effects of site remediation

Location	Distance (km)	Endanger* (mean score)	Std. Dev.	Price change (mean %)	Std. Dev.
Tégláskert	1.54	2.64	0.81	16.62	8.22
Tócó Völgyi	1.75	2.55	0.63	14.02	6.02
Tócóskert	2.24	2.50	0.69	14.94	5.52
Szepes	2.80	2.66	0.50	19.16	7.12
Wesselenyi Ltp	4.06	2.00	0.91	8.71	5.87
Újkert	4.90	1.75	0.87	14.15	9.17
Fényes Udvar	5.04	1.86	0.81	9.50	7.37
Csapokert	6.58	1.90	0.57	12.84	6.64

Note: Endanger is a scale of the respondent's perceived danger to self or family where: 1 = no danger; 2 = some danger; and 3 = high level of danger.

scores suggest that as distance from the site increases, the perceived level of danger decreases. The same pattern is indicated with perceived effect on property value, that is, the predicted change in value decreases with distance from the site. In Tégláskert, 1.54 km from the site, respondents estimated an increase in their property value by an average of 16.62 per cent; whereas in Fényes Udvar, 5.04 km from the site, the perceived average increase in property value was only 9.5 per cent.

Szepes, a small village downstream from the site in terms of surface water and groundwater flow, has the highest mean value for Endanger. Thus, despite a low average income the village has the largest mean predicted price increase (19.16 per cent). This is as expected because there is a high level of concern in the village over potential contamination of groundwater and the villages are totally reliant on shallow private wells for drinking water. In addition, the raised landfills immediately adjacent to the hazardous waste site are visible from the village and, when the wind blows from the north, odours are strong and litter is deposited over the area.

A regression model was developed to examine factors affecting predicted property value changes resulting from site remediation. The dependent variable was predicted property value change following site clean-up. The model indicated that the significant independent variables affecting the predicted price change were location of the property (in terms of kilometres from the hazardous waste site), the perceived level of danger from the site, age and education. Education has a negative value suggesting that as the education level of the respondent increases, the estimated price change resulting from clean-up of the site diminishes. This could be the result of having higher levels of understanding of the likely effects of the site or, perhaps, a realization that clean-up will have little impact on property value in the locations selected due to other factors affecting values. Income is insignificant but the regression coefficient is also negative, suggesting that higher incomes result in a lower predicted price change for clean-up (note that education and income are positively correlated). The model also predicted property price change declines at the rate of 1.4 per cent per kilometre distance from the site over the range 1.5 to 6.6 km.

The analysis indicates that overall there is a perceived effect on property value arising from remediation of the hazardous waste site at Szíkgát. Regression analysis showed that increasing distance from the site does result in a decrease in perceived danger, and a reduction in the predicted percentage change in property value resulting from clean-up. Results suggest that if the Szíkgát site was decontaminated, residents perceive that property values would increase by an average of 16.2 per cent in the area 1–3 km around the site, and an average of 11.3 per cent between 3 and 6.6 km from the site.

The Contingent Valuation Study

Respondents were presented with information on actual and potential environmental impacts of the site, and a hypothetical scenario regarding the potential remediation of the hazardous waste at Szíkgát. The scenario pointed out that some government funds were available but unless there was a local contribution, no clean-up would occur. The proposal was therefore that the city of Debrecen set up a special fund and levy a local tax on residents which would operate over a ten-year period. Households were asked to make a monthly contribution for that period. Respondents were also shown a map indicating the location of the site on the edge of Debrecen and a sketch diagram of the site itself indicating the range of problems. They were then asked for a monthly household contribution to the tax. The sample was split into three groups of 200 and each subsample received a different starting bid. If the respondents agree to pay, they were then asked if they would pay a higher amount. If the answer to the first bid was 'no' they were asked if they would pay a lower amount.

The most influential variables on acceptance of the bid were found to be the size of the bid itself and household income. As bid size increases there is less probability of its initial acceptance. Other influential factors are the expected socio-economic characteristics such as age and gender. Older people are less likely to accept the bid (that is, less willing to pay) and females are more likely to accept the bid than males (that is, pay more). The perception of damage to health from the materials at the site and length of residence in the area also appear to have some influence on the likelihood that the bid will be accepted. Those who are concerned over health defects are more likely to accept the initial bid or pay more. Length of residence in the area results in a lower acceptance rate. One possible explanation is that lower income groups, which in general are less able to move, have been there longer.

A range of statistical models were investigated and the one with the most conservative willingness to pay (WTP) bid, a logistic regression model, was selected. The WTP estimate derived from the logistic model is HUF 288 per household per month (£0.87). As households were asked to make monthly payments over a ten-year period, this amounts to a total of HUF 34 650 per household (£105). This may be an underestimate as there is some suggestion that the starting bids in the CVM survey were set too low. This figure can be viewed as the value of the expected benefits from site remediation which might also reflect some perceived increase in property value on the part of the respondent. However, the WTP was assumed to reflect only the households' income constrained preparedness to pay for an environmental improvement in their neighbourhood.

AGGREGATION OF BENEFITS

Aggregating benefits across the population affected requires defining a boundary between those affected by the clean-up and those who will gain nothing. The distance selected was based on mean scores for the Endanger scale for the different locations (see Table 7.4). Where mean scores drop below 2 this suggests that the majority of the population believe there is 'no danger' from the site. This appears to occur beyond the 4 km point, which was therefore selected as the boundary line. Clearly, any increase or decrease of the boundary will directly affect total benefits.

Aggregation of benefits could be carefully worked out by calculating the number of households and mean property values at various distances from the site and applying a decreasing predicted price change at each kilometre away from the site. However, the household information required was unavailable. Instead an estimate of aggregate benefits was made based on the population living within 4 km of the site. A total figure for improved property values can be derived using the number of households in the area and an assumed average property value of HUF 2 million (mean price of properties within the area).

Property Owner Valuation Survey

Property owners perceive an average increase in value following remediation of 14.7 per cent (HUF 294 000) within 4 km of the site. If we assume 19 500 residential property owners in this area then the total improvement in value is HUF 5.73 billion (£17.32 million).

The Contingent Valuation Survey

Regression models revealed a WTP of HUF 288–357 per household per month for ten years. If the lowest estimate is used, this results in a total payment of 34 650 forints per household (£105). If this value holds over a 4 km radius from the site then the total WTP for clean up is HUF 675.7 million (34 650 × 19 500 households) (or £2.05 million) over the ten-year period.

Implications of the Aggregate Results

These figures suggest that there are potentially extensive benefits to be gained from site remediation whichever approach is utilized. Care must be taken to avoid double counting and the question must be asked about which of these techniques to use. The CVM survey provides significantly lower benefits which would be expected as respondents were being asked to *pay* directly for clean-up rather than being asked, as in the property owner survey, to say what they might *receive* in benefits as a result of site remediation. CVM results are clearly income constrained (and usually discounted which would further decrease the present value of the ten-year stream of payments). The property owner predicted valuation change of HUF 5.73 billion seems very optimistic. Although, if only 7 per cent of this amount is realized, then benefits in terms of improved property values will equal site clean-up costs.

Aggregated WTP results are about 12 per cent of the anticipated property value increase. This would appear to be realistic given the low household incomes, that the CVM scenario spreads the payments over a ten-year period, and that the property owner survey is more explicit in measuring the social benefits which might accrue to the individual household. Based on the results derived above, the environmental benefits to households from the Szíkgát site remediation, in the 4 km area around the site, lie somewhere in the range HUF 675.7 million to HUF 5.73 billion. This may be a conservative estimate as no investigation has been conducted on improvement in agricultural, commercial or industrial property value, or in the potential increase in local taxes that might result from remediation and re-use of the site. Thus, even using the lowest estimates, benefits would appear to outweigh costs of clean-up (estimated at HUF 350–400 million, or £1–1.2 million) by a factor of 2 to 1.

INTEGRATING THE ENVIRONMENTAL BENEFITS DATA WITH THE RISK ASSESSMENT PROCEDURE

The major question to ask at this point is: how should this benefits information be used in the contaminated land programme? The answer is that it should be integrated with the risk assessment to provide decision makers with information on both risks and benefits of proposed remediation actions. A fundamental flaw in the present remediation programme is the risk assessment procedure which ties up a great deal of resources and time through the level of detail required early on in the programme. Many of the data that are collected contain implicit assumptions and there is considerable uncertainty regarding data quality in the existing risk assessment procedure.

What is required is a simplified assessment procedure for use in phase 2 of the remediation programme. This would speed up the number of sites which can be assessed, there would be a reduction in the assessment burden on MERP staff, and this would release resources for more detailed risk assessment – still required in phase 3. As a result, phase 3 could then focus on a much smaller number of sites selected each year for remediation. Such benefit information could be included in the present programme at phases 2 and 3.

In phase 2, initial site visits are made. If this phase were altered to make a preliminary assessment on source(s) of contamination, pathways of potential effects and potential receptors (property, humans, ecosystems), then preliminary benefit estimates could also be provided based on benefit transfer measures from sites elsewhere in Hungary. The danger at this stage is that such a preliminary estimate might miss important impacts and underestimate benefits. The problem with utilizing benefit transfers is that the function selected might fail to cover the range of benefits from clean-up of a particular site (more empirical work is required in Hungary and elsewhere to resolve the relevance of transferring monetary estimates from one site to another). There is a requirement at phase 2 for developing a simplified risk assessment methodology which will allow ranking of risks into broad categories such as high, medium and low. The proposal here is to have two ways of ranking sites, one based on risks to humans, property and ecosystems, and the other based on perceived benefits of decontamination. These ratings would be based on qualitative risk assessment and benefit transfer data in phase 2. This would allow decision makers quickly and easily to identify and prioritize sites with high risks and high benefits for clean-up, leaving low-risk–low-benefit sites for some future date when more resources are available.

If phase 2 resulted in a simplified risk ranking system and benefit measures, then phase 3 could prioritize sites and initially select those indicated as having high risk/high benefits for more detailed investigation. At this phase more highly detailed risk assessments could be carried out along with the use of either benefit transfer information or site-based benefit measures. In addition, in cases where emergency actions have taken place an evaluation could be made of these actions and whether further clean-up is required.

Full remediation benefit estimation would occur in phase 3, utilizing information from a wider variety of sources than the benefit transfer values developed in phase 2. Initial decisions would be required on the most suitable techniques for assessing benefits depending on the individual site characteristics. Benefit transfer information may still play a role but would be supplemented by additional benefit data. Thus, benefit estimation requires, at the least, a preliminary assessment of actual damage and potential risks of future damage. At this stage, phase 2 risk assessment information might be used as a starting-point, to indicate the most suitable techniques for collecting benefit data. Accurate benefit estimates will, however, require a more complete risk assessment, hence the need for improvement and streamlining of the risk assessment process.

CONCLUSIONS

At the present time very little empirical work exists in any of the other transition economies regarding monetary benefits of contaminated land remediation. The research described here is the first attempt at monetary valuation of the social and environmental benefits from decontaminating toxic waste sites in Hungary. This is, therefore, a first step in exploring the application of monetary valuation to the issue. The property owner predicted value approach offers an alternative to the hedonic approach (which will be difficult to implement in Hungary given the data acquisition problems) and the results suggest that a range of social benefits from contaminated site remediation can be captured.

The CVM approach appears to offer considerable flexibility in environmental benefit measurement (as opposed to total social benefits). The CVM attempted to measure what households are prepared to pay for the environmental improvements of site remediation. The total value derived is approximately 12 per cent of the expected property value improvements. A major difference in the two techniques is that one asked respondents to estimate a future gain in benefits at no personal cost while the other asked respondents for a payment in order to receive a future improvement.

Neither of the two methods implemented here have captured all the benefits from contaminated site remediation. Discussions with local farmers and estate agents indicated that improved agricultural land values immediately adjacent to the site were a distinct possibility. In addition, the likelihood of improved commercial and industrial land in the area was not considered, and the re-use of the site for industrial purposes, and consequent contribution to local taxes, was also ignored.

Both techniques rely on the existence of populations nearby to develop site remediation benefits. The property owner approach is particularly dependent, when aggregating total benefits, on numbers of property owners in the area although the CVM technique could be applied in other ways where the local population is small. Application of the property owner technique would clearly place improvements in property value (even though they may be based on improved 'environmental' quality) above improvements in ecological quality in terms of importance. The CVM technique, on the other hand, offers the possibility of capturing a narrower range of values (which may include use, option and bequest values) placed on improved ecological quality, provided it can be adequately measured and described. It also offers the user the possibility of being more selective about which characteristics of an improved site are measured. The property value approach is much more of a broad-brush measure of all the benefits associated with a cleaner local environment.

The questions of interest here are first of all whether environmental valuation data improve decision making in this area, and second whether that improvement is worth the investment required to derive the information. The answer to the first question would have to be a qualified 'yes'. Information on environmental benefits would be extremely useful in both phases 2 and 3 of the contaminated land programme to assist in the prioritization of sites for clean-up. The second question is more difficult to answer. The case study described here revealed some of the shortcomings and difficulties of using monetary valuation methods. These include difficulties with estimating household income, separating the effect of the Szíkgát site from other activities (landfilling, sewage treatment), aggregating benefits, and avoiding double counting issues (understanding which values are included in a CVM or property owner valuation study). Careful research design can reduce the impact of some of these problems but not entirely eliminate them. The 'accuracy' of the derived benefit measures is an issue that must be addressed but it should be borne in mind that the risk assessment procedure itself also makes many assumptions and has various levels of uncertainty attached to the risk ratings produced.

Higher levels of confidence in benefit estimates require more resources and these will always be limited in the transition economies. The aim of phase 2 in the MERP risk assessment procedure should be to develop techniques that will provide an indication of clean-up benefits in terms of orders of magnitude. This should allow quick decisions to be made on which sites are likely to yield the highest benefits for the level of resources invested. For phase 3 more thorough measures can be undertaken, if required, to ascertain the relative merits of alternative remediation techniques.

At present, two estimates of benefits from remediation of one site have been generated. The present study has illustrated that monetary measures of environmental improvement can be obtained in Hungary, though the one site examined here is an inadequate basis upon which to base benefit transfer measures, and little can be said about the reliability of such estimates. The potential scope for utilizing benefit transfer techniques in phase 2 of the remediation programme is enormous as it will side-step the need to develop benefit measures for individual sites. The next step should, therefore, be a study which focuses on developing benefit transfer information and techniques for Hungary.

REFERENCES

Futaki, K. (1997), *Proposed Methodology and Computer Adaptation for the Preparation of the Preliminary Priority List*, Budapest: Mernoki Iroda Kft.
Harvard Institute for International Development (1998), *Development of a Cost-Benefit Approach to Contaminated Land Remediation*, Report submitted to the Ministry for Environment and Regional Policy, Budapest, Hungary.
KMI – Karmentesitesi Programiroda (1997), *Debrecen: Szíkgát Hulladeklerako*, Budapest: Ministry of Environment and Regional Policy.
Lehoczki, Z. (1993), 'Environmental administration in Hungary', unpublished paper.
Magyar Statisztikai Evknonyv (Statistical Yearbook of Hungary) (1996), Központi Statisztikai Hivatal.
Paczi, E. and P. Kaderjak (1997), 'Environmental impacts of industrial privatisation in Hungary', Ch. 3, in P. Kaderjak and J. Powell, *Economics for Environmental Policy in Transition Economies: An Analysis of the Hungarian Experience*, Cheltenham: Edward Elgar.
Regional Environmental Centre for Central and Eastern Europe (1994), *Contamination Assessment and Determination of Prevention Measures for the Sajo Valley*, submitted by CH2M Hill-Unico Environmental Services, Ltd, Szentendre, Hungary.
Research Triangle Institute (1994), *Operating and Managing Communal Solid Waste Landfills in Hungary*, Local Environmental Management Project, USAID Contract No. EUR-0039-C-00-2065-00, Research Triangle Park, North Carolina, USA.
Temesvary, P. (1998), 'Human health risk assessment: Debrecen Szíkgát site', paper submitted to the Harvard Institute for International Development.

8. Combining life cycle assessment and multicriteria evaluation: comparing waste management options in Spain

Giuseppe Munda and Marta Romo

INTRODUCTION

Life Cycle Assessment: Main Characteristics and Problems

There are six stages to conducting a life cycle assessment (LCA): inventory, classification, characterization, normalization, valuation and interpretation. Throughout the consecutive stages the information that is presented is wide-ranging in nature, meaning and usefulness. The inventory stage presents a list of hundreds of consumption and emission measurements of a great number of substances (also termed environmental interventions). Due to the size of this inventory the data are difficult to interpret, and thus of a little direct use. The first phase of impact evaluation occurs under the classification stage. Consumption and emissions are ordered and organized so that the impact categories affected by the system under study are known. However, at this stage the extent to which each category has been affected and the categories that are relevant are unknown.

In the next phase, the characterization stage, the most polluting processes of the system are identified. That is the toxic contribution is estimated from studying the systems potential impacts or 'environmental threats' (Finvenden 1996). One approach under development tries to relate the environmental interactions directly to 'environmental damages' such as death rates, disease, resources consumption and habitat destruction (de Haes and Jolliet 1998). The resulting characterized profile is still difficult to compare with other systems, since such a profile is multidimensional in nature. Next is the optional normalization stage, which is also called 'technical relevancy analysis' by the International Standards Organization (ISO). Here the specific contribution from the system being studied is specified by location and timing.

The relative importance of the impacts of the system under study are estimated in the valuation stage. Subjective values are included, which allow choice between alternatives that score differently on various impact categories (for example, option A is better than option B for avoiding greenhouse gas emissions, but B scores better for reducing acidic deposition and water consumption). The traditional manner of developing this step, as we shall see later on in this chapter, consists of a weighted sum of the impacts on different categories.

The interpretation stage draws out the conclusions and expresses the results of the study in relation to the previously defined objectives. Thus, if the objective of the study were to choose between different functionally equivalent products, the interpretation should provide a detailed justification of the preferred alternative, or perhaps a classification of the alternatives (de Haes and Jolliet 1998). Of course, these conclusions depend on the information obtained in the previous stages. The aim is to avoid the 'garbage in, garbage out' phenomenon (Funtowicz and Ravetz 1990).

Although LCA is widely applied, it still presents some serious methodological and empirical difficulties. For example, impact valuation was absent from many LCA studies prior to 1992 and only the inventory stage has been developed extensively. In recent years, impact valuation has been introduced, mainly thanks to the methodological developments carried out by the Centre of Environmental Science at Leiden University (CML), the Institute of Swedish Environmental Investigation (IVL), a Nordic project (LCA-NORDIC) and the work of the Society of Environmental Toxicity and Chemistry (SETAC) – Europe Impact Assessment Working Group, I and II. This explains why, at the moment, the valuation stage is a focus of scientific discussion inside the LCA community. Some open issues are: missing impact categories, a lack of consensus on some characterization factors, ignorance about impacts due to synergism and antagonism among certain toxic emissions and the difficulty of prioritizing different environmental impacts. This last point is where we believe multicriteria analysis can help and is the topic of this chapter. Multicriteria evaluation concentrates upon the analysis of conflicting situations (that is, where a given alternative A scores better than another alternative B according to some criteria and worse according to others) thus the possibility of using such techniques in the framework of the LCA valuation stage seems potentially fruitful.

In recent years, life cycle assessment has become popular as a tool to support the environmental decision-making process. This produces information which can be used by manufacturers and consumers in their decisions about different products and services (Bailey et al. 1996). LCA as a tool for aiding decision making does not aim to explain natural phenomena, but rather to collect environmental information to aid public resolution of actual environmental problems. One of these environmental problems is related to ecotoxicological damage of pollutants, so the outcomes of LCA, presented as measures of physical impact, are not only a contribution to the greenhouse effect or to resources depletion, but also to human toxicity, terrestrial and aquatic ecotoxicity, three impact categories in a developing state (Jolliet and Crettaz 1996).

As an illustration, this chapter includes human toxicity, an environmental impact often associated with waste management. LCA could be used by ecotoxicology to introduce a wider framework of analysis, since it is a tool that takes into account the whole life cycle of human activities, from the extraction of raw material, energy consumption and production, to disposal of waste. As a consequence, it evaluates potential impacts, rather than spatially and temporally specific impacts. An impact can be broadly defined as any effect on human health and welfare or the environment.

Thus, LCA is a tool for studying the environmental management of flows within a system (see van den Bergh 1997). The application of LCA in ecotoxicological science would involve the analysis of the toxicological effect of whole products or complex systems through their pollutant emissions in different media (air, water, soil and so forth) and temporal stages. This could be an important step, since traditionally ecotoxicology analyses the damage effects to only one substance in only one medium at one determined time.

On the other hand, the relationship between LCA and ecotoxicology is not unidirectional. It can be used by LCA to calculate the relative toxicity of all the substances detected in the entire ecosystem considered and also to determine the way by which these substances may cause their effect. Indeed, the inclusion of pollutant fate and exposure has been recognized as one of the major methodological issues to be addressed in future LCA working groups (Jolliet and Crettaz 1996).

A Brief Introduction to Multicriteria Evaluation

A typical multicriteria problem (with a discrete number of alternatives) may be described in the following way: A is a finite set of n feasible actions (or alternatives); m is the number of different points of view or evaluation criteria g_i ($i = 1, 2, \ldots, m$) considered relevant in a decision problem, where action a is evaluated to be better than action b (both belonging to the set A) according to the ith point of view if $g_i(a) > g_i(b)$. In this way a decision problem may be represented in a tabular or matrix form. Given the sets A (of alternatives) and G (of evaluation criteria) and assuming the existence of n alternatives and m criteria, an $n \times m$ matrix P can be built as shown in Table 8.1. This is called the evaluation or impact matrix whose typical element p_{ij} ($i = 1, 2, \ldots, m$; $j = 1, 2, \ldots, n$) represents the evaluation of the jth alternative by means of

Table 8.1   Example of an impact matrix

Criteria	Units	Alternatives			
		a_1	a_2	a_3	a_4
g_1		$g_1(a_1)$	$g_1(a_2)$	.	$g_1(a_4)$
g_2		.	.	.	.
g_3		.	.	.	.
g_4		.	.	.	.
g_5		.	.	.	.
g_6		$g_6(a_1)$	$g_6(a_2)$	.	$g_6(a_4)$

the ith criterion. The impact matrix may include quantitative, qualitative or both types of information (Munda 1995).

In general, in a multicriteria problem, there is no solution optimizing all the criteria at the same time and therefore the decision maker has to find compromise solutions. As a tool for conflict management, multicriteria evaluation has demonstrated its usefulness in many environmental management problems (see Beinat and Nijkamp 1998). From an operational point of view, the major strength of multicriteria methods is their ability to address problems marked by various conflicting evaluations. Multicriteria evaluation techniques cannot solve all conflicts, but they can help to provide more insight into the nature of conflicts and into ways to arrive at political compromises in cases where preferences diverge, so increasing the transparency of the choice process.

The main advantage of multicriteria models is that they make it possible to consider a large amount of data and a number of relationships and objectives which are generally present in a specific decision problem. That is, the decision problem at hand can be studied in a multidimensional fashion. As mentioned, action a may be better than action b according to one criterion and worse according to another. As a consequence, the validity of a given multicriteria evaluation study depends upon the inclusion of different perspectives as well as the reflexive properties of the system, even though these are difficult to assess. Once the premises of a particular multicriteria approach are known, the decision makers are aware of the consequences of the assumption. This requires transparency in relation to two main factors: (i) mathematical and descriptive properties which make the models used conform to given requirements; and (ii) the way in which such models are used and integrated in a decision process.

The characteristics of being able to tackle conflicts and the emphasis given to the notion of a decision process seem to make multicriteria evaluation a promising methodology to be used in the framework of LCA. There is then a need for empirical corroboration of this possibility. The following section analyses a waste management problem by combining both LCA and multicriteria evaluation. For another study trying to combine these techniques, see Spengler et al. (1998).

MUNICIPAL WASTE MANAGEMENT: A CASE STUDY

The LCA methodology was applied to five different options for municipal waste management in Bizcaia, northern Spain: landfilling with ferric metals recovery, landfilling with energy recovery, landfilling with physical treatment of leachate, incineration and incineration with energy recovery. The aim was to evaluate and compare the environmental impact through the entire life cycle associated with these options.

During the study, a number of critical decisions and hypotheses have had to be made in order to perform the LCA. These were the choice of functional unit and system boundaries. The primary aims were to avoid residues endangering human health, reducing environmental quality and causing nuisances. In recent years, the regulation of waste management in Europe has been moving towards the incorporation of other functions, for example, the material and energy recovery of residues. In this sense, the two systems considered (landfilling and incineration) use the gases generated to produce electrical energy. The functional unit was therefore defined to fulfil all these functions for 25 years, coinciding with the period needed to convert toxic residues into inert residues if they are deposited in a landfill. Thus the functional unit by which the inputs and outputs of the system are measured was a metric tonne of municipal solid waste collected without treatment. In order to define system boundaries around the domestic waste issue, the average composition of household waste was based on the integrated waste management plan of Bizcaia (see Table 8.2).

Stages of the LCA for the Case Study

All the steps, starting from the deposition of the domestic garbage bags into the withdrawal points and arriving at the process of inertization of municipal waste, are taken into account. Materials and construction processes of the facilities needed for the five options are not considered.

LCA Stage 1: Inventory
In the inventory phase of LCA, the inputs and outputs of the system must be quantified. Municipal waste, raw materials and energy are considered as inputs into the system. The outputs to the environment

Table 8.2   Composition of municipal solid waste

Composition	% in weight
Fermentable matter	44.10
Paper carton	25.26
Glass	4.82
Light containers	11.83
RDH*	0.83
Miscellaneous	4.39
Voluminous	2.92
Inert	5.85
Total	100.00

Note: * RDH: Dangerous residues of the household.

Source: Diputación (1997).

include the emissions to the atmosphere, the hydrosphere and the soil (solid waste).

Option 1: landfilling with ferric metals recovery   This involves the elimination of a tonne of municipal residues in landfill, with ferric metals recovery. The following hypotheses on the biogas generation and leachate and emission factors were adopted.

The quantity of generated biogas is 164 kg/t of municipal solid waste. The composition of the biogas is presented in Table 8.3. The leachate is specific to each location and depends on several climatological and compositional factors, in addition to the particular characteristics of the landfill. A soil porosity of 30 per cent is assumed, and the release of leachate is 370 l/t of municipal solid waste (White et al. 1995). The pollutants present in the leachate of landfill and their concentration are shown in Table 8.4. The leachate is submitted to a reverse osmosis treatment, which eliminates 92.4 per cent of chemical oxygen demand, 46.7 per cent of suspended solids, 98.6 per cent of ammoniacal nitrogen (N-NH_3) and 75 per cent of total iron. Using this process, 10–30 per cent concentrated leachate is obtained (Diputación 1996). The energy consumption in the reverse osmosis process was 33.2×10^{-3} MJ per kg of leachate treated. The solid residue that stays in the landfill after the fermentation is 513 kg/t of municipal solid waste.

Option 2: landfilling with energy recovery   This implies the elimination of a tonne of municipal solid waste in landfill, with ferric metals recovery

Table 8.3   *Concentrations of substances detected in landfill biogas*

Components	Concentration (g/kg)	Components	Concentration (g/kg)
CH_4	406.560	Ter-Butil.Benc.	0.076
CO_2	352.800	1,2,4-Trimet.Benc.	0.088
NH_3	0.351	Isobutanol	0.026
Etil.Benc.	0.029	Met.Etil.cet.	0.125
Xileno	0.093	Pipeno	0.131
Butanol	0.008	Etanol	0.075
Met.Iso.But.Cet.	0.021	Isopropanol	0.252
Propanol	0.055	Etil.Acetato	0.016
Tolueno	0.172	H_2S	0.030

Source: CIEMAT (1992).

Table 8.4   *Landfill leachate composition*

Components	Concentration (mg/l)	Components	Concentration (mg/l)
S.S.	47.00	Cd	0.10
COD	910.00	Cr	0.10
NH_4-N	569.00	Ni	0.09
S total	1.41	As	0.06
Al	0.62	Pb	0.11
Fe	6.42	Cu	0.03
Mn	1.31	Zn	0.13
Sn	0.04		

Source: Disputación (1996).

and electrical production by means of the recollected biogas. The following assumptions were made about the energy recovery and emission factors. According to operational experience in different recovery plants, the percentage of ferric metals recovered from the total waste is 0.836 per cent (Romo 1997). We assumed that 40 per cent of the biogas could be used for energy generation in a gas motor. The generation of combustion gas is 10 m^3 per cubic metre of crude gas. During the combustion of the biogas, pollutants are released whose concentration is indicated in Table 8.5. The solid residue that stays in the landfill after the fermentation is 513 kg/t of waste.

Table 8.5   Pollutants emitted to the atmosphere during combustion of biogas

Components	Concentration (g/kg)
CO_2	1470.000
NO_x	0.620
SO_2	0.056
PCDD + PCDF	0.010*

Note: *(μg/kg).

Option 3: landfilling with physical treatment of leachate   This also involves municipal waste disposal with energy recovery although the leachate is treated by physical process and not reverse osmosis. The following hypotheses on biogas generation, leachate and energy recovery and emission factors were adopted. The leachate is submitted to a treatment which allows a reduction by 40 per cent of chemical oxygen demand and also ammoniacal nitrogen. The components do not experience any meaningful change. Total electrical consumption of a conventional plant is averaged at $0.48.10^{-3}$ MJ per kg of leachate to be treated (Calbet 1997). The solid residue that stays in the landfill after the fermentation is 513 kg/t of waste.

Option 4: incineration   This option considers the impact of burning a tonne of residues in an incinerator equipped with a purification system for combustion gases. The hypotheses adopted on the rates of gas and residue generation and emission factors are the following. The rate of gas generation is 5000 normalized cubic metres per tonne of municipal solid waste. Emissions of pollutants into the atmosphere are assumed to be as shown in Table 8.6. We assumed that 0.36 per cent of ammonia is added to the total waste that enters the oven to reduce the emissions of NO_x. The purification of the combustion gases requires 12.66 kg of calcium oxide and water, and 1.333 kg of active coal and lime. The slag and ash generation per tonne of municipal solid waste is 250 and 39.3 kg, respectively. We assumed 50 per cent of the slag would go to landfill and the other half would be used as construction material in civil works. The ashes are made inert and the whole inert solid residue is placed in landfill.

Option 5: incineration with energy recovery   This includes the incineration of the 100 per cent of residues with recovery of energy. The assumptions are the following. For electrical energy production, the steams in the oven must be reheated through the leak gases of a gas turbine. This gas turbine consumes 12 756 MJ/t of municipal solid waste. The gross production of electricity is

Table 8.6   Emission levels from municipal waste incineration

Components	Concentration (mg/kg) German regulation 17BimSchV (dry, 11% O_2)
SO_2	50.00
CO	50.00
HCl	10.00
HF	1.00
NO_x	200.00
Pb + Cr + Cu + Mn + As + Ni + Sb + Sn	0.50
Hg	0.05
Cd + Tl	0.05
COV	10.00
Particles	10.00
PCDD + PCDF	0.10*

Note: *(μg/kg).

764 000 MWh/year. Since the plant self-consumption amounts to 51 000 MWh/year, net electrical energy for export is 11 400 MJ/t of municipal solid waste.

LCA Stage 2: Impact assessment
To carry out this phase of LCA, the following impact categories have been considered: global warming, acidification, eutrophication, ozone layer depletion, smog, human toxicology, energy consumption and solid waste production. In Table 8.7, the inputs and outputs of the inventory are classified into different impact categories.

In order to quantify the potential contribution of an input or output j to the impact i (P_{ij}), the following equation is applied:

$$P_{ij} = A_j W_{ij} \tag{8.1}$$

where A_j is the amount of input or output and W_{ij} is the weighting factor. The total potential contribution from all inputs and outputs (P_i) is calculated as follows:

$$P_i = \sum_j P_{ij} = \sum_j A_j W_{ij}. \tag{8.2}$$

The weighting factors used to quantify the environmental impacts are taken from the evaluation method developed by the Centre of Environmental Science at the University of Leiden (1992). Using these weighting factors and the mass of the emissions, the corresponding potential contributions to the different impact categories have been determined.

For example, in order to calculate the total contribution of option 2 (landfill with energy recovery) to eutrophication, it is necessary to multiply the

Table 8.7   Classification of emissions into impact categories considered

Eutrophication	ammonia, COD, Kjeldahl-N, N-tot, NH_4+, nitrate, NO_x, P, P-tot, phosphate
Ozone layer depletion	CCl_4, CFC-11, CFC-113, CFC-12, CH_3CCl_3, HALON-1301, HCFC-22
Global warming	CFC-12, CFC-14, CH_2Cl_2, CCl_4, CFC-11, CFC-113, CFC-116, CH_3CCl_3, CO_2, HALON-1301, HCFC-22, methane, N_2O
Acidification	ammonia, HCl, HF, NO_x, NO_2, SO_2, SO_x
Smog	1,2-dichloroethane, acetaldehyde, acetone, acrolein aldehydes, alkanes, alkenes, benzaldehyde, benzene, benzo(a)pyrene, butane, butene, CxHy, CxHy aromatic, CxHy chloro, ethane, ethanol, ethene, ethylbenzene, ethyne, fluoranthene, formaldehyde, heptane, hexane, isopropanol, methane, methanol, methyl ethyl ketone, non methane VOC, PAHs, pentane, phenol, propane, propene, propionic acid, toluene, vinyl chloride, xylene
Human toxicity	1,2-dichloroethane, aldehydes, ammonia, As, Ba, benzene, benzo(a)pyrene, Br, Carbon black, CCl4, Cd, CFC-11, CFC-113, CFC-12, CH2Cl2, chlorobenzenes, Co, CO, cobalt, Cr, Cr (VI), crude oil, Cu, CxHy, CxHy aromatic, CxHy chloro, cyanide, cyanides, dichloroethane, dioxin (TEQ), ethanol, ethylbenzene, F, F_2, Fe, fluoranthene, H_2S, HCFC-22, HCl, heptane, HF, Hg, isopropanol, metallic ions, methane, methylene chloride, Mn, Mo, NH_4+, Ni, nitrate, non methane VOC, NO_x, PAHs, Pb, PCDD + PCDF, pentane, phenol, phosphate, propane, propene, Sb, silicates, Sn, SO_2, SO_3, sulphates, toluene, trichloroethene, V, vinyl, chloride, xylene, Zn, VOC, soot, PB + Cr + Cu + Mn + As + Ni + Sb + Sn, particulates, Cd + Tl

inventoried pollutants emitted to the environment by their corresponding contribution factor; and then to add the contribution of all these components: ammonia, chemical oxygen demand, Kjeldahl-N, N-tot, nitrate, nitrogen oxides, phosphorous and its compounds, and total phosphorous. As shown in Table 8.8, the contribution to eutrophication of the pollutant ammonia is then obtained for option 2 as follows:

$$P_{\text{ammonia}} = (0.0344 \times 0.33\ ) = 0.011$$

and the total contribution of option 2 to eutrophication is:

$$P_{\text{eutrophication}} = (P_{\text{ammonia}} + P_{\text{COD}} + P_{\text{Kjeldahl-N}} + P_{\text{N-tot}} + P_{\text{NH}_4+} + P_{\text{nitrate}} + P_{\text{NO}_x} + P_{\text{P}} + P_{\text{P-tot}});$$
$$P_{\text{eutrophication}} = (0.011 + 0.005 + 2.041\ \text{E-05} + 0.00005 + 0.046 - 0.00003 + 0.017 - 1.7564\ \text{E-5} - 4.528\ \text{E-8}).$$

Therefore, by using different weighting factors and the mass of the emissions, the corresponding potential contributions to the different impact categories have been determined. These values are showed in Table 8.9, in which the five options are included. It is clear that this table can be considered as a multicriteria evaluation matrix, to which a multicriteria method can easily be applied.

Table 8.8   Pollutants inventoried of option 2 and respective weighting factors

Species Option 2	A_j (kg)	W_{ij}	P_{ij} (NP kg)
ammonia	0.0344	0.33	0.011
COD	0.224	0.022	0.005
Kjeldahl-N	0.0000486	0.42	2.0412E-05
N-tot	0.000127	0.42	0.00005
NH_4^+	0.14	0.33	0.046
nitrate	−0.000261	0.1	−0.00003
NO_x	0.1303	0.13	0.017
P (air)	−5.74E-06	3.06	−1.756E-05
P-tot (water)	−1.48E-08	3.06	−4.528E-08
phosphate	−	1	−
Eutrophication (Pi)			0.08
Landfilling with energy recovery			

Table 8.9 Environmental impact of five municipal waste management options

Categories	Eutrophication	Ozone layer depletion	Global warming	Acidification	Smog	Human toxicity	Energy consumption	Solid waste production
Units	NP kg	ODP kg	GWP kg	AP kg	POCP kg	HCA/HCW	MJ	kg
Landfilling with ferric metals recovery	0.09	0.02	935	0.24	0.54	1.53	145	707
Landfilling with energy recovery	0.08	0.01	633	0.04	0.22	0.72	−905	689
Landfilling with physical leachate treatment	0.11	0.01	632	0.03	0.22	0.71	−933	617
Incineration	0.16	0.00001	948	1.14	0.04	0.996	5.690	173
Incineration with energy recovery	−0.26	−0.0002	172	−7.91	−0.14	−12	−14.900	−178

Notes
NP: Nutriphication potential. Phosphate is the reference substance.
ODP: Ozone layer depletion potential. CFC-11 has been adopted as reference substance.
GWP: Global warming potential. This potential has been calculated on a 20-year period, and the reference substance is CO_2.
AP: Acidification potential. The reference substance is SO_2.
POCP: Photochemical ozone creation potential. Ethylene is the reference substance.
HCA/HCW: Human-toxicological classification values for air and water. The human toxicity potential indicates the effect of a substance by potential exposition (determined through a simple distribution model and its mean lifetime) and its toxicity (MTL, maximum values tolerated in air and water).

Applying the NAIADE Multicriteria Method

The 'novel approach to imprecise assessment and decision environments' (NAIADE) is a discrete multicriteria method whose impact (or evaluation) matrix may include crisp, stochastic or fuzzy measurements of the performance of an alternative with respect to an evaluation criterion. This makes it very flexible for actual applications. The aggregation procedure of NAIADE is summarized next (further details can be found in Munda 1995).

A pairwise comparison of all the alternatives on the base of the set of evaluation criteria is carried out. For each pair, a preference index is determined by two factors. One is the number of criteria in favour of each alternative (for example, in a parliamentary process, the number of criteria in favour of a given alternative is given by the number of votes in favour of a proposal or alternative in our case). The second factor is the intensity of preference for each single criterion, measured by the credibility that a given alternative is better than another.

After the pairwise comparison, there is still a need to derive a ranking of the alternatives taken into account. For example, consider a soccer championship. After a set of matches (pairwise comparisons) for each team (alternative) we know the number of teams that it has defeated and the number of teams that have defeated it. We also know the intensity of its competitive quality, that is, the goals received and the ones given. This concept of strength and weakness of each alternative is used in NAIADE for obtaining a final ranking of the alternatives. This ranking can be a complete pre-order (among the alternatives only relations of preference or indifference exist) or a partial pre-order (also incomparability relations may exist). Some indicators of the uncertainty and compensability introduced in the aggregation process are also employed.

Equity and distributional issues in NAIADE are introduced by means of conflict analysis procedures and can be integrated with the multicriteria results. This allows policy makers to seek decisions that can reduce the degree of conflict (in order to reach a certain degree of consensus) or that could have a higher degree of equity for different income groups. NAIADE uses a fuzzy conflict analysis procedure. Starting with a matrix showing the impacts of different courses of action on each different interest/income group, a fuzzy clustering procedure is used to indicate those groups whose interests are close.

Summarizing, NAIADE can give the following information:

1. ranking of the alternatives according to the set of evaluation criteria (that is, compromise solution/s);
2. indications of the distance of the positions of the various interest groups (that is, possibilities for convergence of interests or coalition formations); and
3. rankings of the alternatives according to actors' impacts or preferences.

From a technical point of view, NAIADE has several important characteristics. A constructive decision aid framework is implied by the need to communicate with the decision maker to elicitate different relevant parameters. The method is based on some aspects of the partial comparability axiom in particular, a pairwise comparison between alternatives is carried out, and incomparability relations are allowed. Intensity of preference is taken into account, and this implies that a certain degree of compensation between criteria is allowed. Given the characteristics of the method it may be classified among partial compensatory methods. For the indifference relation no transitivity is implied, and the preference relation is max–min transitive. Finally, a partial (or total) order of feasible alternatives is supplied. The final ranking is a function of all the alternatives considered which implies that, if a dominated or a dominating action is introduced, the ranking may change. Moreover, if the best action is eliminated, the ranking of the other alternatives may also change. Thus NAIADE does not respect the independence of an irrelevant alternatives axiom.

Given that, in our specific case study, the multicriteria evaluation matrix is quantitative in nature (see Table 8.9), a wide range of possible aggregation procedures may be chosen (Nijkamp et al. 1990; Roy 1996). In order to explore the possibility of combining LCA with multicriteria evaluation, the NAIADE method was chosen. This has some advantages. First, most of the criterion scores coming from an LCA study are characterized by uncertainty and are therefore most realistically dealt with as fuzzy numbers. Second, in actual management situations, the technical information coming from an LCA study has to be combined with socio-economic criteria. This normally implies the presence of mixed information (quantitative/qualitative) which can easily be dealt with in the framework of NAIADE. The ability of NAIADE to take distributional issues into account allows a more complete framework analysis.

By applying the NAIADE method to the impact matrix shown in Table 8.9, the results shown in Figure 8.1 are obtained. As one can see, the final ranking is very stable. No incomparability relation exists (since the two pre-orders are equal). Incineration with energy recovery is clearly the best option. If one looks at the pairwise comparisons between this first option and the second one in the ranking (that is, landfilling with physical leachate treatment), see Figure 8.2, this statement is further corroborated. In fact, five of the eight criteria confirm that incineration with energy recovery is the best option. An indifference relation could exist for only one criterion (with a credibility degree of 40 per cent). None of the criteria support the landfilling option.

The evaluation is less clear-cut, as Figure 8.3 shows, if one looks at the comparison between the second option (landfilling with physical leachate treatment) and the third one (landfilling with energy recovery). Almost all the criteria have good credibility, so there is little difference between the two

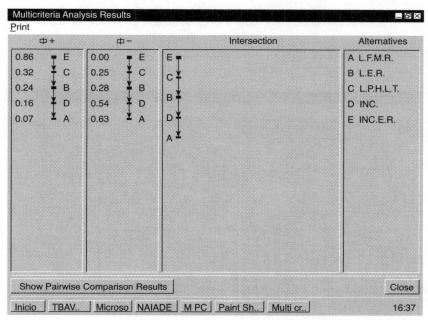

Figure 8.1   Rankings of options given by the NAIADE method

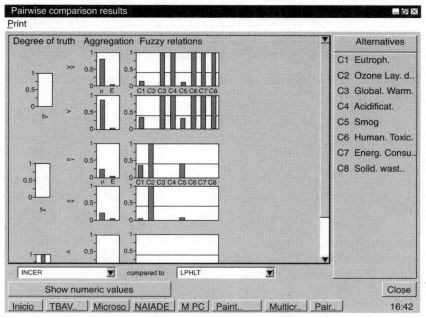

Figure 8.2   Comparison between the first and second options in the ranking

options. Only one criterion (solid waste) is clearly in favour of the second option. The second position in the ranking of landfilling with physical leachate treatment is therefore due to this criterion and to the additional information given by the relationship between this option and all the others.

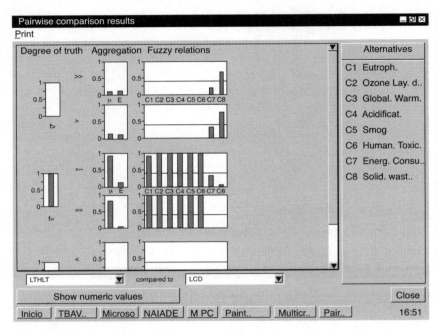

Figure 8.3 Comparison between the second and third options in the ranking

CONCLUSIONS

This chapter can be considered as a first step towards the integration between LCA and multicriteria evaluation. From the theoretical analysis of these two methodologies, it is possible to derive the conclusion that this integration seems desirable. LCA is very useful for generating environmental impact criteria with a reduced degree of arbitrariness. On the other hand, multicriteria analysis can greatly increase the degree of transparency of the valuation step of LCA. This theoretical statement has been corroborated empirically by the case study presented.

We should like to conclude this chapter by saying that multicriteria evaluation can be a very useful tool for a variety of approaches in ecotoxicology. The main difference between multicriteria evaluation and cost–benefit analysis is the possibility of taking into account conflictual incommensurable dimensions without any monetary reductionism. Monetary valuation is often very difficult since many environmental issues involve 'mixed information', that is, both quantitative and qualitative elements. Moreover, this information is often uncertain, where uncertainty may be stochastic or fuzzy in nature. This suggests the use of flexible evaluation tools such as qualitative multicriteria evaluation. For a systematic comparison between cost–benefit analysis and multicriteria evaluation, see Munda et al. 1995.

REFERENCES

Bailey, P., C. Gough, M. Chadwick and G. McGranahan (1996), *Methods for Integrated Environmental Assessment: Research Directions for the European Union*, Stockholm: Stockholm Environment Institute.

Beinat, E. and P. Nijkamp (eds) (1998), *Multicriteria Evaluation in Land-use Management: Methodologies and Case Studies*, Dordrecht: Kluwer.

Calbet, A. (1997), Consorcio del Riu Besòs. Personal communication.

Centre of Energy, Environmental and Technological Innovations (CIEMAT) (1992), *Electrical Autogeneration in Artigas Sanitary Landfill: Current State of Project*, Madrid: Ministry of Industry and Energy.

de Haes, U. and H.Y. Jolliet (eds) (1998), 'Preparation document for SETAC', European Working Group on Life Cycle Assessment, Bordeaux.

Diputación Foral de Bizkaia (1996), *Estudio de la situación ambiental de los vertederos de RSU de Bizkaia*, Madrid: Department of Medio Ambiente y Acción Territorial.

Diputación Foral de Bizkaia (1997), *Plan Integral de Gestión de los Residuos Sólidos Urbanos del Territorio Histórico de Bizkaia*, Madrid: Department of Medio Ambiente y Acción Territorial.

Finvenden, G. (1996), *Valuation Methods Within the Framework of Life Cycle Assessment*, Stockholm: Swedish Environmental Research Institute (IVL).

Funtowicz, S.O. and J.R. Ravetz (1990), *Uncertainty and Quality in Science for Policy*, Dordrecht: Kluwer Academic Publishers.

Jolliet, Oliver and Pierre Crettaz (1996), 'Critical surface-time 95', in *A Life Cycle Impact Assessment Methodology including Fate and Exposure*, Lausanne: École Polytechnique Fédérale de Lausanne (EPFL).

Munda, G. (1995), 'Multicriteria evaluation in a fuzzy environment', in *Theory and Applications in Ecological Economics*, Heidelberg: Physica-Verlag.

Munda, G., P. Nijkamp and P. Rietveld (1995), 'Monetary and non-monetary evaluation methods in sustainable development planning', *Economie Appliquée*, **48**(2): 145–62.

Nijkamp, P., P. Rietveld and H. Voogd (1990), *Multicriteria Evaluation in Physical Planning*, Amsterdam: North-Holland.

Romo, Casasola M. (1997), 'Avaluació del Cicle de Vida d'abocadors de Residus Sòlids Urbans. Proyecto' (unpublished), Licenciatura en Ciencias Ambientales, Universidad Autònoma de Barcelona.

Roy, B. (1996), *Multicriteria Methodology for Decision Analysis*, Dordrecht: Kluwer.
Spengler, T., J. Geldermann, S. Hähre, A. Sieverdingbeck and O. Rentz (1998), 'Development of a multiple criteria based decision support system for environmental assessment of recycling measures in the iron and steel making industry', *Journal of Cleaner Production*, **6**: 37–52.
van den Berg, N.W. (ed.) (1997), *Beginning LCA: A Guide to Environmental Life Cycle Assessment*, Rotterdam: Humanitas.
White, P., M. Franke and P. Hindle (1995), *Integrated Solid Waste Management: A Life Cycle Inventory*, London: Blackie.

9. Cost-effectiveness analysis for nitrate pollution control in the European Union

Floor Brouwer

INTRODUCTION

While nitrogen is an essential nutrient to enhance plant growth, in many regions of Europe the quantity applied to agricultural land far exceeds crop requirements. Furthermore, excessive quantities of nitrogen are often fed to livestock – which is then simply excreted. Nitrates in drinking water are considered a serious threat to human health, as nitrates are transformed in the body into nitrites – a process that can limit transformation of oxygen through the body. Young babies are particularly vulnerable to this and may develop a condition known as 'blue baby syndrome' (although the nitrate level would have to be far in excess of the current EU standard of 50 mg per litre). Furthermore, nitrites react with compounds in the stomach, which may subsequently cause cancer in animals. However, there is no scientific evidence to link nitrites and cancer in humans (European Commission 1998). High nitrate levels can also lead to eutrophication of fresh and coastal waters, causing algal blooms and fish deaths. Eutrophication of surface waters is a particular problem in some of the marine and coastal areas of Europe – such as the coastal zones of the North Sea, the Baltic Sea and the Mediterranean.

The high external costs of excessive nitrogen application have led to several EU directives designed to prevent and control such pollution. In meeting the consequent environmental and human health standards, adjustments are required by the agricultural sector in the European Union. A wide variety of adjustment processes need to be considered, given their implications for the economic viability of farming. Operational constraints can either be on-farm or off-farm, and they range from targeting measures at pollution sources (fertilizer management and nutritional management) to end-of-the-pipe measures (processing and treatment of livestock manure, requiring storage facilities and equipment for transport of livestock manure). Measures which are most promising are those which achieve the targets on nitrogen emissions cost-effectively.

In this chapter, we review the nitrate pollution problem in Europe and cost-effectiveness of policy options. In the next section, we outline the nature of the nitrate problem in various European countries and the policy response in the form of various EU directives. Then in the third section, we discuss the cost-effectiveness of measures to control nitrate pollution. Specifically, we consider the implications of the regional distribution of the nitrate problem for the efficacy of policy measures at an EU and/or national level. We then consider the cost-effectiveness of measures at a farm level – input reduction versus more sustainable farm management practices. Finally, we present conclusions.

NITRATE POLLUTION IN THE EUROPEAN UNION

There are various sources of anthropogenic nitrogen entering the agricultural system – including mineral fertilizers, nutrients from organic sources (for example, effluents from livestock, in particular animal manure), biological fixation of nitrogen and enhanced organic matter through mineralization in soils. Similar to phosphate and potassium, plants require nitrogen in relatively large amounts, whereas other nutrients such as copper and iron are needed in smaller quantities. In order to be utilized by plants, nitrogen must be 'fixed' in chemical compounds, such as ammonia (NH_3) and nitrates (NO_3). Livestock also require sufficient amounts of dietary protein with nitrogen as the main component.

However, in recent years, excess amounts of nutrients have been applied to land in large areas of Europe, both from organic and inorganic sources. Excessive quantities of nitrogen have been fed to livestock which is also simply excreted. According to Stanners and Bourdeau (1995), leaching of nitrates exceeds the EU standard (50 mg per litre of groundwater) on 22 per cent of the agricultural land in Europe and exceeds 25 mg per litre on 87 per cent of the land. Nitrate levels in drinking water resources are still increasing in parts of Europe. This implies that some water treatment plants may have to close down. In other plants, costs of water treatment may need to increase before water can be used as drinking water or as a raw material for the food-processing industry.

In order to quantify the nitrogen input from the agricultural sector, a system known as 'nitrogen balances' has been developed in many regions of the European Union – at least at a national level. These nitrogen balances help identify whether or not nitrogen is being used in excess of crop requirements. The quantity of nutrients applied at a field level is compared to the uptake by crops. In Table 9.1, we show the main sources of N inputs in different EU countries and also the difference between N inputs and uptake. The relative importance of fertilizer and manure as a source of N inputs varies between countries. In every country, a positive surplus N is recorded, and is especially high in Belgium, Denmark and the Netherlands. However, in most countries, there has been a downward trend in N surplus over the last ten years.

Table 9.1   Nitrogen balances in 1995

Country	Nitrogen inputs (% of total input)			Total nitrogen	Nitrogen uptake	Surplus
	Fertilizers	Manure	Other input	(1000 tonnes)	(1000 tonnes)	(kg N/ha)
Austria	30	46	24	411	269	57
Belgium	39	49	12	434	195	177
Denmark	52	36	12	647	270	138
Finland	65	25	10	274	121	59
France	55	35	10	4155	4048	4
Germany	50	26	23	3411	2288	66
Greece	47	41	12	713	484	45
Ireland	47	45	8	854	613	55
Italy	44	30	26	2010	1229	48
Netherlands	40	56	4	1005	472	272
Portugal	36	48	16	371	137	59
Spain	41	41	18	2229	1540	25
Sweden	54	28	17	380	268	35
United Kingdom	45	31	24	3041	1751	76
EU-14*	47	36	17	19938	13685	46

Note: *Excluding Luxembourg.

Source: OECD (1997).

The relationship between nitrogen surpluses and the actual leaching of nitrates to soils and water is not direct since it depends on soil conditions and the weather. For example, leaching might be much more dramatic during unfavourable weather conditions such as extreme rainfall. However, much of the current nitrate problem is not so much due to current conditions as to agricultural practices from past decades (Hanley 1997). Furthermore, scientific knowledge remains limited on the link between nitrogen surpluses and nitrate concentrations in the available drinking water resources.

Detailed information on the individual input and output components of the nitrogen balance is available for the Netherlands (Olsthoorn and Fong 1997). The balance they present is based on the framework of the farm gate approach, wherein the nitrogen content of farm inputs is compared with the outputs supplied (Table 9.2). At a national level, the most important inputs are imported raw materials, that is, those used as compound feed (485 million kg N) and mineral fertilizers (406 million kg N). The EU is a very large net importer of animal feed and the Netherlands accounts for about 30 per cent of imports of raw material for the production of compound feed.

Table 9.2   Nitrogen balance of agriculture in the Netherlands in 1995 (million kg of nitrogen)

Input	974
Imported raw material to produce compound feed	485
Imported compound feed	11
Stocks from previous period	22
Mineral fertilizers	406
Other	18
Deposition	32
Output	291
Livestock products	147
Export of compound feed	48
Crop products	50
Export of manure	22
Other	24
Surplus	683
Ammonia	104
Other	563

Source: Olsthoorn and Fong (1997).

However, national figures tend to obscure the regional problem of nitrate pollution. Nitrate pollution problems are largest in regions with a high density of livestock population. Supply of nitrogen from animal manure exceeds 100 kg per hectare in Belgium, Denmark, parts of Germany, some coastal regions of Spain (Galicia and Cantabria), the western part of France (Brittany), the Po Valley area in Italy (mainly the region of Lombardia), Luxembourg, the Netherlands and the western part of the United Kingdom (Figure 9.1). Large variation around the average results from factors such as farm structure, cropping plan, livestock composition and management practices. Nitrogen surpluses are observed to be most critical on pig and poultry holdings as a result of their high stocking density compared to the nitrogen requirements of the available farmland.

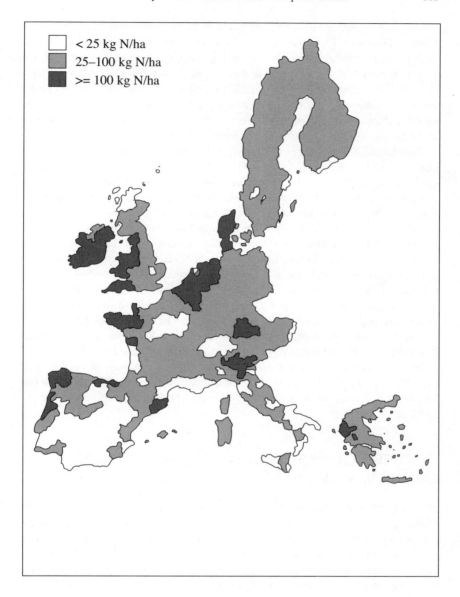

Source: Farm structure survey (FSS) (1989/90), adaption LEI Agricultural Economics Research Institute.

Figure 9.1   Supply of nitrogen from livestock manure in the EU (kg N/ha)

The policy response to the nitrate problem has mainly been through the EU Nitrates Directive. Directives are the main legal instruments used by the EU to implement policy and these are legally binding for member states. They inform member states of goals and the time frame for their achievement. However, implementation is left to each member state and thus there is some scope for achieving the common goal of unity in ways that recognize the national character of agricultural systems. There can be significant differences in the legislation across different countries in the EU.

The detail of the Nitrates Directive is outlined in the appendix. Its main objective is to 'reduce water pollution caused or induced by nitrates from agricultural sources and preventing further such pollution' (European Commission 1991). Member states were requested to designate 'vulnerable zones' within which codes of good agricultural practice would apply. Standards are specified that limit the application of N from livestock manure. By mid-1997, five member states (Denmark, Germany, Luxembourg, the Netherlands and Austria) identified their whole territory as zones vulnerable to the leaching of nitrate. Ireland identified no zones and the United Kingdom identified five zones (both these decisions are presently being examined by the Commission). The other eight member states have not identified any zones as vulnerable and are delaying their implementation of the Nitrates Directive.

The Directive concerning Integrated Pollution Prevention and Control (96/61/EC) is also relevant. With regard to agricultural activities, the directive states requirements for installations for the intensive rearing of poultry and pigs. Finally, there is also a proposal for a new directive on water policy in the EU. More information on the various relevant EU directives is outlined in the appendix.

COST-EFFECTIVENESS OF NITRATE POLLUTION CONTROL MEASURES

In this section, we consider two types of 'cost-effectiveness' with regard to reducing nitrate pollution. First, we consider the implications of the spatial distribution of nitrate pollution for taxation policies applied at a European or at a national level. Second, we consider the relative cost-effectiveness of control options at a farm level. The farmer can affect nitrogen surpluses by reducing intensity on the farm or by changing management practices.

Policy Implications of Regional Distribution of the Nitrate Problem

As has been discussed in the previous section, conditions vary greatly between countries with regard to the extent of the nitrate problem. Brouwer et al.

(1999) show that even between regions with a significant nitrate problem, there are considerable differences in the nature of the problem and potential solutions. For example, in the Netherlands, the high intensity of production methods necessitates greater reliance on costly 'end-of-pipe' measures than in many other regions. Only a small part of the pig manure can be applied on the holding within the limits set by the Nitrates Directive. As a consequence, a large part (about 90 per cent) of it must be transported at a high cost. Differences in the scale and the nature of the problem imply that the relative cost-effectiveness of options varies considerably between countries or regions. Another implication of regional differences in the nitrate problem is that changes in policy at a European level will have very different impacts across regions.

One possibility to achieve the environmental standards stipulated in the Nitrates Directive would be to introduce a fertilizer tax in European countries. Economists often advocate the use of such an approach because of the potential efficiency advantages of such a policy. In comparison with a standard, farmers have greater flexibility in the extent to which they reduce fertilizer input. Farmers with lower returns from the use of fertilizer will show larger relative reductions in its use. This gives rise to the oft-cited efficiency gain. One of the few examples of a study that assesses the impact of such policies across Europe is that by Kleinhanss et al. (1997). They explore the economic and environmental impact of agricultural and environmental policy changes on nitrogen surpluses from agriculture. The analysis is based on a regional production and nutrient balance model – a neo-classical simulation model. They examine the potential impacts of introducing economic instruments such as a fertilizer levy. The model suggests that a fertilizer levy would induce lower intensity of crop production and a substitution of livestock manure for mineral fertilizers. The expected reductions in input use are substantial in this model. For example, a fertilizer levy of 50 per cent would induce reductions in the use of fertilizer by 20 per cent and 50 per cent in Italy and the Netherlands, respectively. However, although nitrogen surpluses would be reduced considerably, this would take effect mainly within regions with only intermediate levels of nitrogen surplus and with an emphasis on dairy farming. This type of policy has hardly any impact within the 'hot spot' areas, where farms are generally engaged in intensive livestock production and nitrogen surpluses exceed 200 kg per hectare. Thus, effectively reducing nitrate pollution requires more targeted measures.

Rather than introduce product taxes, another option would be to impose a tax on nitrogen surpluses. The idea of nitrogen surpluses was briefly introduced in the previous section. In several European countries, various types of farm-level mineral book-keeping systems have either been introduced or have been proposed. One option for policy makers would be to tax the estimated nitrogen surplus. Helming (1997) considers this option, along with several other policies in the context of the Netherlands. The study is based on a spatial equilibrium model, which uses a set of linear regional demand and supply functions to describe the most important regional input and output markets of the agricultural sector. In this model, the national profit from agriculture is maximized subject to the constraint that demand equal supply in each regional market. In this framework, it is possible to investigate the impact of taxing inputs (for example, fertilizers or animal feed) versus taxing nitrogen surpluses. In this model, the demand for mineral fertilizers is very price inelastic. Thus a very high levy is required to reduce nitrogen surplus. The analysis shows that taxing nitrogen surpluses is more cost-effective than a product charge. This finding seems intuitive since the policy is more carefully targeted on holdings which are the source of the problem.

Cost-effectiveness of Options at the Farm Level

Aside from the question of what policies are cost-effective given the regional nature of the nitrate pollution problem, there is also a question of how farmers might respond to any policy. What are the options available and how can farmers respond in a cost-effective manner? In general, farmers can respond either by altering intensity of production or by changing farm management techniques. Brouwer and Hellegers (1997) discuss the various farm management options available to individual producers. For example, one possibility is to use organic manure more effectively as a nutrient – by applying manure during the spring, when crop demands are high (and vulnerability of soils to leaching is relatively low). This can benefit producers financially if organic fertilizer is a good substitute for inorganic sources. Another management option that can reduce nitrate pollution is alteration in feed strategies. Such strategies include the use of feed supplements and the modification of feeding systems (for example, phase feeding, reduced dietary feeding systems). Brouwer et al. (1999) argue, on economic and environmental grounds, that such nutritional management measures offer an effective method to prevent nitrate pollution and to comply with European legislation.

Often sustainable management systems are equally, if not more, effective in reducing pollution than reduction of input use. For example, in Table 9.3, nitrogen surpluses of regular dairy production units are compared with holdings that operate under sustainable management practices and are guided by research. Although farms in the sustainable management scheme are on average slightly smaller than the other holdings (in terms of hectares and number of dairy cows), structural features indicate that in some respects they are relatively more intensive. However, better nutrient management practices

Table 9.3   Nitrogen surpluses of regular dairy farms with farms that operate under a sustainable management scheme, 1995

Feature	Sustainable management	Regular holdings
Farm size (ha)	31	38
Number of dairy cows	55	67
Stocking density (LU/ha)	2.6	2.5
Milk production per cow (kg)	7 607	7 111
Milk production (kg milk/ha)	14 687	12 601
Input (kg N/ha)	440	515
Compound feed	121	120
Mineral fertilizer	226	279
Other	93	115
Output (kg N/ha)	115	92
Surplus (kg N/ha)	273	359

Source: Brouwer and Hellegers (1997).

on such holdings are leading to lower surpluses. This illustrates the importance of good management practices.

An analysis by Schleef (1996), based on German data, also considers the various possible management options that farmers may use to control the nitrate problem. The analysis also allows one to identify the holdings that would be most affected by legislation implemented as a consequence of the Nitrates Directive. Using a linear programming methodology, Schleef examines the effect of different policies to encourage farmers to reduce nitrate pollution. There are various ways in which farmers may respond to the constraints imposed by the Nitrates Directive: transportation of manure to regions with less pressure on the manure market; increasing the available land resource (for example, through renting); changing the feed diet of livestock (for example, lowering the protein content of feed). The analysis shows that most of the holdings have options to dispose of their excess manure without necessitating reduction in livestock numbers. The encouragement of better nutrient management can effect a significant substitution of organic for inorganic nitrogen.

Brouwer et al. (1999) also argue that farm management practices can be very cost-effective in responding to the requirements of directives. The cost-effectiveness of better nutritional management largely arises from the fact that it is based on preventative measures. Protein levels in feed can be reduced without affecting performance. The closer correspondence between feed and animal requirements leads to reduced nitrogen excretion. Changes in EU agricultural policy have made this 'nutritional' option more attractive. The reform to the Common Agricultural Policy in 1992 reduced the intervention price of cereals and this changed the price ratio between energy and protein crops – making lower protein diets more attractive. However, it can still be argued that by international standards, the protein content of the typical pig diet in Europe is too high. In Europe the protein content is 17 per cent whereas in the US this figure is 14 per cent. A further lowering of cereal prices will strengthen the incentive to reduce the protein content of feed.

Thus, alteration of management practices rather than reducing the intensity of production are often relatively more cost-effective in meeting emission targets. In general, it seems desirable to encourage preventative measures to reduce nitrate pollution, rather than rely on the very costly 'end-of-pipe' measures. Preventative measures include the adoption of nutritional management in livestock production; using inputs more efficiently in crop production; and adoption of sustainable farm management practices in which inputs are used in a more efficient and effective manner.

CONCLUSION

There is enormous regional variation in the extent and nature of the nitrate pollution problem across the different regions in Europe. In particular, this is a major issue in the 'hot spots' of intensive livestock production units (mainly pigs and poultry), although there can still be large variation within these regions due to factors such as farm structure, cropping plan, livestock composition and management practices.

The EU Nitrates Directive is the major European legislation that attempts to control the nitrate pollution problem. Many member states have formulated policies to reduce pollution by improving farming practices and adjusting farm structures. In addition, action has been taken to achieve a balance between input and output flows from agricultural sources, including transport and treatment of livestock manure. Various types of mineral book-keeping systems either are in operation or have been proposed in an effort to keep mineral surpluses under control.

The uneven distribution of the nitrate pollution problem means that product charges might have only a limited impact on nitrogen surpluses in the most nitrate-intense regions. Another alternative considered has been a tax on nitrogen surpluses – which is feasible if some form of farm-level mineral accounts is maintained. It is possible that some form of tax based on nitrogen surplus could be a more efficient way to reduce pollution than various product charges.

At the farm level, control options include reducing input use (that is, livestock intensity or fertilizer use) or adopting alternative management practices. Several research papers have shown that various types of 'sustainable management practices' provide much scope to reduce the nitrate problem, without necessarily reducing input use. Changes in EU agricultural policy may be expected to reinforce some of these management options such as more careful nutritional management and lower protein feeds.

REFERENCES

Brouwer, F. and P. Hellegers (1997), 'Nitrogen flows at farm level across European Union agriculture', in E. Romstad, J. Simonsen and A. Vatn (eds), *Controlling Mineral Emissions in European Agriculture: Economics, Policies and the Environment*, Wallingford: CAB International, pp. 11–26.

Brouwer, F., P. Hellegers, M. Hoogeveen and H. Luesink (1999), *Managing Nitrogen Pollution from Intensive Livestock Production in the EU: Economic and Environmental Benefits of Reducing Nitrogen Pollution by Nutritional Management in Relation to the Changing CAP Regime and the Nitrates Directive*, The Hague: Agricultural Economics Research Institute (LEI-DLO), Rapport 2.99.04.

Commission of the European Communities (CEC) (1996), *Communication from the Commission to the Council and the European Parliament for a Framework Directive on European Community Water Policy*, Brussels: Commission of the European Communities, COM (96) 56, Final.

European Commission (1991), 'Council Directive of 12 December 1991 concerning the protection of waters against pollution caused by nitrates from agricultural sources', *Official Journal of the European Communities* (91/676/EEC), No. L 375/L, 31.12.91.

European Commission (1998), 'Execution of Directive 91/676 by the Council concerning the protection of waters against pollution by nitrates from agricultural sources', Report of the Commission to the Council and the European Parliament.

Hanley, N. (1997), 'Externalities and the control of nitrate pollution', in F. Brouwer and W. Kleinhanss (eds), *The Implementation of Nitrate Policies in Europe: Processes of Change in Environmental Policy and Agriculture*, Kiel: Wissenschaftsverlag Vauk, pp. 11–22.

Helming, J. (1997), 'Impacts of manure policies for the Netherlands', in F. Brouwer and W. Kleinhanss (eds), *The Implementation of Nitrate Policies in Europe: Processes of Change in Environmental Policy and Agriculture*, Kiel: Wissenschaftsverlag Vauk, pp. 235–51.

Kleinhanss, W., H. Becker and K.-H. Schleef (1997), 'Impacts of agri-environmental policy measures on nitrogen emissions from agriculture', in E. Romstad, J. Simonsen and A. Vatn (eds), *Controlling Mineral Emissions in European Agriculture: Economics, Policies and the Environment*, Wallingford: CAB International, pp. 137–55.

Olsthoorn, C.S.M. and N.P.K. Fong (1997), 'Anthropogenic nitrogen cycle in the Netherlands', paper published in the Proceedings of the International Workshop on

'Dissipation of N from the human N-cycle, and its role in present and future N_2O emissions to the atmosphere', Oslo, Agricultural University of Norway, 22–25 May.

Organisation for Economic Cooperation and Development (OECD) (1997), 'Agri-environmental indicators: stocktaking report', document submitted to the Joint Working Party of the Committee for Agriculture and the Environment Policy Committee, Paris: OECD.

Schleef, K.-H. (1996), *Impacts of Policy Measures to Reduce Nitrogen Surpluses from Agricultural Production – An Assessment at Farm Level for the Former Federal Republic of German*, Braunschweig: Bundesforschungsanstalt für Landwirtschaft, Institut für Betriebswirtschaft, Arbeitsbericht 2/96.

Stanners, D. and P. Bourdeau (eds) (1995), *Europe's Environment: The Dobri_ Assessment*, Copenhagen: European Environment Agency.

APPENDIX

The Nitrates Directive

This directive concerns the protection of waters against pollution caused by nitrates from agricultural sources. It was issued by the Council of Ministers of Environment in December 1991 (Directive 91/676/EEC). The objective of this directive (Article 1) is to 'reduce water pollution caused or induced by nitrates from agricultural sources and preventing further such pollution' (*Official Journal of the European Communities*, 1991). Article 3 of the Nitrates Directive states: 'Waters affected by pollution and water which could be affected by pollution if action ... is not taken shall be identified by the Member States in accordance with the criteria set out in Annex 1'. Member states were to designate 'vulnerable' zones, which would include the following:

- Surface waters that contain more than 50 mg/l nitrates per litre (or that could contain more than this if action is not taken) – in particular those used or intended for the abstraction of drinking water.
- Groundwater that contains more than 50 mg/l nitrates or that could contain more than 50 mg/l nitrates if action is not taken.
- Natural freshwater lakes, other freshwater bodies, estuaries, coastal waters and marine waters which are found to be eutrophic or could become eutrophic in the near future if action is not taken.

Codes of good agricultural practices were expected to be formulated by member states before the end of 1993, in order for farmers to fulfil the objectives of the Nitrates Directive. The majority of the member states have now completed this exercise. Such codes should specify the following items (Annex (ii) of the Directive):

- Periods of the year when the application of fertilizer is inappropriate.
- Regulations concerning the land application of fertilizer taking account of factors such as soil conditions, soil type and slope; climatic conditions, rainfall and irrigation and so on.
- The conditions for land application or fertilizer near watercourses.
- The capacity and construction of storage vessels for livestock manure, including measures to prevent water pollution by runoff and seepage into the groundwater and surface water or liquids containing livestock manures and effluents from stored plant materials such as silage.
- Procedures for the land application (including the rate and uniformity of spreading) of both chemical fertilizer and livestock manure that will maintain nutrient losses to water at an acceptable level.

Member states may also include the following items in the Code(s) of Good Agricultural Practices:

- Land use management, including the use of crop rotation systems and the proportion of the land area devoted to permanent crops relative to annual tillage crops.
- The maintenance of a minimum quantity of vegetation cover during (rainy) periods that will take up the nitrogen from the soil that could otherwise cause nitrate pollution of water.
- The establishment of fertilizer plans on a farm-by-farm basis and the keeping of records on fertilizer use.
- The prevention of water pollution from runoff and the downward water movement beyond the reach of crop roots in irrigation systems.

One of the main features of the directive concerns limitations on the application of nitrogen from livestock manure. This should not exceed 170 kg per ha. This standard should be met by the end of the year 2002. During a transition period, which started in late 1998, the application of nitrogen from livestock manure should not exceed 210 kg per ha.

The directive is also designed to achieve a balance between the nitrogen requirements from the crops and nitrogen supply from the soil and from fertilizers. Therefore, mineral balances provide insight into flows of nitrogen through the agricultural sector – at farm, regional and sector levels.

Integrated Pollution Prevention and Control (IPPC)

The purpose of Council Directive 96/61/EC of 24 September 1996 concerning Integrated Pollution Prevention and Control is to achieve integrated prevention and control of pollution arising from the activities listed in Annex I of the directive. Emissions from industrial installations in the Community into air, water and soil need to be prevented wherever this is practicable, and where it is not, to minimize them with a view to achieving a high level of environmental protection. This applies to certain installations of energy industries, production and processing of metals, mineral industry, chemical industry, waste management and other activities. With regard to agricultural activities, the directive is applicable to installations for the intensive rearing of poultry and pigs with more than (a) 40 000 places for poultry; (b) 2000 places for production pigs (over 30 kg), or (c) 750 places for sows. IPPC is applicable only to new buildings during the first couple of years. As of 2005, it will be applicable to all livestock production units with minimum size levels mentioned before.

In the context of this directive, measures are designed to prevent or (where this is not practicable) to reduce emissions in the air, water and land from categories of industrial activities – including measures concerning waste. Permits are required for new installations, which meet the requirements of the directive. The directive requires the application of best available techniques (BAT) adapted to local circumstances and taking into account contribution to transboundary air pollution.

Proposal for a Framework Directive on Water Policy in the EU

The European Commission recently proposed a Framework Directive on Water Policy in the EU to the Council and the European Parliament. According to the Communication (CEC 1996), the Commission is considering that the Nitrates Directive and the proposed Integrated Pollution Prevention and Control Directive move into the Directive on Water Policy. The principles of European Community Water Policy are likely to include the following:

- High level of protection.
- Precautionary principle.
- Preventative action.
- Damage to be rectified at source.
- Polluter pays.
- Integration.
- The use of available scientific and technical data.
- The variability of environmental conditions in the regions of the Community.
- Costs/benefits.
- The economic and social development of the Community and the balanced development of its regions.
- International cooperation.
- Subsidiarity.

These principles are also set out in Article 130R of the Treaty, which requires the integration of the environment into other community policies. Some general principles of environmental policy are established in this Article.

10. Pesticide policy design and decision making in the United Kingdom: information, indicators and incentives

Katherine E. Falconer and Ian D. Hodge

INTRODUCTION

Since the 1947 Agriculture Act, and the subsequent adoption of the Common Agricultural Policy in Europe, great efforts have been made in the UK (as in most other European member states) to increase agricultural productivity. This drive to increase food production has given rise to environmental concerns, particularly with regard to the use of agrochemicals (McLaughlin and Mineau 1996; Campell et al. 1997). Following the implementation of the 1980 European Drinking Water Directive, there has been increased monitoring and awareness of the pesticide problem (Ward et al. 1993). Pesticide issues have remained high on the policy agenda.

The reliance on the pesticides approval and registration system in most member states has come under increasing criticism in recent years, suggesting that policy needs to develop further to protect the environment from the adverse effects of regular, legal pesticide usage. There is now widespread agreement across Europe that pesticide use should be reduced wherever feasible, particularly in countries such as the UK where usage is relatively intense. The Fifth EU Environmental Action Programme proposed a reduction in the use of plant protection products as a major objective to be pursued for the agricultural sector. In this context, it is important to identify the economic approach that is most appropriate for assessing the environmental problems and making progress in improving environmental quality. For example, in the context of a policy to reduce pesticide use, the types of chemical on which reductions are focused has important implications for the environmental outcome and for cost-effectiveness.

Progress will be made by targeting usage reductions on those chemicals perceived as causing most damage to the environment. However, the identification of such chemicals is far from straightforward. The nature of pesticide impacts depends on a wide range of factors: the amount of active ingredient applied; the mode of application; the toxicity properties of the chemical; its persistence; local environmental characteristics; and species presence and vulnerability. The question is what approach might be acceptable and useful, given the gaps in knowledge and understanding.

Environmental-economic theory suggests that policy should be designed so that the marginal social costs of a particular activity are just balanced against the marginal social benefits. Economists are a long way from being able to produce reliable estimates of the social costs of pesticide usage, so Pigovian approaches to policy design (for example, in the sense of an 'optimal' tax) are infeasible. Some other basis for decision making needs to be developed and implemented.

The precautionary principle is an important criterion in European environmental policy making, and embodies the notion that harm arising from actions such as pesticide use should be prevented despite the lack of full scientific knowledge and understanding of ecological consequences. However, the principle cannot mean complete prevention of harm, since many activities would then be required to cease completely. Thus, there is a need for a basis by which to determine the extent of reduction in an activity.

Ecotoxicological data provides a useful starting-point. In this chapter, we assess the use of environmental indicators based on such data. Issues relate to the contribution that such models or indicators can make and to their operationability. The focus here is on the management of adverse environmental effects relating to agricultural field usage of pesticides. The structure of the chapter is as follows. The next section covers the nature of the pesticide problem. In the third section, we define environmental indicators and discuss their potential role. Then in the fourth section, we discuss some of the issues involved in constructing indicators for pesticide impacts. In the fifth section, we develop an illustrative pesticide indicator. The potential application of this indicator in policy making is assessed. The final section concludes.

THE NATURE OF PESTICIDE PROBLEMS

Criteria have not yet been developed by which pesticide risks and impacts can be measured and monitored systematically and rigorously. However, concerns about current levels of chemical use have been characterized along a number of dimensions – for example, the contamination of groundwater, surface water, soils and food (with consequent impacts on wildlife and human health Reus et al. 1994), as well as the potential health consequences for farm workers from continued exposure in the field. In a number of European countries, water contamination has been a particular focus of attention, following the implementation of strict limits on the amount of pesticides in drinking water under the 1980 Drinking Water Directive. Monitoring in the UK has shown that there are low concentrations of a wide range of pesticides in many 'environmental' waters, although generally not at sufficiently high concentrations to have an immediate adverse effect (DWI 1994). However, the long-term effects are still unknown.

Environmental impacts can be considered from several perspectives: current and future; actual and potential; direct and indirect; and in terms of their effects on different ecological components. Very careful definition of 'impact' is needed. Furthermore, it is essential to distinguish between 'hazard', 'risk' and 'impact' (see Figure 10.1). 'Hazard' relates largely to pesticide properties *per se*, and ecotoxicological properties in particular. For an indicator to move beyond simple hazard assessment towards quantification of impacts, there needs to be an assessment of how the chemical affects the environmental resource of concern. This requires an understanding of how the chemical is dispersed in the environment, prediction of chemical concentration and the exposure of different ecological components. 'Risk' relates to the probability of harm from pesticide exposure. The 'impact' is the consequence of actual exposure, in terms of physical ecological changes (for example, in terms of the number of a species present), or in terms of changes in the economic value of the resource. Ideally, a pesticide use damage function would be constructed with the following information:

● how emissions relate to concentration in the environment;
● the relationship between pollutant concentrations and physical damage; and

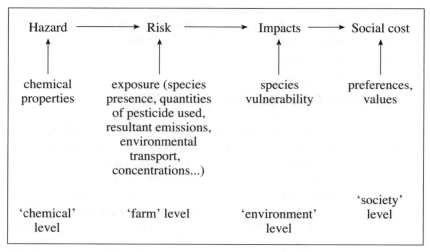

Figure 10.1   The links between hazard, risk, impact and social cost

- the relationship between physical data and social welfare loss (through economic valuation).

The fundamental problem is the lack of knowledge relating to the magnitude, and even the direction, of a range of potential ecological consequences associated with different products. There are a large number of routes through which pesticides affect the environment: leaching through soils; surface runoff (following adsorption to soil particles and rain); residues on crops; ingestion or inhalation by wildlife and humans; and vaporization into the atmosphere.

Some general characteristics of the pesticide problem can be summarized as follows:

- There are a large number of potential contaminant sources (field applications, spillages, disposal and so on) and multiple aspects of pesticide usage affecting impact (the quantity of pesticide applied, its type, the area treated, the method of application and so on).
- The costs of measuring dispersed (non-point) emissions and of identifying polluters are prohibitively high, especially where there is more than one potential source. In addition, information is asymmetric: the farmer knows more about his/her actions than the regulator.
- Multiple contaminants arise from a large number of heterogeneous compounds. The impact may be gradual and cumulative over time, as well as highly site specific.
- Stochastic influences affect contaminant behaviour: for example, variable weather conditions pose a challenge to accurate prediction of environmental quality at any given time. Systems are also dynamic: parameters such as environmental capacity and assimilation vary over time.
- There are a large number of dimensions of risk and impact, which may be direct and indirect. These operate in complex ecological systems where thresholds, irreversibility and non-linearities may be important.
- There are also potential synergies between different pollutants, with consequent problems in untangling the chain of causation and attributing damage to one substance rather than another.
- There is often a lack of understanding of the risks posed and of the effects of contaminants on ecological components. This is also among the difficulties in attempting to place economic values on ecological impacts.
- A large number of potentially affected parties, a proportion of which may be located far away from emissions, imply very high costs of conflict resolution.

THE ROLE OF ENVIRONMENTAL INDICATORS

Some of the above problems make it very difficult to identify, prioritize and measure the ecotoxicological impacts associated with agricultural production and thus to assess potential areas for improvement. Consequently, among policy makers, interest has been growing in the development and use of environmental indicators – in an attempt to make environmental policy problems more tractable from the perspective of both policy design and policy evaluation (OECD 1997; Moxey et al. 1998).

Levitan (1997) defines environmental indicators as measures or estimates of the consequences of an action for one or more environmental parameters. The role of an indicator is to make complex systems more tractable, thus providing some guidance to policy makers – for example, with regard to the relationship between input usage in agricultural production and ecological change; helping to determine where a system is in relation to policy goals. Generally environmental indicators synthesize information collected by other types of impact assessment methodologies, forming potentially useful decision aids. The aim is to provide a means of coping with a surfeit of information, given limited capacities to absorb knowledge, in both public and private decision making. Given the numerous challenges to estimating pesticide damage functions, progress can be made through characterizing ecotoxicological impacts through related, more measurable parameters, such as the volume of inputs used and their quantifiable properties.

The OECD (1997) suggests that indicators can be evaluated according to policy relevance, analytical soundness, measurability and appropriate level of aggregation. Other considerations when choosing an indicator are as follows:

- the range of ecological components and effects considered in the analysis;
- data available for operationalization (that is, that which can be assembled at reasonable cost);
- adjustability in the light of new information;
- transparency and the ease of use of the final model: for example, it must be understandable to the general public and to the farming community.

Inevitably, indicators represent compromise designs, involving trade-offs between their ease of application and the cost of development (for example, in terms of the measurability of their components in quantitative terms), scientific validity, transparency and relevance to users (Moxey et al. 1998). The crucial question is how to make indicators readily comprehensible without loss of critical content. It is necessary to select and digest information, and determine how it can it be best used. Areas where data are incomplete at present also need to be considered. Furthermore, Moxey et al. suggest that for an indicator to have relevance to an intended user, the decision maker must perceive some capability to monitor the indicator and/or to influence the value of the indicator through (deliberate) action. If the indicator is perceived to be beyond the influence of the decision maker, it is unlikely to be useful (for example, if impacts were thought to be primarily influenced by the weather).

There are several uses to which such indicators could be put in policy. Indicators could provide a framework in which to assess the social and environmental impact of damage. 'Valuing' the impact of pollution is particularly difficult in the case of pesticides. The range of values attached to the 'environmental goods' affected by pesticides varies greatly (in addition to great uncertainty about how pesticides affect the environment). There are many methodological difficulties in establishing people's preferences for environmental goods. Some dimensions of the economic impact of changing pesticide use are more readily evaluated – such as the opportunity cost of production. Even in this case, there are problems of adjusting prices to reflect the social opportunity costs, given distortions in the markets for inputs and outputs. However, though potentially useful, knowledge of such costs does not address how impacts such as health risks, damage to wildlife habitats and so on should be valued. The environmental indicator approach is an easier way of starting to assess the various environmental and social dimensions of damage which may be attributed to pesticide application.

A primary application of pesticide indicators is to compare pesticide use strategies in terms of their potential for adverse effects from an ecotoxicological perspective (O'Bryan and Ross 1988). Indicators could be designed to reflect the relative hazards of different products, or preferably their risks and potential impacts (if sufficient data were available). At present, once a pesticide has passed the approvals process, it is above the safety threshold required of all pesticides. There is no special indication of the most hazardous pesticides. If indicators were developed, allowing comparison of pesticides, the resulting ecotoxicological rankings could form a basis on which to differentiate taxation or regulation of diverse products. Currently, the actual use of pesticide ranking models at the strategic policy-making level is very limited, although they are being considered in Australia (Penrose et al. 1994).

Indicators that allow examination of the *relative* ecotoxicological hazards of different products would potentially be very useful for pesticide users. Although it is possible to obtain the technical information used in the pesticides approval process, this is often very difficult for non-experts to interpret. If producers had better information on the different hazards and risks associated with different compounds, they might be encouraged to substitute high-impact for low-impact compounds, particularly where these are marketed at the same price. Indicators might also be useful in 'green labelling' accreditation schemes: for example, in specifying a quantitative benchmark by which produce can be more formally classified as complying with 'acceptable' pesticide usage or integrated pest management in terms of the inputs used in its production (Penrose et al. 1994).

Indicators may also be used in policy evaluation. For example, an agricultural pesticide index was developed in the US to assess whether regulatory policies had succeeded in reducing pesticide risk since the revision of legislation in 1972. Two indices of pesticide risk were derived from acute and chronic toxicity indicators for mammals and linked to actual pesticide usage data. The results suggest little change in pesticide risks to public health over the period under study (Levitan 1997). There have been various other applications. For example, Verhoeven et al. (1994) discuss the integration of an environmental yardstick for pesticide use in an economic farm model to monitor changes under different price and policy conditions. They develop a model to compare the effects of two control systems for pesticide use in arable farming in the Netherlands: the governmental system focusing on the amount of active ingredients used per hectare, and an alternative based on the detailed environmental criteria of the yardstick.

Janssen et al. (1995) use an indicator-type approach to investigate the relationship between environmental burden and pesticide usage per hectare. They question the usefulness of the Dutch pesticide 'volume' policy since they do not find a proportional relationship between use and environmental burden. Webster et al. (1995) apply an impact indicator in a study comparing different methods of producing crops. The damage index resulting from wheat produced under the integrated farming system (IFS) is estimated as under half that resulting from the conventional production of wheat. This is due to a lower number of active ingredients used in the former system, as well as use of less-damaging active ingredients.

CONSTRUCTING AN INDICATOR FOR PESTICIDES

Two broad approaches to the development of environmental risk indicators can be identified (Davis 1997). The first involves the construction of an indicator that reflects the *presence* of pesticides in the environment. This might be based on monitoring data reflecting the 'real world' use rather than just 'approved' use – for example, from the Wildlife Incident Investigation Scheme in the UK, or from water quality data. However, a detected presence of pesticides in the environment does not necessarily equate with damage.

The second approach involves the construction of an indicator based on the pattern of pesticide use – for example, kilograms of active ingredient applied per hectare. A disadvantage is that such a measure would only pick up impacts allowed by the approvals policy (users would be assumed to adhere to conditions of use) and would not take account of impacts that arise through accident or misuse, such as water contamination from pesticide spillage (Davis 1997). Furthermore, given the qualitative differences between pesticides from an ecological perspective, reductions in use (as measured by per-hectare-doses or weight in kilograms) may not necessarily be environmentally beneficial. Chemical type must also be taken into account. However, this latter approach has been the focus of many efforts to develop indicators to date.

A review of the literature on environmental indicators for pesticides highlights both differences and similarities in the degree of detail and the scope of analysis (Falconer 1997). For example, Higley and Wintersteen (1992), Kovach et al. (1992) and Reus and Pak (1993) all consider parameters related to toxicity and to exposure (for example, presence in soil, leachability to groundwater or runoff potential). Of the studies reviewed, only Taylor et al. (1995) take exposure itself into account, through the development of a complex ecological algorithm. Levitan et al. (1995) develop a continuum of approaches ranging from anecdotal assessments, through composite impact rating systems, to detailed assessments combining economic and site-specific parameters. Indicators can be subjective (Penrose et al. 1994), quantitative (Kovach et al. 1992), or mathematical and predictive (Gustafson 1989). The general issues in constructing indicators can be discussed under several headings: data availability and assumptions; the timescale of impacts and spatial variability; levels of aggregation and weighting components; and incorporating economic information.

Data Availability and Assumptions

The biggest challenge in developing environmental indicators for pesticides is the lack of knowledge and understanding of the links between pesticide use, emissions, environmental concentrations and any adverse effects on biodiversity. Indicators can only be constructed using whatever information is available and in this sense they are unavoidably biased (Ward 1995). Furthermore, indicators can express only what is quantifiable, either cardinally or ordinally.

Generally, assessment of the ecological consequences of pesticide usage through actual measurement is a lengthy, expensive process, requiring detailed surveys and laboratory studies. Levitan et al. (1995) comment that surprisingly few data on the ecological effects of pesticides are available in the scientific literature, possibly because much of the testing required for pesticide registration is now carried out in private laboratories. Even then, some of the existing 'ecological effects' data are inappropriate for assessing the impacts of particular pesticides because they were not collected using standardized testing protocols, rendering them incomparable (Levitan 1997). Furthermore, ecotoxicological studies are typically for a single species, despite the importance of the interactive effects of pesticide inputs at the community and ecosystem levels (Campbell et al. 1997). Limited understanding of ecological interactions means that indirect impacts are unpredictable and extremely difficult to quantify accurately.

Environmental indicators for pesticides have so far tended to concentrate on chemical or physical variables, as such data are usually more readily available. However, even so, the selection of quantitative data is not straightforward. For example, there are a number of different measures of toxicity: acute, chronic, and definitions based on reproductive, teratogenic, mutagenic and oncogenic effects, and perhaps others such as on nervous and immune systems.

Indicators may be criticized with regard to their structure, and particularly the assumptions made about the characteristics of variables or their interactions. Most constructed indicators assume linearity between pesticide application and environmental impact (Falconer 1997). For example, Kovach et al. (1992) construct a model under the assumption that doubling the quantity of pesticide applied in agriculture leads to a doubling of 'environmental impact'. This assumption overlooks the strong possibility of non-linear dose-response curves, ecological thresholds and interaction effects.

However, the relationship between indicator values and meaningful break-points in biological, ecological or other impacts is rarely known and is often ignored by assessment procedures. Arbitrary scoring criteria are common (Levitan 1997). The criteria for establishing hazard categories are commonly based upon orders of magnitudes rather than on biophysical or ecological responses to threshold doses (for example, the World Health Organization pesticide hazard classification system). Scores are generally step functions (rather than continuous) and numerical intervals between categories do not correlate with measured differences in toxic effect between benign and dangerous chemicals. Dushoff et al. (1994) concede that it is very difficult to see how else researchers can meet the goal of assigning a number to any combination of pesticide applications. An alternative to additive aggregation methods would be an exponential or multiplicative approach, although there is not yet any firm scientific basis for this.

The Time-scale of Impacts and Spatial Variability

An important issue relates to the time-scale of analysis. There may be a long time lag between pesticide application and resulting ecotoxicological consequences. For example, chronic health effects may occur following low exposure to chemicals over long time spans. Thus, damage in one period may be related to emissions in previous years or even decades. It is difficult to construct indicators that reflect the dynamic, cumulative aspect of potential damage, given the newness of many pesticide compounds and uncertainty about their long-run effects.

Risks and impacts are also likely to vary spatially across ecosystems. This implies that models should also be differentiated between sites (or at least regions), either in terms of their structure, or of the data on which they are calibrated. A trade-off must be resolved: assessments with fewer parameters may offer broadly applicable guidelines and ease of use but little site-specific reliability; more complex assessment systems, which consider site-specific conditions, are narrowly applicable and difficult to use, requiring intensive data input and technical capacity. The approach taken depends on the objectives of the decision-making system, as well as on the data available. Differences in environmental circumstances may not be relevant if the aim is to compare pesticides on a relative basis (rather than knowing absolute damage) – for example, in terms of product hazard. However, it is questionable whether the ordering of products on the basis of ecotoxicological impacts is robust to differing circumstances of their use.

Levels of Aggregation and Weighting Components

Since many different parameters affect pesticide impact, one question is whether it is more useful for indicators to be 'composite' or disaggregated. Given that the impacts of pesticide use are multidimensional, a composite approach may allow for easier comparison across compounds or products (a principal aim of many indicators). However, there are at least three general criticisms of such an approach (Midmore et al. 1995):

- Detailed understanding is needed for each process represented by an element of the indicator. If these processes and their interactions are not understood, then elements may be chosen which when combined, will not reflect true environmental quality.
- Reducing all elements to a continuously based scale tends to favour discrete, measurable pollutants for which standards have been established.
- The weighting of variables is a subjective process, which puts value judgements into the hands of technicians rather than elected representatives.

The decision depends on the use to which an indicator is to be put and the transparency of its structure. For some users, it may be more helpful to have a composite indicator since it would take a lot of time to weigh up a large number of different indicators.

Among composite indicators, a distinction can be drawn between 'scientific', mathematical and '*ad hoc*' indicators. The former are based on natural science and aim explicitly to predict a *specific* type of environmental response or effect of pesticide usage: for example, the quantity that will leach into water from the soil. Furthermore, they can in principle be validated. In contrast, *ad hoc* indicators are more general and may include such factors as product cost and social valuations of the impacts of usage. Falconer (1997) notes some basic similarities used in the construction of *ad hoc* indicators in the literature. A common approach in many studies is assessment of environmental impact on the basis of parameters related to toxicity and exposure (such as their half-life in soil, and their leachability to groundwater).

A critical issue when developing composite or aggregated indicators is the way in which different aspects are combined and the relative significance given to each in the overall indicator. The relative significance of different components in any indicator may depend on the specific context. For example, if a farm has a large number of ditches or is adjacent to surface water, most importance will probably be attached to the risk of pesticide application to water organisms. There is always some subjectivity in how various components are combined: multiattribute indicators will always embody judgements about the relative importance of different factors. Weighting is an unresolvable issue for economists at present, since the relative importance of different factors will depend on largely unknown social preferences, knowledge and perceptions. Economic valuation could play a role, if findings from studies on preferences are applied (Foster and Mourato 1997), but much more work in this area is needed.

There are several possible ways of coping with the weighting problem in the absence of knowledge about social preferences. One approach could be to examine whether one set of chemicals dominates another across all of the dimensions of impact. This 'Paretian type' approach means that there will be an environmental gain if the impact to one ecological component is reduced, while holding constant the level of impacts. However, such unambiguity is unlikely in practice. Another approach could be to disaggregate indicator scores into their component physical parameter values, allowing decision makers to apply their own weights. This has the attraction of flexibility, but political safeguards may be needed to ensure transparency. Finally, one could conduct a sensitivity analysis to examine whether the selection of weights makes a significant difference to the implications of applying the indicator.

Incorporating Economic Information

The development of environmental indicators fills in some gaps in knowledge when making decisions about the use of environmental resources. Ideally, information on social preferences for resource allocation would be used as a basis for decision making. However, such information is lacking for non-marketed resources. Attempts have been made by economists to improve the information available relating to social values – for example, through the application of contingent valuation techniques.

A criticism of many environmental indicators is that they generally ignore 'cost' factors and do not translate physical measures of impact into monetized impacts using economic valuation techniques. Indeed, there are few economic studies relating to the valuation of pesticide impacts. Pimental et al. (1992) is one of the few examples. They seek to estimate the environmental and social cost of pesticide use across the US, using, for example, the cost of damage remediation through water treatment.

Higley and Wintersteen (1992) report on a contingent valuation study which was undertaken to establish the monetary value farmers might place on risk reduction associated with pesticide use. Specifically, they classify field crop insecticides into four risk categories and ask farmers to indicate their willingness to pay to avoid different levels of risk associated with these categories. However, the methodology produces results of dubious validity. For example, farmers are chosen as the relevant survey population: since farmers are influenced by a wide range of factors relating to agricultural production, they are unlikely to be representative of the general population. Another approach is to use contingent ranking to apply monetary weights to the different aspects of environmental degradation. For example, Foster and Mourato (1997) show that UK consumers are on average willing to pay about six times as much to reverse the decline in one species of farmland bird as to prevent a single case of short-term human morbidity resulting from pesticide exposure. However, a particular change in the state of the environment may not easily be interpreted as either beneficial or harmful in all cases, as judgements on environmental quality are affected by social attitudes, which are dynamic over time.

Some researchers do not favour the 'translation' of environmental impacts into a monetary measure of social welfare loss. For example, Levitan et al. (1995) argue that it is crucial to evaluate environmental and economic considerations separately because environmental impacts are not reduced or recompensed as a result of the economic benefits resulting from pesticide usage. In this context, environmental indicators and the findings of economic valuation studies can fulfil different functions in assisting decision making. Moreover, they are not mutually exclusive.

To avoid 'confounding' environmental rankings, economic costs could be expressed in financial terms, with environmental impacts expressed using a non-monetary rating system. A graphical approach is used by Hoag and Hornsby (1992) to demonstrate the trade-off between product cost and groundwater risks. A pesticide should be rejected for usage if it has both higher cost and the same or a greater hazard than another one. Falconer (1997) assessed the trade-off between farm income and environmental hazard levels (as measured by an ecotoxicological indicator for pesticides) under different pesticide tax policy scenarios. However, such an approach becomes less straightforward if several environmental factors are included since the trade-off is harder to evaluate. None the less, the capacity to summarize useful information without pre-empting the judgement of users and policy makers can be considered an advantage of the approach (Dushoff et al. 1994).

AN ILLUSTRATIVE PESTICIDE INDICATOR

To illustrate and develop the environmental indicator methodology, the construction of a simple pesticide hazard indicator is outlined below (further detail available in Falconer 1997). The aim is for the indicator to be quick and easy to use as a preliminary decision tool.

In the UK, most arable crops are protected from pests and disease by the application of high levels of pesticide. The most widespread decline in birds is believed to have occurred in intensive arable regions (Campbell et al. 1997; Greig-Smith et al. 1992). Using an indicator approach, a selection of the most commonly used arable pesticides are ranked on the basis of their environmental potential, as represented by a simple ecotoxicological indicator. A composite score is derived for each pesticide – on a scale of one to ten. Higher scores indicate that the pesticide poses a greater hazard.

The first step is the definition of the ecotoxicological components of interest. In the UK, all products are labelled with conditions of use, including environmental precautions, as stipulated by the Pesticides Safety Directorate. These conditions should be a good summary of current knowledge since they are based on all of the available information used in the government pesticide approvals and registration process. Nine different ecological and human-health dimensions are identified from product label information and special environmental precautions contained in the 'Green Book' of pesticides (Ivens 1994). An extra 'general' (or unknown) hazard dimension is also included, since no pesticide can be assumed to be entirely hazard free, given their nature as biocides. Figure 10.2 summarizes the components.

A simple summary indicator for each chemical is constructed through the arithmetic aggregation of scores for each ecotoxicological dimension. The

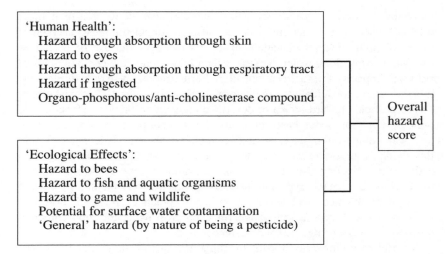

'Human Health':
  Hazard through absorption through skin
  Hazard to eyes
  Hazard through absorption through respiratory tract
  Hazard if ingested
  Organo-phosphorous/anti-cholinesterase compound

Overall hazard score

'Ecological Effects':
  Hazard to bees
  Hazard to fish and aquatic organisms
  Hazard to game and wildlife
  Potential for surface water contamination
  'General' hazard (by nature of being a pesticide)

Figure 10.2   Hazard indicator components

scores for each dimension are based on whether the pesticide has been assessed as 'irritating', 'harmful' or 'dangerous'. The number of 'units' applied (where one unit is one application at the standard (labelled) dose per hectare) is multiplied by the hazard score to give a per-hectare score for any given crop. Further information on the method of scoring is outlined in the appendix.

In this approach, different types of impact are given the same weight – which can itself be regarded as an implicit weighting procedure. For example, the characteristic 'extremely dangerous to fish' is given the same weighting as 'dangerous to skin'. However, efforts have been made to ensure consistency: for example, different hazards to farmworker health are weighted in the same way. This is deemed a reasonable approach in the absence of any information on weightings. The weights are also easy to change should such information become available.

The aim of this indicator development is to enable some guidance as to the relative environmental 'nastiness' of different pesticide products – for example, to allow an ordering or categorization. Although simple and unavoidably subjective, orderings or groupings of products based on the above hazard scores may be more closely related to ecotoxicological impact than variables such as the volume of active ingredients of a typical per-hectare dose or its cost. Also, the ability to disaggregate the hazard along different dimensions is useful. This allows identification of the nature and extent of trade-offs between the use of products with different characteristics.

As discussed above, there are limitations to such an approach. The hazard indicator is based on linear aggregation and can take no account of indirect effects caused by interactions between different dimensions. No account is taken of environmental management efforts (such as the use of pesticide-exclusion strips along watercourses), which may reduce the ecotoxicological risks and impacts of pesticide application. Furthermore, given data limitations, it is impossible to validate the indicator with regard to actual ecological effect.

The pesticide hazard indicator described above was linked to an economic policy evaluation model, based on a farm-level linear programming model for a typical arable farm in the East Anglian region of the UK (Falconer 1997). In this model, a pesticide usage strategy is defined for each arable production activity in terms of the type of chemicals available for use and the number of units used of each type per hectare for each crop (including 'current commercial practice' and several 'low-input' practices for each crop). A pesticide hazard score is calculated for each crop using the environmental dimensions and scoring system described above.

A series of optimization (profit-maximizing) runs of the model allows the trade-offs between environmental hazard reduction and agricultural production/incomes to be observed for different scenarios. Different pesticide tax specifications are evaluated. The study shows how taxes targeted on different products according to an ecotoxicological indicator would reduce environmental hazards at lower cost (in terms of farm income) than alternative regulatory mechanisms.

The link between volume of pesticide use, financial cost of inputs and ecological hazards is also examined, at the chemical level and at the crop level. The correlation between these parameters has important implications for policy design. A high correlation between per-hectare spray expenditure, pesticide application in physical units (kilograms of active ingredient), and the ecotoxicological score arising from pesticide usage implies that the level of all such indicators falls steadily as tax rates increase. This effect will be observed regardless of whether the tax is linked to spray costs (for example, if it is implemented on an *ad valorem* basis), or to quantities such as the number of units used, or differentiated according to the adverse environmental potential of the product.

However, in reality, the correlation between these parameters is far from perfect. The impact of the tax can be quite different, depending on the parameter to which it is linked. For example, a levy on the kilograms of active ingredient applied should reduce the total volume of pesticide used in the optimal farm plan, but it may not necessarily reduce the total hazard score of the plan. Similarly, a spray tax might reduce total spray expenditure, but physical pesticide usage or environmental hazard may fall to a much smaller extent. The effect depends on how farmers adjust to the tax by substitution of different types of chemical or by a change in the cropping mix. Changing the chemical composition of pesticides means that while some 'damage impacts' decrease, others could increase as a result of this substitution. Thus, it is conceivable that an *ad valorem* tax on pesticide expenditure could be counter-productive.

Crop-level correlations are derived from the farm model to give some indication of the likely outcomes of different policies (Table 10.1). The relatively high correlation between spray units and the hazard indicator score per crop hectare suggests that a pesticide tax based on spray units would have a closer impact to one based on the hazard score than it would to one based on spray expenditure.

Correlations at the level of the individual pesticide chemical are stated in Table 10.2 (for those included in the model). The very low correlation between hazard score and kilogram per unit suggests (far more strongly than the crop-level correlations) that incentives based on the weight of pesticide applied would not be the most appropriate way to reduce environmental hazards from pesticides. The negative correlation between pesticide price and its ecotoxicological potential suggests that an *ad valorem* tax would give an incentive for farmers to substitute towards the cheaper product, which has a greater ecotoxicological hazard. This would clearly be a highly undesirable policy outcome.

Table 10.1   Correlation matrix for crop-level variables (per hectare) in the arable farm model

	Spray expenditure	Number of spray units	Hazard score	Total sprays by weight	Gross margin
Spray expenditure	1	0.747	0.628	0.454	0.297
Number of spray units		1	0.869	0.704	0.235
Hazard score			1	0.526	0.294
Total sprays by weight				1	0.359
Gross margin					1

Table 10.2   Chemical-level correlations

	Hazard per unit	Kilogram per unit	Price per unit
Hazard per unit	1	0.125	–0.442
Kilogram per unit		1	–0.138
Price per unit			1

Knowledge of the ecotoxicological trade-off between different ecological and health dimensions is very important. For example, it may be impossible to adjust pesticide usage on a farm so as to reduce hazards to bees without increasing hazards to fish – in which, case environmental priorities must be set. An analysis of the ecotoxicological scores for the hundred or so most commonly used chemicals in arable farming in the UK gave a correlation coefficient of 0.496 between total human-health and total ecological hazard scores. The moderate level of this coefficient implies that there is a trade-off to be made between these dimensions in deciding how to reduce pesticide use.

SUMMARY AND CONCLUSIONS

In the context of agri-environmental policy development, a credible mechanism or indicator with which to gauge movement towards improved environmental safety is needed. An analysis of the use of environmental indicators, taking agricultural pesticides as a case study, has been presented here as a practicable approach to policy analysis.

The role of an indicator is to make complex systems more transparent, and to help determine where a system is relative to its goals. Establishing a link between pesticide use and environmental impacts is extremely complex. It will, for example, depend on many location-specific factors. Progress can be made by considering the ecotoxicological parameters of different active ingredients to develop indicators of their relative potential for adverse effects.

The indicators reviewed above vary in their construction, although several common themes are detected. *Ad hoc* composite indices based on scoring and ranking are most typical. Such indicators may lack scientific validity, but nevertheless may be useful presentational tools, summarising the available ecotoxicological information.

A particularly important issue relates to the ability of an indicator to represent the social cost of ecotoxicological impacts, that is, the economic impacts on ecosystems and on human health. It is necessary to aggregate individual components of 'impact' to compare scenarios. The weighting of impacts is controversial. One might consider schemes that weigh components according to social preferences. However, there are methodological problems in revealing social preferences for different ecological states. For biodiversity impacts, another approach might be to weigh impacts according to species scarcity – on the assumption that value rises with scarcity. Any approach needs to be flexible and adjustable. For example, it should be possible to incorporate improved understanding of social preferences by adjusting the weights given to different components.

This chapter illustrates how indicators might be used to look at the trade-off between agricultural production and environmental risk. The development of environmental profiles for pesticides, to highlight differences between chemicals, could be very useful for policy design and evaluation, and perhaps in decision support for agricultural users. A problem in agri-environmental systems is that there are myriad decision makers operating at different levels, so there is unlikely to be one indicator that will be accepted universally. Different indicators will be needed for different purposes, and for use by different decision makers. Transparency is important, especially with issues where the underlying science is complex and there is a significant degree of processing of the raw data. However, all indicators are used normatively, to fulfil the particular purpose of decision making in any given context, and so organizational and political imperatives are as important as technical aspects of indicator design (Moxey et al. 1998). In the absence of other bases for decision making, such ecotoxicological indicators may play a useful role in environmental policy development. Given the high ecological complexity, great caution is needed in their development and application; there are great demands for further work.

REFERENCES

Campbell, L.H., M. Avery, P. Donald, A.D. Evans, R.E. Green and J.D. Wilson (1997), *A Review of the Indirect Effects of Pesticides on Birds*, Joint Nature Conservation Committee (JNCC) Report 227; Peterborough: JNCC.

Davis, T. (1997), 'Developing pesticide indicators', Pesticides Forum memorandum PF29, London: Department of Environment, Transport and Regions.

Drinking Water Inspectorate (DWI) (1994), *Drinking Water 1993: A Report by the Chief Inspector for Drinking Water*, Department of the Environment/Welsh Office, London: HMSO.

Dushoff, J., B. Caldwell and C. Mohler (1994), 'Evaluating the environmental effect of pesticides: a critique of the environmental impact quotient'. *American Entomologist*, **40**, 180–83.

Falconer, K.E. (1997), 'Environmental policy and the use of agricultural pesticides', PhD dissertation, Department of Land Economy, University of Cambridge.

Foster, V. and S. Mourato (1997), 'Behavioural consistency, statistical specification and validity on the contingent ranking method: evidence from a survey on the impacts of pesticide use in the UK', Centre for Social and Economic Research on the Global Environment (CSERGE) Working Paper, London.

Greig-Smith, P., G. Frampton and T. Hardy (1992), *Pesticides, Cereal Farming and the Environment: The Boxworth Project*, Ministry of Agriculture, Fisheries and Food, London: HMSO.

Gustafson, D.I. (1989), 'Ground-water ubiquity score: a simple method for assessing pesticide ubiquity', *Environmental Toxicology and Chemistry*, **8**: 339–57.

Higley, L.G. and W.K. Wintersteen (1992), 'A novel approach for environmental risk of pesticides as a basis for incorporating environmental costs into economic injury levels', *American Entomologist*, **39**: 34–9.

Hoag, D.L. and A.G. Hornsby (1992), 'Coupling groundwater contamination with economic returns when applying farm pesticides', *Journal of Environmental Quality*, **21**: 579–86.

Ivens, G.W. (1994), *UK Pesticide Guide 1994*, Farnham: CAB International/British Crop Protection Council (BCPC).

Janssen, H., A.J. Oskam and R. Vijftigschild (1995), 'Pesticide use environmental burden and economics of arable farms in the Netherlands', in A. Oskam (ed.), *Proceedings, Workshop on Pesticides*, Wageningen, August, pp. 1–23.

Kovach, J., C. Petzoldt, J. Degri and J. Tette (1992), 'A method to measure the environmental impact of pesticides', *New York's Food and Life Sciences Bulletin*, **139**: 1–8.

Levitan, L. (1997), 'An overview of pesticide impact and assessment systems', Organization for Economic Cooperation and Development Workshop on Risk Indicators, Copenhagen, 21–23 April.

Levitan, L., I. Merwin and J. Kovach (1995), 'Assessing the relative environment impacts of agricultural pesticides: the quest for a holistic method', *Agriculture, Ecosystems and Environment*, **55**: 153–68.

McLaughlin, A. and P. Mineau (1996), 'The impact of agricultural practices on biodiversity', *Agriculture, Ecosystems and Environment*, **55**: 201–12.

Midmore, P., S. Russell and T. Jenkins (1995), 'Developing an holistic approach to the concept of environmental quality', a report for Scottish Natural Heritage, University of Wales, Aberystwyth.

Moxey, A., P. Lowe and M. Whitby (1998), 'Environmental indicators for a reformed common agricultural policy: monitoring and evaluating policies in agriculture', Report to English Nature, Centre for Rural Economy, Department of Agricultural Economics and Food Marketing, University of Newcastle-upon-Tyne.

O'Bryan, T.R. and R.H. Ross (1988), 'Chemical scoring system for hazard and exposure identification', *Journal of Toxicology and Environmental Health*, **25**(1): 119–34.

Organization for Economic Cooperation and Development (OECD) (1997), *Environmental Indicators for Agriculture*, Paris: OECD.

Penrose, L.J., W.G. Thwaite and C.C. Bower (1994), 'Rating index as a basis for decision-making on pesticide use reduction and for accreditation of fruit produced under IPM', *Crop Protection*, **12**: 146–52.

Pimental, D., H. Acquay, M. Biltonen, O. Rice, M. Silva, J. Nelson, V. Lipner, S. Giordano, A. Horowitz and M. D'Amore (1992), 'Environmental and economic costs of pesticide use', *Bioscience*, **42**: 750–60.

Reus, J.A.W.A. and G.A. Pak (1993), *An Environmental Yardstick for Pesticides*, Med.Fac. Lanbouww, University of Gent. 58/2a: 249–55.

Reus, J.A.W.A., H.J. Weckseler and G.A. Pak (1994), 'Towards a future EC pesticide policy: an inventory of risks of pesticide use, possible solutions and policy instruments', CLM paper 149, Centre for Agriculture and Environment, Utrecht.

Taylor, M., T.P. Milsom, P. Smith, S.A. Field and A.D.M. Hart (1995), *Final Report on Project CSA 2146: The Costs and Benefits of Pesticide Usage. Annex 1: Assessment of Environmental Effects*, Central Science Laboratory, Ministry of Agriculture, Fisheries and Food, London: HMSO.

Verhoeven, J.T.W., G.A.A. Wossink and J.A.W. Reus (1994), 'An environmental yardstick in farm economic modelling of future pesticide use: the case of arable farming', Netherlands, *Journal of Agricultural Science*, **42**(4): 331–41.

Ward, N. (1995), *An Evolutionary Perspective on Pesticide Use and Water Pollution in Europe*, in A. Oskam (ed.), *Proceedings, Workshop on Pesticides*, Wageningen, 24–27 August.

Ward, N., J. Clark, P. Low and S. Seymour (1993), 'Water pollution from agricultural pesticides', Research Report, Centre for Rural Economy, University of Newcastle-upon-Tyne.

Webster, J.P.G., M.J. Himms and R. Clare (1995), *The Costs and Benefits of Pesticide Usage*, Final Report to Ministry of Agriculture, Fisheries and Food, Project No. CSA2146, London: HMSO.

APPENDIX 10A   SCORING SYSTEM FOR INDICATORS

The pesticides 'Green Book' (Ivens 1994) is used as a basis for hazard assessment. The information contained in this is taken from statutory product labels and conditions of use. Environmental and special precautions are listed; these are assumed to have the advantage of taking into account all available information in pesticide risks and impacts used in the approval process. Therefore, the resulting yardstick should be a fair summary of current knowledge about pesticides.

Nine different ecological and human-health dimensions are identified from product label information and precautions, along with an extra, 'general (or unknown) hazard' dimension: no pesticides are assumed to be entirely hazard free. Scores for each component are based on the qualitative information contained in the manual (that is, according to whether the pesticide is 'irritating', 'harmful' or 'dangerous'). The different components are given a weight of between 0.33 and 1 (see Table 10A.1).

Thus we compute a simple summary yardstick for each chemical on the basis of an arithmetic aggregation of scores given for each hazard dimension. All pesticides receive a score between 1 and 10 (chosen as an easily manageable range) – higher scores indicating that the pesticide poses a greater hazard.

Table 10A.1   Scoring system for the indicator

		Scoring components		
1.	General hazard (by virtue of being a pesticide)	Pesticide = 1	–	–
2.	Special warnings, e.g. if product contains an organophosphate or is on the red list	Warning = 1	–	–
3.	Hazard to water	6m buffer zone required = 1	–	–
4.	Skin	Irritating = 0.5	Harmful = 1	–
5.	Hazard from swallowing	Irritating = 0.5	Harmful = 1	–
6.	Hazard to eyes	Irritating = 0.5	Harmful = 1	–
7.	Hazard to respiratory system	Irritating = 0.5	Harmful = 1	–
8.	Hazard to game and wildlife	Harmful = 0.5	Dangerous = 0.5	–
9.	Hazard to bees	Harmful = 0.33	Dangerous = 0.66	Extremely dangerous = 1
10.	Hazard to fish and aquatic organisms	Harmful = 0.33	Dangerous = 0.66	Extremely dangerous = 1

Index